Nehemiah Wallington

Historical notices of events occurring chiefly in the reign of Charles I.

Edited from the original MSS. with notes and illus. Vol. 2

Nehemiah Wallington

Historical notices of events occurring chiefly in the reign of Charles I.
Edited from the original MSS. with notes and illus. Vol. 2

ISBN/EAN: 9783337204136

Printed in Europe, USA, Canada, Australia, Japan

Cover: Foto ©ninafisch / pixelio.de

More available books at **www.hansebooks.com**

NEHEMIAH WALLINGTON'S

HISTORICAL NOTICES.

HISTORICAL NOTICES

OF EVENTS OCCURRING CHIEFLY IN

THE REIGN OF CHARLES I.

BY NEHEMIAH WALLINGTON,

OF ST. LEONARD'S, EASTCHEAP, LONDON.

EDITED FROM THE ORIGINAL MSS. WITH NOTES AND ILLUSTRATIONS.

IN TWO VOLUMES.

VOL. II.

LONDON:
RICHARD BENTLEY, NEW BURLINGTON STREET,
Publisher in Ordinary to Her Majesty.
1869.

PRINTED BY WILLIAM CLOWES AND SONS, DUKE STREET, STAMFORD STREET,
AND CHARING CROSS.

CONTENTS OF THE SECOND VOLUME.

CHAPTER XXIII.
PAGE
Of Petitions, and the Manner of their Coming 1

CHAPTER XXIV.
Of the Passages of several Things in the Week in Parliament . . 22

CHAPTER XXV.
Of the Plots of the Wicked against the Godly 34

CHAPTER XXVI.
A Preservation of Four Worthy and Honourable Peers of this Kingdom, and some others. Of the Plots of the Wicked against the Godly (*continued*) 54

CHAPTER XXVII.
Copy of a Letter from Hull. Sir John Hotham's Speech to the Knights' Meeting at York. The King declareth himself on Heworth Moor. A Letter from York. Heavy and Sad Times with the Poor People of God. God gives Victory to His People 65

CHAPTER XXVIII.
Pillaging and Plundering. The Setting up of the King's Standard at Nottingham. The Mercy of the Wicked is Cruelty; what then is their Cruelty? God's Wonderful Preserving some Houses from Burning. Great Cruelty and Plundering. That Malignant Party is further strengthened 85

CHAPTER XXIX.

Skirmish at Worcester. God's Wonderful Preserving the Town of Manchester. A Few to overcome Many. Heavy and Sad Times in Plundering and Pillaging 104

CHAPTER XXX.

Marlborough's Miseries. Plundering of the Counties of Northampton and Warwick. Bibles and other Good Books burned at Reading. Prince Rupert's Taking of Cirencester 127

CHAPTER XXXI.

A Memorial of Great Storms of Rain, of Thunder, and Lightning. Strange Sights in the Air 148

CHAPTER XXXII.

The Wonderful Work of God in the Guidance of Bullets. Battle of Edge Hill 152

CHAPTER XXXIII.

Plunderings and Pillagings (*continued*). Cruelty used to Prisoners at Oxford. Ireland and the Irish Rebels. More Savage Cruelties and Extreme Miseries 158

CHAPTER XXXIV.

Savage Cruelties in Bristol. Of the Cruel Plundering and Firing the Town of Ockingham, in Berkshire 178

CHAPTER XXXV.

Notes. Of openly Profaning the Lord's Day by Prince Rupert and the Cavaliers 192

CHAPTER XXXVI.

The Miseries of Ireland since the Cessation. Ireland and the Irish Rebels. Ireland's Lamentation for the late Cessation . . . 195

CHAPTER XXXVII.

A Judgment upon Organs 211

CHAPTER XXXVIII.

Cruelties and Miseries. The Cruelty of the Irish shewn to the Inhabitants of Bristol. More Cruelties and Miseries . . . 213

CHAPTER XXXIX.

Of the Cruelty of the King's Army in the West. Of the Sad and Heavy Condition of Many of God's Children in Lincolnshire and Lancashire. Of the Miseries in Staffordshire. Of the Great Fire in Oxford. Notes 228

CHAPTER XL.

Parliament Occurrences. Some Part of the Life and Plots of the Lord Macguire. The Cruel Plundering of the Town of Birmingham. Outrage on a Minister in the Pulpit. Wickedness and Cruelty in our own Armies. Cruelties in Skellum Grenville's Armies 244

CHAPTER XLI.

Cruelly Plundering Progress 255

CHAPTER XLII.

Goring's Cruelty in Devonshire. Sad Condition of the People in Cornwall. Sad News from Ireland 273

CHAPTER XLIII.

Beheading of the King 279

APPENDIX 281

NEHEMIAH WALLINGTON'S
HISTORICAL NOTICES.

XXIII.

OF PETITIONS, AND THE MANNER OF THEIR COMING.

AFTER intelligence was given to *Buckinghamshire*[1] men that Mr. *Hampden*, being Knight of that Shire, the Lord *Mandeville*, Mr. *Pym*, Sir *Arthur Haselrigg*, Sir *Denzil Hollis*, and Mr. *Stroud*, were impeached of high treason by His Majesty, moreover that His Majesty intended to have them committed to the Tower thereof, they were all unanimously resolved to petition to the King and Parliament on the behalf of them all; the news was transported into the Shire, but last *Friday*, late at night, and warrants being given out to certify the county of the same, five thousand were presently assembled, and presented themselves submissively to go with the petition to *London*; and, if they had longer time, there would

---

[1] From a pamphlet entitled "The Parliament's Answer to the Petition of the County of Buckingham. . . . With the manner of their coming through London to the Parliament House.—Printed the 13th of January 1642."

have been three times more. But the petition being made, and these men ready attending the same, approaching near the aspect of the city of *London*, where they came through *St. Leonard's Shoreditch*, through *Bishopgate*, and so through *Cheapside* onward to *Westminster*, there was above three thousand on horseback, every man with his protestation in his hand, intimating that they had a petition to present to the Honourable Court; the others were on foot; but they reached in all from the Exchange to *Newgate*, three and four in a rank, coming to *Westminster*; they acquainted the House of their petition, and humbly presented it unto them, where they had afterward at the conference of both Houses a correspondent answer given to them respectively.

On *Thursday* the 20*th* of *January*, the humble petition of the Knights, Gentlemen, Ministers, and other Inhabitants of the County of *Essex*, was delivered into the House of Parliament, wherein, after their acknowledgement of our care and pains, they desired a happy Reformation in Religion, And, because they conceived that the Popish Lords, Bishops, and others, were a chief hindrance of the success, they desired that their votes might be taken out of the Lords' House. This was delivered in the House with a long speech by a lawyer of that County, with the tender (of) laying down their lives and estates for the defence of the privileges of Parliaments, when they should be thereunto required; the Speaker was ordered to call them in, and to give them thanks for their expression of care and affection;

to say that we will be as ready to forward the Reformation of Religion, and their freedom and liberty, and that with all convenient speed, will take their petition into consideration.[2]

There was likewise a petition from *Gloucester* complaining of the disturbance of trade in clothing, to the impoverishing of many thousands, by reason of the present distractions; this petition was likewise read, and they answered that, in due time, it should be taken into consideration. Many thousands flock to *London* to deliver many petitions of this nature.

Monday, the 24th of *January*, both Houses of Parliament met at *Westminster*, and there were several petitions preferred, as, namely: the petition of the Knights, Gentlemen, Ministers, and other inhabitants of the county of *Essex*; and a petition of the Barons, Justices, and Gentlemen of the County of *Devonshire*,[3] which [had] above two thousand hands to it of the Gentry and Freeholders; and a petition of the Mayor, Aldermen, and Common Councilmen of the city of *Exeter*. Another from the county of *Middlesex*,[4] and another from *Somersetshire*,[5] all of them being to this effect, humbly praying and desiring that the Bishops and Popish Lords might have no votes in the Lords' House, and that a Reformation in Religion might go forward; and to maintain the privilege of Parliament, the putting of the kingdom into a posture of

---

[2] See *Diurnall Occurrences.* [3] See *Perfect Diurnall.*
[4] Ibid. [5] Ibid.

defence, the securing the Cinque Portes, and the speedy sending of aid to *Ireland*, the liberty of the subject, and the King's prerogative.

Tuesday, the 25th of *January*, the Parliament received a petition from the County of *Hertford*,[6] above four thousand of the Knights, and Gentry, and Freeholders of that County, desiring that evil counsellors may be removed from His Majesty, the Popish Lords and Bishops out of the Lords' House, the Papists disarmed throughout the kingdom, the kingdom put into a posture of defence, the forts and strength of this put into safe hands, and the speedy sending of relief to *Ireland*. And that they would be ready to hazard their lives and estates for the defence of the King and the Parliament, and would maintain the privileges of the same, and, in special, those noble Lords and gentlemen in both Houses now happily met, whose endeavours are all for the public good, and the safety of the king and kingdom, and withal desiring that those Lords and gentlemen may have liberty to protest against all those enemies to this kingdom and State, who refuse to join with those honourable Lords and House of Commons for the putting of the kingdom into the way of safety under the command of such persons as the Parliament shall appoint; which petition was received with many thanks from both Houses, and promising with all conveniency to give them answer thereunto.

There was also a petition preferred by the Lord

[6] See *Perfect Diurnall*.

Mayor and Aldermen, and Common Councilmen of *London*[7] to the House of Commons, which petition was of great weight, laying open many great grievances now undergone by them, which were unsupportable; this petition was carried up to the Lords by a conference, where Mr. *Pym* did declare to the Lords the whole substance of the petition, making a speech of an hour long upon it, for which he was much applauded.

Monday, the 31st of *January*, a petition from the Inhabitants of the County of *Suffolk*,[8] to the number of fifteen hundred, against the votes of Popish Lords and Bishops in the House of Peers, was delivered, and an answer given approving their care and endeavour for the public good, with a promise that the House of Commons will use all their endeavours for the obtaining their desires. Another petition of a thousand poor people, tradesmen in and about *London*, to the effect of the former, shewing that the distractions and fears conceived by the not going forward of the Reformation intended, was the cause of the decay of trading, whereby they were not able to get bread for themselves and family, was delivered, and answered that the House of Commons were in consideration of those things whereof they complained. The poor people replied that they doubted not the care of the House of Commons; but they heard that all stuck in the House of Lords by reason of the votes of Popish Lords and Bishops there, and they desired to know the names of those Peers that

---

[7] See *Perfect Diurnall.*   [8] See *Diurnall Occurrences.*

hindered the good agreement betwixt the good Lords and the Commons. This they pressed with such earnestness that they unwillingly did withdraw, while the Commons' House were in consultation. Afterwards, they were called in, and this answer given, That the House of Commons have endeavoured, and still continue, and they doubt not but when they have represented their petition and speeches to the Lords, which the House of Commons promised presently to do, the causes of their evil will be found out, and some speedy course resolved upon for their relief; desiring them with patience to attend a further answer.

"The same day in the Lords' House there was a petition delivered to the Lords by a company of women, containing their wants and necessities, by reason of the great decay of trading, occasioned by the present distempers and distractions of the State, and composing of differences between the two Houses of Parliament; that the Commons' House they conceive have done what in them lay to relieve them, and redress their grievances; but, that such opposition being made in the Lords' House, which is a great hindrance to their real intentions in their proceedings to perfect the same, that religion may be established, and present aid and assistance transported into *Ireland* for the relief of the distressed Protestants."[9]

"In the afternoon there came to the Lords' House one of the Sheriffs of *London*, with a message from

[9] From *True Diurnall Occurrences*, Averred by R. P. Clerke. London, 1642. See Appendix, Note AAA.

the Lord Mayor of the city, intimating they had received intelligence from *France* that the French King had commanded all the havens and ports of that kingdom to be shut, and that all the English ships on that coast should be stopped."[10]

Wednesday, February the 2nd. In the House of Commons was delivered a humble petition of fifteen thousand poor labouring men, known by the name of porters, and the lowest members of the city of London; this petition was much like the former.[11] The next day was brought two men, who were abettors of the tumult, when *Cheapside* Cross was defaced, and were committed.[12]

Thursday, the 3rd of *February*, a great number of Knights, Gentlemen, Ministers, and others of the Inhabitants of the county of *Surrey*,[13] came into *London* with petitions to both Houses of Parliament, who presented them to the Committees in *Merchant Taylors' Hall*; but they were deferred until the next day, the Parliament sitting then at *Westminster*. And then the petitions for the County of *Surrey* were delivered, for taking away of Bishops and their Government, the sequestering of Romish Lords from the Lords' House, a form of service in the Church enacted and established, as may be convenient for the preservation of the purity of religion, and the abolishment of superfluous ceremonies; the settling their country in a posture of war, for the defence and safety thereof.

---

[10] From *True Diurnall Occurrences*.
[11] See *Diurnall Occurrences*.
[12] Appendix, Note BBB.
[13] See *Diurnall Occurrences*.

Mark the judgement of God upon one that stood in defence of plays, and to maintain them.

This *Thursday* the 3rd of *February*, in the House of Commons there was a complaint made against play-houses, and a motion made for the putting of them down. Then stood up Sir *Peter Lighs* and said that he would spend his blood in defence for the plays, before they should go down, or some words to the like effect; then afterwards, he, being at a play, he hurled a piece of tobacco-pipe at a man, thinking he had known him; but, being mistaken, they fell out in words, and so challenged one another, and he was slain presently. And so you may see his being at a play was the cause of his blood to be shed.

Tuesday, the 8th of *February*, a petition from the Knights, Gentlemen, and Freeholders of the County of *Kent*[14] was brought to the House, acknowledging the great care and pains of the House of Commons for their liberties in Religion and estates. And also, a copy of another petition to the Lords, praying their conjunction with the House of Commons in the removal of the Popish Lords and Bishops out of the House of Peers, and evil counsellors from the King, and the redeeming of the privileges of Parliament. Both which were read aloud, and they thanked for their care, and their tender of service of defence with their lives and fortunes, and these petitions were ordered to be entered into the Journal Book.[15]

---

[14] See *Diurnall Occurrences*.
[15] See *Rushworth*, part iii. vol. i. p. 135.

These Kentish men I did see myself come up *Fish Street Hill*, many hundred of them, on horseback, with their protestations sticking in their hats and girdles; they came in order, three in a rank, first the Knights, and Gentlemen, then about twenty Ministers, then the other horse and footmen.

Wednesday, the 9th of *February*, a petition was delivered to both Houses by the clothiers of *Suffolk*[16] and part of *Essex*, about a thousand coming with them, which, for the most part, was consonant to the Kentish petition delivered the day before, and received answer alike, for they prayed also that scandalous Ministers and the Popish Lords and Bishops voted in the Lords' House might be removed.

A petition was delivered to the House of Commons from the inhabitants of *Cleveland*, in *Yorkshire*, concerning the securing of the papists, and settling of the Militia for defence. The House was turned into a Committee to go on with the Bill for securing of the papists, and the nomination of places for their confinement.

Thursday, the 10th of *February*, a petition was presented to the House by the inhabitants of the county of *Lincoln*.

Another petition from the Knights, Gentlemen, Ministers, subsidy-men, and Free-holders of the county of *Oxford*,[17] with a copy of another to be presented to the Lords.

Another petition from *Northamptonshire*[18] was presented by Knights and Gentlemen of that county,

---

[16] See *Diurnall Occurrences*, No. 6.   [17] Ibid.   [18] Ibid.

with the copy of another to be presented to the Lords, to all which thanks were given for their care of the general good, and particularly for their respect to the House of Commons, with promise of their endeavours to fulfil their desires.

Their petition was, as the former petitions, for the redress of grievances, as removal of scandalous Ministers, and placing others in their room, for the disarming of papists, &c., which, being read and somewhat scanned, answer was given to the preceding.

Friday, the 11th of *February*, was a petition delivered to his Majesty at *Greenwich*, "by the clothiers of *Suffolk* and *Essex*, complaining of the deadness of trade, in respect they had no vent for their clothes, having many thousand pounds worth lying upon their hands, to the great impoverishing of themselves, and the poor of those counties, whom they daily employed. His Majesty himself gave answer unto the petition, That he had considered of their petition, and hath sent it to the Parliament."[19]

Friday, the 11th of *February*, "both houses being met, the members sent by them to his Majesty, who returned answer that his Majesty was pleased to give way to the passing of the Bills concerning the Bishops, votes, and pluralities, and touching their desire of the removing of the Lieutenant of the Tower, and the Militia of the Kingdom, because he would remove the fears and jealousies of his subjects."[20]

[19] See *Diurnall Occurrences*, No. 6.   [20] From *Diurnall Occurrences*.

Saturday, the 12th of *February*, the Company of silk throwsters presented a petition to the House declaring the obstructions of their trade through the distractions of the times.

The Bailiffs, Citizens, Portreeves, and others, of the city of *Ipswich* presented a petition to the House of Commons of like nature to the former petition. And the Seamen and Sailors to the number of two thousand and eight hundred of *Ipswich*, presented another petition to the House, both which were read, approved, and they received thanks by the Speaker, and a promise to take the particulars of their petition into a speedy consideration.

Another petition brought to both Houses by the Knights, Esquires, Gentlemen, and Freeholders, and many Thousands of the Inhabitants of *Warwickshire* and the City of *Coventry*, tending much to the same effect as the former; some of the chief being admitted into the House, had thanks given them, promising this petition should be taken into consideration.

The Knights, Citizens, and Burgesses, are ordered to bring in the Names of Ministers of every County, who are to consider of the means and ways to settle the Government of the Church, and the rites[21] and ceremonies thereof.

Tuesday the 15th of *February* there was delivered a petition from the County of *Leicester* (near a thousand of that County being come to Town that day) which petition for the most part insisted, as former

[21] Rights.

petitions, upon a Reformation of Abuses in Religion, and putting the Kingdom into a posture of defence, and when after some debate thereupon they gave answer that as much as in them lay, and with what expedition they could, redress should be had.

"The Committee of the Lords and Commons appointed to discover and prevent evil Counsellors about his Majesty, voted certain heads which were reported and voted in the House of Commons.

"1. That his Majesty be desired that all privy counsellors and great officers of state (except such as had their places by inheritance) be removed.

"2. That his Majesty would be pleased to receive none into those places but only such as shall be recommended by the humble advice of both Houses of Parliament.

"3. That all whose names shall be presented to his Majesty by both Houses of Parliament, shall have access to the persons of the King and Queen.

"4. That Mr. *William Murray*, *Endimion Porter*, Lord *Digby*, Mr. *William Crofts*, and Sir *John Winter*, be removed from the persons of the King and Queen, as conceived to give dangerous counsel." [22]

Thursday, 17th *February*, Divers from the county of *Sussex* [23] (near upon three thousand being come to town) delivered petitions to both houses, wherein they prayed, the fortification and guard of the sea coast and forts in those parts, lying naked to an invasion, with other things agreeable to former

---

[22] From *A Continuation of the True Diurnall of Passages in Parliament*.   [23] Ibid.

petitions, as reformation of abuses in the Church, which took up some time to consider of.

That day, "An Act for suppressing of Divers innovations in Churches and Chapels in and about the worship of God, the abolishing of superstitious and idolatrous practices, the better observation of the Lord's Day, and for setting up of preaching and preachers, &c., being read the second time, was committed."[24] I myself did see the coming of these *Sussex* men up *Fish Street Hill.* There was about three thousand of them in all, most of them on horseback.

On *Saturday* the 19th of *February,* "A petition was delivered to the house by the Knights, Gentlemen, Ministers, and freeholders of the County of *Dorset*, against Popish Lords and Prelates, &c., which was read, reported, and thanks given to them for their care and respect of the public good of the kingdom, and for the expression of love to the House."[25]

Praise the Lord, and call upon His Name, declare His Works among the people: Remember His marvellous works that He hath done. He is the Lord our God, His judgements are through all the earth. —1 *Chron.* xvi. 8.

Praise ye the Lord for the avenging of *Israel*, and for the people that offered themselves willingly.— udges v. 2.

As the people of the Lord hath fasted and petitioned to the great God of Heaven and earth for a

---

[24] From *A Continuation of the True Diurnall,* &c.   [25] Ibid.

Reformation both in Church and Commonwealth, so now here are the names of those petitions that I do keep by me for the generations to come, that they may see and behold what our God hath done in the stirring up the people of all counties, and of all sorts, high and low, rich and poor, of both sexes, men and women, old and young, bond and free, both in the cities and countries, for to go up to *Westminster*, to both the Houses of the Honorable Court of Parliament with their petitions for the removing of those great obstacles [26] that lie in the way (as are evil Counsellors about the King, and Popish Lords and Bishops out of the House of Peers, and such like) which hinders that blessed Reformation both of Church and Commonwealth, which we have so long hoped and laboured for.

This is the work of the Lord, and it is marvellous in my eyes.

1. First, this city of *London* petition, in *December* the 11th, 1641, subscribed with the names of above twenty Thousand, by Aldermen, Aldermen's Deputies, Merchants, Common Councilmen, and many others of great rank and fashion to the number of four hundred, who were selected to deliver the petition; all riding out of the City of *London* in fifty coaches or thereabouts, to the Parliament House. The House hearing of their coming, gave admittance to a hundred of them, and did receive the petition of Mr. *Fookes*, Merchant, who related to the Honorable Assembly that he could have brought them as

[26] Obstrocticklcs.

many persons as there were hands to the petition, but that he judged it not fit to come thither in a tumultuous manner. And he did declare some interruption was given them by ill affected persons in *London* about subscribing of hands; and so withdrew themselves. In the interim, the petition was read in the House. And then they were called in again; they being come in, the Honorable Assembly certified unto them that their petition was very lovingly and thankfully accepted of, with reality of affections; promising them that they would take the several branches of their petition into consideration, giving them order (likewise) to present the Names of such ill-affected persons as did hinder or discourage them in seeking to redress their grievance in so lawful a way, and a strict order should be taken with them.

2. In *December* the 20th, 1641, there was a petition of sundry Ministers.

3. In *December* the 23rd, 1641, there was a petition of the Apprentices, and those whose time of Apprenticeship are lately expired in and about the City of *London*.[27]

4. In *January* the 5th, 1641, Divers Knights and Gentlemen and Freeholders of *Buckinghamshire* men met, about five thousand, to go up to *London*. Coming to *Westminster*, they acquainted the House of their petition, and humbly presented it unto them, where afterward they had an Answer given to them respectively.

[27] See Appendix, Note YY.

5. *Essex* petition.
6. *Gloucester* petition.
7. *Devonshire* petition.
8. The City of *Exeter* petition.
9. The County of *Middlesex* petition.
10. The County of *Hertford* petition.
11. The Lord Mayor, Aldermen, and Common Councilmen petition.
12. *Suffolk* and *Deacham* petition.
13. *Langham* in *Essex* petition.

[A gap here occurs in the MS.; the next numbers are as follow.]

58. The petition of the Lords and Commons to the king.
59. *Nottingham's* petition to the king, subscribed by four thousand, five hundred, and forty, hands of Knights, Esquires, &c.
60. The County of *York* petition to the king, April 7, 1642.
61. Petition of both Houses of Parliament to the king, *April* 18, two of them.
62. The petition of the County of *Kent* to the Lords and Commons.
63. The petition of *Cornwall* to the parliament.
64. The petition of *York* to the king.
65. The petition of the County Palatine of *Chester* to the king.
66. The petition of the County of *Stafford* to both Houses of Parliament.
67. The petition of the Kingdom of *Scotland* to his Majesty's Privy Council, 31st of *May* 1642.

68. The petition of the inhabitants of the County of *York* to the king, *June* 3.

69. The petition of the County Palatine of *Lancaster* presented to the king at *York* the last of *May.* Subscribed by 42 Knights and Esquires, 55 Divines, 740 Gentlemen, and of Freeholders and others above 7000.

70. The petition of *Leicester* to the king, *June* the 18th, 1642.

71. The petition of the captains and soldiers in *Essex* to the parliament, *June* 10, 1642.

72. The petition of *Watford*, in the County of *Hertford*, to the Commons.

73. The petition of *Southampton* to the Lords in Parliament, *July* 5.

74. The petition of *Cumberland* and *Westmoreland* to his Majesty, *July* 9.

75. The petition of the captains and soldiers of *Warwick* to the parliament, *July* 12.

76. The petition of the Parliament in *Ireland* to the King's Majesty, *July* 15.

77. The petition of the Lords and Commons in Parliament here to the king, *July* 16.

78. The petition of many thousands of the inhabitants of *Norwich* to the parliament, *July* 25.

79. The petition of the captains and soldiers of *Buckingham* to the parliament.

80. The petition of the parliament to the king at *York*, *July* 29.

81. The petition of the parliament to the king, sent by the Earl of *Holland*, *July* 29.

82. The petition from the County of *Leicester* unto the king, *August* 1.

83. The petition of the County of *Lincoln* to the parliament.

84. The petition of *Kendal* in the County of *Westmoreland* to the parliament.

85. The petition of *Ireland* to the Assembly in *Scotland*, in *July* 1642.

86. The petition of the City of *Chester* to the parliament.

87. Two petitions to the king, one from *Southampton* and from *Suffolk*.

88. The petition of *Nottingham* to the king, *September* 6, 1642.

89. The petition and resolution of *Kent* to the parliament, *August* 30.

90. The petition of the Lords and Commons to the king, *September* 5.

91. The petition of *Chester* to the Commissioners of Array.

92. The petition of the Lords and Commons to the king, *September* 25.

93. The petition of the Commissioners of *Scotland* to the king, *September* 9.

94. A petition of *York* to the Lords and Commons, *June* 3, 1641, with a copy of letter of Sir John Bourchier from *York*.

95. A petition of the knights and gentlemen and freeholders of *York*, unto the king, *November* 25, 1642.

96. A petition of all the Inhabitants of old

Brentford, (to) the Honourable House of Commons, November 27, 1642.

[Three numbers are missing here.]

100. The petition of the County of *Berks* to the king.

101. Two petitions of the Kingdom of *Scotland* to the king, *January* 1642.

102. *England's* petition to their king, *May* the 5th, 1643.

103. The petition of the Lord Mayor, Aldermen, and Common Council to the parliament, *May* the 16th, 1644.

1646. *May* 26. — A Remonstrance from the Lord Mayor, Aldermen, and Common Council, was presented to the parliament, one to the Lords, and another to the Commons, and their petition unto them.

May 29.—The humble petition of the Ministers of the Counties of *Suffolk* and *Essex*, concerning Church Government, presented to the Right Honourable the House of Peers.

June 2.—The Cross Petition of divers Inhabitants in and about *London* (called by the Name of Independent) presented to the Commons of *England* assembled in Parliament.

The Names and Number of those Petitions that I have by me.

14. A thousand poor people's petition.
15. The Women's petition.
16. The fifteen thousand poor porters.
17. The County of *Surrey* petition

18. The County of *Kent* petition.
19. *Suffolk* and part of *Essex* petition.
20. *Huntingdon* petition.
21. *Norfolk* petition.
22. *Cleveland* in *Yorkshire* petition.
23. *Oxford* petition.
24. *Northamptonshire* petition.
25. *Lincoln* petition.
26. *Ipswich* in the County of *Suffolk* petition.
27. *Warwick* and *Coventry* petition.
28. The Seamen of *Ipswich* petition.
29. Silk Throwsters' petition.
30. The County of *Leicester* petition.
31. The County of *Sussex* petition.
32. The County of *Dorset* petition.
33. *New Sarum* and the County of *Wilts*.
34. The County of *Berkshire* petition.
35. The County of *Somerset* petition, with a speech of Sir *Thomas Wroth*.
36. Poor Tradesmen in and about *London* and *Westminster*.
37. The County of *Salop* petition.
38. Petition and Articles Exhibited in Parliament, against Mr. *Fuller*, Vicar of *Giles Cripplegate*.

[One number wanting.]

40. Two petitions of the Lords and Commons to his Majesty, *February* 2, with his Majesty's Answer and his Message, *February* 14.
41. A petition of the Lords and Commons to his Majesty, *February* the 18th.
42. The humble petition and Resolution of both

Houses of Parliament, presented to the King's Majesty, *March* the 1st.

43. The Commons' petition to the king, in defence of Mr. *Pym*.

44. The County *Southampton* petition.

45. The petition of the Parish of *Shoreditch* against *John Squire*, Vicar of the said parish.

46. The County of *Worcester* petition.

47. The County of *Derby* petition.

48. The County of *Bedford* petition.

49. The City of *London* petition.

50. The County of *Rutland* petition to the king.

51. The County of *Lincoln* petition to the king.

52. The petition of the Citizens of *York* to the king.

53. The County of *Rutland* to the Peers and to the House of Commons. A petition.

54. The petition and protestation of all the Bishops and Prelates.

55. The humble petition of the Kingdom of *Ireland*.

56. The petition of both Houses of Parliament, and the petition of the Noblemen in *Ireland* to the King and the King's Answer.

57. The County of *Derby* petition to the king.

XXIV.

OF THE PASSAGES OF SEVERAL THINGS IN THE WEEK IN PARLIAMENT.

Now to return again to some few chief heads of weekly passages in the parliament.

February 21, 1641. *Monday.*—The new Remonstrance[1] and Declaration of the state of the kingdom was read in the House of Commons, setting forth the dangers, obstructions and fears the kingdom now labours under, the discouragement, discountenancing, and displacing of well affected Members of State for their free, ingenious, and clear discovering of Delinquents. The same Declaration sets forth likewise the Remedies of these evils to be these: That his Majesty would be pleased to remove all his Privy Council, and make choice of such again as should be humbly recommended to him by the advice of his Parliament; to discover and declare those that have of late infused evil counsels into his gracious ears; to remove the Popish Lords out of the House of Peers, and from the privilege of giving their votes

---

[1] "There was drawn up a Declaration of the State of the Kingdom by Mr. *Pym*, and by the appointment of the House he went up with it to the Lords, consisting of twelve heads, being the summe of the generall causes of our grievances that we groane under, and twenty-foure remedies for prevention of the same, and a worthy and applauded Speech made by him in illustration thereof."—*A True Diurnall.*

or suffrage there, and that such good Members and well affected persons as have been zealous and serviceable in discovering Delinquents, might be admitted to their place and offices again.

This day there was a petition drawn up by divers great Citizens to be presented to the Parliament, and another to his Majesty, disapproving of the Election made by the Common Council, according to the order of the house, for the ordering of the militia of the City; which Election was confirmed by the parliament; but now these citizens petition against it, desiring the Lord Mayor might be Lieutenant, to order the Militia according to the ancient custom. This petition was found with one Mr. *Gardner*, a rich citizen, having about some three hundred hands to it. And the next day this Mr. *Gardner* was sent to the Tower.

Wednesday, February the 23rd, the Monthly Fast was solemnly to be kept over the whole land. And the Lords and Commons kept this day's Fast at *Margaret's* in Westminster, Mr. *Calamy* and Mr. *Marshall* again preaching before them.[2]

---

[2] See *Perfect Diurnall*. The Rev. Edward Calamy, B.D., of Pembroke-Hall, Cambridge, was driven out of the diocese of Ely by Bishop Wren, and subsequently appointed to Aldermanbury, where he became very popular. He refused a bishoprick, and died of grief on seeing the ruins of London after the Great Fire. He was one of the Smectymnuans. See Neal's *Puritans*, vol. iv.

Stephen Marshall, B.D., the celebrated incumbent of Finchingfield, Essex, was born at Godmachester, and graduated at Cambridge. He was frequently referred to by the Long Parliament in matters of religion. He was buried with due solemnity in Westminster Abbey, but at the Restoration his body was dug up again, with those of Pym and Strode

Thursday.³—A bill was read in the House of Commons for attainting of Sir *Edward Herbert*, the King's Attorney General, of great misdemeanours, for drawing a scandalous paper, containing articles of high treason against the Lord *Kimbolton*, a Member of the House of Peers, and against the five Members of the House of Commons, by which bill the said Sir *Edward Herbert* forfeits all his goods and chattels and the profits of his lands for his life, and Imprisonment during the king and parliament's pleasure.

"This day there was a petition of his Majesty's loving subjects in the City of *Sarum* and County of *Wilts*, delivered with thousands of the hands of the Gentry and others there inhabiting to it, and another to the Lords, shewing much affection to our Commonwealth, redress of grievances had, and aid to them that lie languishing, whose throats are exposed to the sword of the savage and barbarous foe."⁴

Friday, February 25.⁵—" In the Court of Wards there sat a Committee concerning popish reliques,

---

(two of the Five Members), May, the historian of the Long Parliament, Elizabeth Cromwell, mother of the Protector, and Elizabeth Claypole, his daughter; and some others. See Neal's *Puritans*, vol. iv.; London. Mr. Marshall was also one of the authors of Smectymnuus (a word composed of the names of the authors), a treatise published in reply to Bishop Hall's 'Humble Remonstrance to the High Court of Parliament' in defence of Episcopacy.

³ Rushworth assigns Saturday, Jan. 15, as the date of the Impeachment of Sir Edward Herbert.

⁴ From *A Continuation of the True Diurnall*, &c.

⁵ From *True Diurnall of Passages in Parliament*, No. 7.

as the Book of Canons, Crucifixes, Organs, and Pictures in Churches; it is ordered by the House that betwixt this time a perfixed[6] day of *May* all these reliques shall be taken down; and in case of the Churchwardens' neglect therein, any 2 Justices of Peace, within the country, shall have power to execute the parliament's commands."[7]

"This day [Saturday, February 26] were letters presented to Mr. *Pym* and Mr. *Hollis*, which was delivered by a Merchant of *London*, that they received intelligence in letter from beyond the sea, that the French Fleet is ready to set sail, and manned with French and Irish, which is suspected to be for the Rebels' assistance."[8]

Saturday, February 26th.—The petition of the Lord Mayor and Aldermen and other citizens of *London*, was taken into consideration, in which it did appear that this petition was plotted, contrived, and solicited by some malignant persons, intending thereby to breed differences and dissensions in their fellow citizens to the disturbance of the peace and quiet of the City, by proofs it appeareth that Mr. Recorder advised the framing and presenting of the said petition. That Master *Bradburn* and Mr. *Binion*[9] were earnest solicitors and promoters

---

[6] *i.e.* predetermined.—*Halliwell.*

[7] ". . . . some were so zealous in taking down Crosses and Crucifixes, as they took down the *Sign of Charing Cross*, being the sign of a Tavern, near that place where *Charing Cross* stood."—Rushworth's *Historical Collections.*

[8] From *True Diurnall of Passages*, &c.

[9] "One or two most pragmaticall spirits among them, were chiefe agents and active instruments openly and audaciously appearing and per-

thereof, who have now deserted the same, and craved pardon for such their indiscretion.

On *Monday*, the last of *February*, and *Tuesday*, *March* 1, the Lords sent a Message to his Majesty for a Militia of the kingdom, but he will not grant nor yield unto [it], and some other things they do request of the king for his own safeguard, and the good of the whole kingdom, which his Majesty will not consent nor condescend unto. So that now this is a heavy time with us.[10]

Wednesday, March the 2nd.—There was brought to the House of Commons a petition with about two hundred hands to it, of those citizens that subscribed to the petition, for the ordering of the Militia of the City by the Lord Mayor, declaring their hearty sorrow for that business. And that they had no hand in the framing or advising of that petition, but were drawn to subscribe thereunto by the other citizens, desiring to be excused for their error therein. To which petition they had answer given them by the Speaker, that the House of Commons will take care to make a difference between the Authors and chief Actors in that petition, and those that were drawn to subscribe thereto.

"That afternoon [Wednesday, March 2] they received a petition from *Staffordshire*, setting forth

sisting in it, namely, one Mr. *Binion*, a silkman in Cheapside."—Vicar's *Jehovah Jireh*; London, 1644. The author goes on, however, to speak of Mr. Binion as adhering to his " foresaid insolencies and misdemeanours " and being, in consequence, fined 3000*l.*, as " an example of terrour to the rest." [10] See *True Diurnall*.

that they were in such fear of the papists rising in that country, that every man was constrained to stand upon his guard. And that they durst not go to Church unarmed. And it was moved that this petition might be also sent to his Majesty." [11]

Thursday, March 3rd.—"They received a petition from *Worcestershire*, with many thousand hands to it, giving thanks for the happy and constant concurrence of both houses, and to desire the putting of the kingdom into a present posture of defence, that Delinquents may be suddenly brought to condign punishment, the votes of Popish lords taken away, and that Religion may be suddenly settled according to the Rule of God's word. This petition the Committee received with many thanks, promising to take the same into consideration in due time." [12]

Friday "there was a petition brought to the House from *Berkshire* and another from *Norfolk, Norwich,* and *Lynn*, with many Thousand hands to them, tending to the same effect as the former. To which they had answer given to them as to the former.[13]

Saturday "there was an ordinance of parliament drawn up and voted for the ordering of the Militia of the kingdom by the authority of both Houses, which was sent to the Lords, and they agreed in it," [14] and to take order for the sending of the same presently to his Majesty.

Monday the 7th of *March*, "there was brought a petition to the House with ten thousand hands to it, of the Inhabitants of the County of

[11] From *A Perfect Diurnall.* [12] Ibid. [13] Ibid. [14] Ibid.

Salop, excusing their backwardness, in their presenting of it no sooner, occasioned by their living at so great a distance from the parliament, desiring according to the former petitions, that the votes of the popish lords may be taken away, delinquents brought to condign punishment, and the kingdom presently put into a posture of defence, which petition was very well approved of by the Commons." [15]

Wednesday, March 9th.—They received a petition from the County of *Lemster*, wherein they prayed that the accusers of the Members of the House, being a breach of Parliament, might be made examples; Whereupon the House giving them many thanks for their great care, consulted about sending a petition to his Majesty, containing the same.

Thursday, March the 10th.—" There was a petition brought to the Lords, and another to the Commons, from the Inhabitants of *Southampton*, tending to this effect, That his Majesty may be petitioned by both Houses to reside near the parliament with the prince, and that the kingdom may be put into a present posture of defence both by sea and land, giving hearty thanks for the happy concurrence that hath already been between both Houses in the settling of many worthy things in this government." [16]

That day the House of Commons received a petition from *Hampshire*, it importing as former petitions, for the Relief of *Ireland*, and it was then sent up to the Lords to consider of it.

[15] From *A Perfect Diurnall*.   [16] Ibid.

On *Monday* the 14th of *March* were read several Bills in the House of Commons, one for restraining the corporal bowing at the Name of Jesus, being merely an outward badge of Popery. Another Bill for the abolishing popish relics, as the Cross in Baptism, Organs, singing any part of Divine service, Candlesticks and Basons to be removed from the Communion Table, and the Communion Table to be placed in the Body of the Church. Likewise all inscriptions upon Tombs and monuments, importing any ways to Superstition, as praying or invocating upon Saints or Angels, to be defaced or demolished, also all crosses in and about Churches. And this to be done by the Churchwardens in every parish, and in default or neglect of the Churchwardens' duty herein required, the two next Justices of Peace to see the same done, according to the true intent and meaning of this Bill, and if both the Churchwardens and Justices neglect the execution thereof, then the King's Attorney for every Circuit is to make enquiry thereof by the Grand Jury, and upon finding them negligent or unwilling therein, to prefer an information in His Majesty's name against them as Delinquents, and so to pay Fine and Ransom according to the further Declaration of the said Bill.

The same day in the House of Commons a Committee sat touching Recusants, where one Mr. *Bradshaw* and some others of quality, were examined touching an information given against them of their combination together, for the making of a certain number of Balls of wildfire, to set on fire some towns in *Lancashire*, and having correspondence with the Rebels, who [were] to land some forces out of *Ireland* on that coast, upon the executing of such design.

"Then there was a petition delivered to the House of Commons from the County of *Rutland*, humbly craving a sudden course to be taken with the papists inhabiting there, of whom they were very much afraid, both in respect of their number, as also by reason of threatening words, daily proceeding from them tc their terror, insomuch that without some speedy remedy, it is in danger of a commotion, by reason of the discord and variance daily arising betwixt. This petition was signed unto by ten thousand housekeepers' hands, and presented to the House by Sir *Edward Nicholls*." [17]

This 14th of *March* was delivered to the House, The humble petition of divers Baronets, Knights, Esquires, Gentlemen, Ministers, Freeholders, and others of the County of *Derby* [18] to the number of seven thousand seventy and seven, Which gave thanks to both Houses for their great care of the kingdom's safety in disposal of the Militia, a settlement of the Religion establishment, with other things concurring thereunto. Which being read, was thankfully accepted by the House, and special order given for the recording of it, with the petitions of several other counties.[19]

---

[17] From *A True Diurnall*.   [18] Darby.
[19] See *A True Diurnall*.

Tuesday the 15th of *March*, there was presented to the House of Commons a petition from the Knights, Esquires, Gentry and Commons, Inhabitants of the County of *Cambridge*, for which they were received with thanks.[20]

"There was another petition, from the high Sheriff, Knights, Gentry, and yeomen of the County of *Bedford*, one to the Lords, and another to the Commons, presented by Sir *John Burgoyne*,[21] Baronet, who was entrusted with the delivery of this petition; [he] had further direction personally to declare their particular thanks to the Lords for their concurrence with the House of Commons in the late ordinance concerning the militia, together with a desire that the same may speedily be put in execution forthwith, especially as for the rest in general. Their Lordships returned them hearty thanks.

"It was ordered by the Commons' House that Master Speaker, in the Name of the House, shall take particular notice, and give the Gentlemen of *Bedfordshire* thanks for their desire of the King's return, and of their desire to have the ordinance of the Militia speedily put in execution. There were above two thousand hands to it:"[22] I myself did see I think, above two thousand of these men come riding from *Finsbury fields*, four in a rank, with their protestations in their hats.

On *Wednesday* the 16th of *March*, "there was a petition delivered from the Counties of *Hampshire*

---

[20] See *A Perfect Diurnall*.   [21] Burgon.
[22] From *A True Diurnall*.

and *Berkshire*, jointly, requesting that the parliament would take into consideration the great hindrances made against their good endeavours, because of the popish lords' contradiction. They therefore most humbly craved a speedy course might be had, that their votes in either House might be taken away."[23]

Thursday the House received a petition "from the town of *Cambridge* for the placing of a Lecturer there."[24]

Friday the 18th of *March*, upon the meeting of both Houses, there was a petition delivered from the City of *London*, complaining of a surreptitious copy of their petition (delivered to the Houses in *February* last) printed and dispersed through the kingdom, by which they conceived themselves much scandaled, and desired the Authors thereof might receive condign punishment. Which being read was well approved of by both Houses.[25]

"Then there was a petition brought to the Lords, and another to the Commons, from the County of *Cornwall*, wherein they request that his Majesty may be petitioned by both Houses, to reside near his parliament with the Prince, and that the kingdom may be put in a posture of defence, both by sea and land, giving hearty thanks for the happy concurrence that hath already been betwixt both houses, in the settling of many worthy things in this Government."[26]

[23] From *A True Diurnall*. [24] Ibid. [25] See *A Perfect Diurnall*.
[26] From *A True Diurnall*.

Saturday, March 19th, " came news to the House that the French king hath sixty sail of men-of-war at sea, hovering between the coast of *Devonshire* and *Britain*, manned with many thousand of land soldiers."[27] As likewise forty thousand Danes, to be landed at *Hull*, to serve the King.

[27] From *A True Diurnall.*

XXV.

OF THE PLOTS OF THE WICKED AGAINST THE GODLY.

Now first to begin with that great Grand Plot in *Ireland* that hath been in some years a plotting, for you know the (common) proverb is—

> "He that will *England* win,
> Must first with *Ireland* begin."[1]

The Lord Deputy *Wentworth* (in his life time) disarmed the Subjects there, as I have in some part shewed you before.

[1] A correspondent of 'Notes and Queries' says:—"The original saying is to be found in Hall's and Holinshed's *Chronicles*, and is also quoted in Shakspeare's *King Henry V.* Hall gives it at the conclusion of the Earl of Westmoreland's speech, as 'the old auncient prouerb used by our forefathers, which saieth—

> 'He that will Fraunce wynne,
> Must with Scotlande first begyn.'

"The earliest reading of the modern version known to us occurs in Fynes Moryson's Itinerary, 1617, fol. part ii. p. 3, where, under the year 1577, he tells us that 'religion rather than liberty first began to be made the cloke of ambition, and the Roman locusts, to maintain the pope's usurped power, breathed everywhere fire and sword, and were not ashamed to proclaim and promise Heaven for a reward to such cutthroats as should lay violent hands on the sacred persons of such princes as opposed their tyranny. Amongst which, this famous Queen (Elizabeth) being of greatest power, and most happy in success against them, they not only left nothing unattempted against her sacred person and her crown of England, but were encouraged by the blind zeal of the ignorant Irish to popery, or animated by an old prophecy—

> 'He that will England win,
> Must with Ireland first begin,' &c."

And their first design and plot was to take the castle in the City of *Dublin*: For one *Friday* the 22nd of *October* 1641, Owen *O'Connally*,[2] servant to *John Clotworthy*, at nine of the clock in the night, came and discovered a plot for the seizing of the Castle of *Dublin*, and making themselves Masters of the whole kingdom.

The Lords of the Council caused all the parts of the city to be strongly guarded. And in the morning we went to search for the Lord *Macguire* at his lodging, from whence we found he was departed, but searching narrowly in his lodging we found several skenes, headless hatchets and hammers, in abundance, and in the end we found him secretly hid in a cockloft.

The Discovery of the Plot.

Owen O'Connally, who is servant to Sir *John Clotworthy*, came to Dublin to the lodging of *Hugh Ogmack*[4] his friend, and *O'Connally* with his friend going to the lodging of the Earl of *Macguire*, understood there had been great store of Noblemen and strangers, but they were all gone abroad, whereupon they returned back again to the lodging of the said *Ogmack*, where *O'Connally* had not been any long space, but *Ogmack* declares to him a plot which

---

[2] Ockanellee.
[3] Hugh Oge Mac-Mahon, Esq. (Grandson to the Traitor *Tyrone*), a Gentleman of a good Fortune in the County of *Monaghan*. . . . This Mac-Mahon had been abroad, and served the King of *Spain* as a Lieutenant-Colonel.—*Rushworth*.

was intended, swearing that *O'Connally* should not go out of his house till it had been executed, which was, that the Jesuits, popish priests, and other papists, together with two sects of Irish, and amongst the rest the said *Hugh Ogmack*, and *Bryan O'Neale*, with others, should have come and seized upon the Castle at *Dublin*, and the Earl of *Macguire* should be governor thereof; which when they had attained unto, they should have shot at the chimneys, and by that means have tried if they could have brought the City in subjection; but if shooting at chimneys could not prevail, then they should have shot down their houses about their ears, and at one hour, and one moment of time, to have murdered all the English and Protestants in the kingdom of *Ireland*, and to have murdered the two Lords Chief Justices, and all the Privy Council of *Dublin*, and at the same time to have seized on all his Majesty's Castles, forts, and magazines throughout the whole kingdom, and all persons that should be refractory to have destroyed with the sword... *O'Connally* finding his opportunity, leaped over the pales in the yard, and made an escape, and went to Sir *John Burlacy* and Sir *William Parsons*, and discovered the whole matter.

Now amongst other remarkable deliverances of divers and sundry persons from time to time by the power of the Almighty, let this take your serious thoughts, for one, not of the meanest, but among the greatest, this party, *Owen O'Connally*, who was servant to Sir *John Clotworthy*, being suspected by some of the conspirators, who were sworn to secrecy therein, to have discovered this plot, by his divers times persuading them to desist from their devilish intentions, telling them what a heinous matter it was to cause rebellion in their native country, and the dangerous evils that might happen to their own persons and their present estates, and their posterity after them. These conspirators, finding this party cold in the business, one among the rest breaks out in a passion, and swore to the rest of the company that the aforesaid party had revealed their plot, and, without any more advice, pulls forth a pistol (for all of them have swords and pistols) which was charged with a brace of bullets, and set it to this *Owen's* breast, intending to shoot him through at that instant, which was prevented by the Divine power in that the flint did not strike fire. Some of the company, being affrighted at this sudden assault, asked this party, *Randal*, that would have shot him, how he could prove that *Owen* had spoken of it to any party, or in any kind betrayed their cause, to which *Randal* could give no certain answer, but only this, that he did surmise, and his heart did think so. "Nay," then said the rest, "you are to blame to offer this, as you have done." This, no sooner appeased, but another in the same passion, and of the aforesaid company, seconds the former's motion, whose name was *Nicholas*, who urged *Owen O'Connally* that he was the man, and only he that the cause was betrayed. Which the aforesaid *Owen* denying, with many protestations and with manlike courage. Nevertheless, the said *Cusock* made at

him with another pistol charged with a brace of
bullets also, but, whether the powder in the pan
was damp, or the flint not good, thanks be to God,
he missed his intent; this was the second deliverance. Now being still in the aforesaid house, and
not suffered to stir, but watched and guarded for
fear of his escape, words grew, insomuch that a
party amongst them ran a tilt at him with his
naked sword, which was put aside by one in the
company who was behind him, and stayed his arm.
To be short; ten or twelve hours being thus spent,
about ten or eleven o'clock at night . . . . *Owen*
having an opportunity, leaps over the pale in the
yard, twice his height, and over a brick wall as
high, and so into the high way, and runs into the
city, which was half a mile distant from the house,
and there reveals the whole plot to Sir *John Burlacy*, and other Justices of the Peace, who forthwith
raised the city, and came to the place, and found
some of these conspirators, which they apprehended,
others of them ran away and hid themselves; some
of them, being examined, partly through fear, others
to get favour, confessed they were to have an army
of seventeen thousand from several parts of *Ireland*,
which should be all papists and Jesuits, that should
surprise all the castles and forts, but especially the
castle of *Dublin*, cut the throats of the chiefest
noblemen, gentry, and others of that kingdom that
were there present; and this, being thus discovered
by *Owen O'Connally*, he was dispatched with letters
into *England* to make known to the Lords now pre-

sent in Parliament what he had discovered, who, for his good service and fidelity therein, the honourable House hath thought fit to give the said *Owen* five hundred pounds and two hundred a year for ever, and to be preferred to one of the chief places under the Deputy in *Ireland*.

A Gunpowder Plot in Ireland for the blowing up of the chiefest Church in Dublin, when the Lords and others were at sermon on the Lord's Day, October the 31st, 1641.

In a letter from *Ireland* from the Lords Chief Justices, declaring that the papists and popish priests had undermined the chiefest Church in *Dublin*, and there placed great store of faggots, and barrels of gunpowder, intending, when the Lords and Privy Council in *Ireland* had been at Church, to have blown them all up at once, and at that time to have set upon all the rest of the Protestants in *Dublin*, and to have massacred them, had they not been miraculously prevented.

The first rising was in the county *Fermanagh*, the Lord *Macguire* being the chief Agent in their rebellion, who lived about thirteen miles from *Belturbet*, northward towards *Enniskillen*, which Lord *Macguire* is since taken, and now prisoner in the Castle at *Dublin;* he is of the blood of that great traitor *Macguire*, the General of *Tyrone's* army, that great rebel to Queen *Elizabeth*.

[The treachery of *Mark Davo*[4]] "is now discovered, for, upon the 20th of December, 1641, he marched out, with the assistance of Lord *Care* with two thousand foot, and two thousand horse. They marched towards *Feather*, about ten miles from him, a walled town, most inhabited with Irish, and as soon as he came thither with his forces, the gates were presently opened; but as soon as he was entered, they presently massacred the Protestants. And, taking Mr. *Low*, the Minister, they cut out his tongue, flaying the skin off his head and back, saying that they would make a drum-head of his skin, that the heretics might hear the sound of it; and hanged his quarters on the gates."[5]

December the 10th, 1641.—About the space of six miles from *Dublin*, there is a town inhabited with Irish, called *Rockall*. About a mile from *Rockall* dwelleth one *Patrick Locke*.[6] He hath also, since the first intent of rising of the rebels in *Ireland*, entertained fourscore men, who by the rebels have been set on work to vault the said hill of *Rockall* round about. The passage over this hill is a great road, through which they pass from *Dublin* to the chiefest part of the country towards *Munster*, so that, when the King's Majesty's army had been come into *Ireland* from *England* to relieve the Protestants against the rebels, this hill was the direct and ready road for them to pass over in

---

[4] See page 302, Vol. I.
[5] From *The Happiest News from Ireland*, &c.
[6] See page 302, Vol. I.

the valley whereof, which they had digged for that purpose.

William Raster, that was taken by Col. *Carot Topey*, discovered this plot, and confessed that their purpose was, if they could take *Athy* and the castle, then they knew that when the King's forces came to *Dublin*, they would immediately move that way, because the way doth lie directly over the said hill *Rockall*, and with the said powder in the hill they had determined to blow them as they passed by.

And he discovered that Mr. *Ochashen*, of *Azabe*, in *Queen's* County, together with Sir *Florence Fitzpatrick*, of *Castletown*, should have come by night with five thousand armed men to the Fort of *Leise*, and lie as soldiers that were to ward[7] the papists within had agreed, and were appointed to let in certain company of the rebels, appointed for that purpose to burn and batter down the town.

Hereupon Captain *Picket* went forth to meet that company with five hundred men, who fell upon them, and slew three or four hundred of the rebels, and the rest flew into the woods.

Himself sustained the loss of sixty men slain and dangerously hurt.

Now, all these plots in *Ireland* are but one plot against *England*, for it is *England* that is that fine, sweet bit which they so long for, and their cruel teeth so much water at. And therefore these blood-thirsty papists do here among us in *England* plot what

---

[7] *i. e.* to keep guard.

may be for our overthrow, to bring in their damnable superstition and idolatry amongst us. I will give a touch of some of their devilish plots and designs among us, as here followeth, that all the world may see that they are of their father the devil, for he hath been a murderer from the beginning.—*John* viii. 44.

A bloody plot brought to light by God's providence, wherein was intended a great insurrection and rising of the papists in divers counties of this kingdom.[8]

On *Thursday, October* the 18th, 1641, one Mr. *Beal*, overheard their discourse, which is related according to the true copy by him presented to the Parliament. On *Monday*, about one or two o'clock in the afternoon, this Mr. *Beale*, walking in the fields beyond the Pest-house,[9] hearing the discourse, perceived their names the one to be *George*, the other *Philip*. But this plot being too tedious, as some other plots and designs will be, I wanting both time and paper, will commend you to those copies at large lying by me.

In *November* the 12th, 1641, another great discovery of a damnable gunpowder plot, at *Ragland* Castle, in *Herefordshire*; the chief agent in this hellish plot is the Earl of *Worcester*. It was found out by one *John Davis*. I will give you a hint of this plot. This *Davis* saith when he was in the castle, in the Earl's stable, the groom of the stable

---

[8] See Appendix, Note CCC.
[9] In the parish of St. Luke's, Old Street.

shewed him to the number of threescore horses prepared for war. After he had shewed him all in that stable, he led him into a vault under the ground which went round about the castle, where was made an obscure stable, in which he perceived about twelve light horses. He was going further into that stable underground, to have seen the rest of the horses there, which was, as he saith, about forty, but it was so dark, that he was fearful to go any further, for fear of danger.

In another place underground, he shewed him furniture for about six or seven score of horse. In which place was furniture also for about two thousand men, with great store of match and powder, and other ammunition belonging to war, in abundance. One of these stables I guess to be about sixscore feet in length, and twenty-four feet in breadth. "He told me," saith he, "that his master, the Earl of *Worcester*, gave notice privately that any man who would be entertained should have sixteen pence a day, good pay, from him in case they would be true to him, and to press me, as I conceived, to have some desire to serve him, he told me that his master had at this time seven hundred men under pay; but I, being nothing at all pleased with this discourse, hasted away to return to my own business at home."

Upon this discovery of this plot, the Parliament hath caused a strong guard of men to be set about the Earl of *Worcester's* house, here in *London*. As also they have caused another strong guard to be set about the French Ambassador's house in *Lincoln's-Inn-Fields*, supposing he hath some hand in this business, and to be a chief agent in this damnable plot.

The 16th of *November*, 1641, there was a cruel and wicked plot discovered about the city of *London*, which was intended against some of the chief members of the High Court of Parliament, and brought to light by a religious man. Therefore it was commanded by the House of Commons that great search should be made for the finding out of two Frenchmen, who were supposed to be the chief agents in this wicked design. This that I have now written of, I will shew more plainly :

The information of *Thomas Beal*, a tailor, (which I named before) living in *White Cross Street*, delivered in Parliament on *Tuesday, November* the 16th, That he, on the Sabbath day last, late at night, passing through *Moorfields*, near the city of *London*, overheard certain fellows talking and whispering together about their intended plot, the one of them saying that he had received forty shillings in hand to murder divers persons, eminent in the House of Parliament, which he would shortly accomplish, and another of them made report that he had also received a larger sum to do the like enterprise upon some persons of the higher House, which pretended plot of theirs, they verily expected should have taken effect on the *Thursday* following, had not the providence of Almighty God prevented those bloody designs of those cruel and merciless papists (but they, espying the man in the dark, fearing by him to be discovered, made at him to have killed him, had not God, of His mercy, prevented them, by his escaping from them). In which conference of theirs, he also overheard them to whisper about some great plots or treacheries in *Wales*, now intended against *England*, and that the three next shires adjoining to *Ragland Castle* were lately come in with all their forces to the assistance of the Earl of *Worcester*.

And the said young man, coming before the Parliament house, really and truly did relate the said former passages with great modesty and honest confidence, moreover alleging that they intended the murder of many Protestant Lords, with many other gentlemen, such as Mr. *Pym* and the like, and the papists in *Wales* intend to seize into their hands all the strongholds of *Cheshire* and *Lancashire*, with the adjacent parts, And that in that hurly burly and combustion, the plot was laid and contrived that by the papists at the same instant, the City of *London* should have been surprized, and all the Protestants' throats cut.

Upon which relation the Houses of Parliament sat very late on *Monday* night last, and the Lords and others of both Houses were conducted to their lodgings and houses by most of the trained Bands in *Middlesex* the same night. There was great search made for the apprehending of the persons of Father *Jones* and Father *Andrews*. There was an order made by the High Court of Parliament that all papists throughout *England* should be disarmed, which command the private officers in *Cheshire* went about to obey; but the papists there were so resolute that they told them plainly they would not be disarmed; which answer being carried to the Mayor of the City, he commanded the Train bands to go search, each one charging his Musket with a Bullet, and those papists which would not yield presently, to shoot them. The next day, being the 20th of *November* 1641, the papists gathered themselves together to the Lord *Toomes* his house. The chief leader was one Mr. *Henry Starkey*, and in the night some of the watch discovered fifteen in arms, battering down the City walls. The watchmen went in the city and cried " Treason, treason," upon which the Citizens presently did arise, the Train bands presently in readiness, but 13 of these Traitors escaped away, but two of them were taken and confessed that the others were run to the Lord *Toomes* his house, who, being pursued, were taken, were carried to prison. And a strong guard being left at the Lord *Toomes* his house, that none of the papists might issue out there. So soon as those fifteen were laid fast, the Train bands came to the Lord *Toomes* his house, and commanded the door to be opened, but they were denied to have any entrance. Then ten of the Train bands discharged their Muskets, at which the aforesaid Lord made an escape by a postern door, which opens into the fields. The Train band, most of them, went into the house and searched it, wherein they were all like to have been slain, for coming into a private wood house there stood fifty Papists with Muskets ready charged, and so soon as they saw the Train band they discharged altogether, and slew twenty-five of the Protestants, and then ran out at a back door, but being met by the rest of the Train band which were without, between whom grew a bloody skirmish, and nineteen of the Papists were slain, and *Starkey*, their leader, was wounded and sent to prison. All being still, the aforesaid *Starkey*, the leader of the Rebels, was examined, being ready to die by reason of his wounds; who confessed what their intents were, being urged thereunto by the Lord *Toomes* to have beaten down privately the greatest part of the City walls, that so the Papists in *Lancashire* and *Cheshire* should have had an advantage to use the Protestants as they pleased themselves; and so he died.[10]

A Plot against Norwich to burn the City.

Upon the 27th day of *November*, there was a great uproar in *Norwich* concerning the Papists arising there, they being intended to burn the whole city without any remorse, two being appointed privily for the same purpose, one to begin at one end of the City, and the second at the other

---

[10] For details of this plot, and of the following one against Norwich, see "Foure Wonderfull, Bloudy, and Dangerous Plots discovered, and brought to light, by God's Providence. London. Printed for *John Gilbert*, 1642. 4to. pp. 8."—*King's Pamphlets.*

end. The one was discovered being about to set fire to a thatched house, the other he set the house on fire joining to *High Bridge* Street, which was burnt to the ground, to the great astonishment of the whole City.

A Plot against London by Colonel LUNSFORD *the Papist.*

When Sir *William Balfour,* Lieutenant of the Tower, went to *Ireland,* having a great estate there in great danger to be lost; then Colonel *Lunsford* he obtained letters of many popish lords, and so did get of the king to be elected to be lieutenant of the Tower. Then the papists' resolutions were thus moulded; when as Colonel *Lunsford* should have free liberty in the Tower, divers of the guard should be suborned, having great sums of money given them to conceal their counsels, and about the dead time of the night they should place the ordnance lower, and being charged should incontinently blow up the city. About which time of the night the other papists would provide a sudden Army, and sufficient number of men to set *Westminster* and the Parliament house on fire. And at the same time they would provide shipping for the Archbishop of *Canterbury,* Bishop *Wren,* and many other popish Doctors, who should have been all transported into *Spain.* Their design was sealed with an oath that every one should be constant to *Rome,* and put this new hatched conspiracy into execution with all possible care and expedition. Whereupon eight of the guard were sworn to their machination, the ordnance were in agitation to be suddenly placed lower in the tower against the City, and shipping was in great preparation for the Arch-prelate and the other popish Doctors. But mark the successless event of their wicked intentions, and consider the miraculous providence of the Mighty and Almighty God, who delivered us from their cruel hands. The Apprentices having great suspicion (as indeed they had great cause) of some treacherous plot which might ensue upon the City, did forthwith rise, and presented themselves unto the parliament, totally and universally petitioning against the papists, and the Colonel that was a papist in the Tower, shewing what great danger the City was in. Thus they went to *Westminster* to the parliament house three or four days together, and were then unanimously resolved to pull him out of the Tower, which induced the king and parliament immediately to displace him.[11]

A Great Conspiracy of the Papists against the Worthy Members of both Houses of Parliament; and also, against the City of London, and generally the whole Kingdom. Discovered by divers Wicked and Bloody Letters, which by God's Providence came to light, and was read in the House of Commons, the 10th and 11th of January 1641.

" To the worshipful and honourable friend, *Orlando Bridgeman*, Esq., &c., Burgess of the parliament, at his Chamber in the Temple :—

---

[11] See *Rushworth*, part iii. vol. i. pp. 459–462.

"We are your friends, these are to advise you to look to yourself, and to advise others of my lord of *Strafford's* friends, to take heed lest they be involved in the common calamity; our advice is to be gone, to pretend business till the great hubbub be passed; withdraw, lest you suffer among the puritans. We entreat you to send away this enclosed letter to Mr. *Anderton*, enclosed to some trusty friend that it may be carried safely without suspicion, for it concerns the common safety. So desire your friends in *Covent Garden, Jan. 4.*"

"To the worshipful and my much honoured friend, Mr. *Anderton*—

"Sir—Although many designs have been defeated, yet that of *Ireland* holds well. And now our last plot works as hopeful as that of *Ireland*. We must bear with something in Man, his will is strong enough, as long as he is fed with hopes. The woman is true to us; her counsel about her is very good. I doubt not but to send you by the next very joyful news. For the present, our rich enemies, *Pym, Hampden, Strode, Hollis, Haslerigg*, are blemished, challenged for no less than Treason; before I write next, we doubt not but to have them in the Tower, or their heads from their shoulders. The Solicitor, and *Fiennes* and *Earle* we must serve with the same sauce. And in the House of the Lords, *Mandeville* is touched, but *Essex, Warwick, Say, Brooke*, and *Paget* must follow, or else we shall not be quiet. *Falkland* and *Culpepper* are friends to our side. The protestants and puritans are so divided, that we need not fear them; the protestants in a greater part will join with us, while the puritan is suppressed. If we can bring them under, the protestants will either fall in with us generally, or else, if they do not, they are so indifferent, that either by fair or foul means we shall be able to command them.

"The mischievous Londoners and Apprentices may do us some hurt for present, but we need not much fear them, they do nothing orderly, but tumultuously. Therefore we doubt not but to have them under command after one brunt, for our party is strong in the city, especially *Holborn*, the *New Buildings*, and *Westminster*. We are afraid of nothing but the Scots appearing again; but we have made a party there, at the King's last being there, which will hold their hands behind them, while we act our parts at home. Let us acquit ourselves like men, for our Religion and Country, now or never. The King's heart is a protestant, but our friends can persuade him, and make him believe anything; he hates the puritan party, and is made irreconcilable to that side. So that the Sun, the Moon, and Stars are for us. There are no less than twenty thousand Ministers in *England*, the greater half are for us, to avenge the Bishops' dishonour. Let our friends be encouraged; the work is more than half done.

"Your Servant,
"*R. E.*"

Another Letter sent to a Papist of London.

The Grand Committee of the Parliament sitting at *Grocers' Hall*,[12] about the weighty affairs of the state of the Kingdom, there was notice brought in to them of a letter directed out of *Ireland* to a great personage of this city, a papist; which letter by God's providence coming into the hands of a woman, and the housekeeper of this papist, upon great suspicion of some evil accidents that might thereby happen, caused the said letter to be opened, whereby by the great providence of God the secret thereof was disclosed. The contents thereof was to this effect :—

"Worthy Sir—Out of the care of your welfare, I make bold to advertise you for your good, that you would be pleased speedily to convey yourself and family out of the City, and that you repair as far northward as conveniently you may, for there is a terrible and sudden blow expected to be given shortly against the City of *London;* for though I am of opinion, the King's Majesty be a good Protestant in his heart, yet I am persuaded that by the persuasions of the Queen's Majesty, and the advice of the Catholic Lords and other Gentlemen, the wished design may take full effect. The truth of which premisses was delivered to the Court of

---

[12] See "The Jesuites' Plot discovered, against the Parliament and City of *London* very lately. . . . With the just cause of the Parliament removing from *Westminster* to *Grocers' Hall* the 18 and 19 day of *Januarie.*" Printed 1641; small 4to. pp. 8.—*King's Pamphlets.*

Aldermen, and Common Council of the City of *London* from the Committee."

There was a letter brought to Mr. *Pym*, with an odious plaster, taken from a plague sore, saying, "If this will not do, then a dagger shall;" and, as I did hear very credibly, one standing by him, looking over his shoulder upon it, took a conceit[13] at it, and sickened, and died presently.[14]

[13] *i. e.* apprehension.—*Halliwell.*
[14] See Appendix, Note DDD.

XXVI.

A Preservation of Four Worthy and Honourable Peers of this Kingdom, and some others— Of the Plots of the Wicked against the Godly (*continued*).

A Preservation of Four Worthy and Honourable Peers of this Kingdom, and some others. Who should have been poisoned (by a Frenchman) at a Supper at the Earl of Leicester's House in Martin's Lane, near Charing Cross, January 11th, 1641.[1]

The Earl of *Leicester*.
The Earl of *Essex*, Lord Chamberlain.
The Earl of *Holland*.
The Earl of *Northumberland*, and some others.

The Earl of *Leicester* having invited four Honourable Lords and Peers of this Kingdom, with some other great personages to a supper, and being all at supper, there came in a bloody minded fellow, a Frenchman; backed unto that wicked intention by some of the popish faction, which may well be conjectured by the sequel which followeth.

[1] "This day was a *French* Cooke (as supposed) brought before the Lords, who had undertaken to poyson divers of both Houses at an intended Feast they were to be invited to, the Earle of *Leicester* and others, and upon examination was sent to *Newgate*, there to answer it."— *Diurnall Occurrences.* This account is abridged from "A Happy Deliverance, or Wonderfull Preservation of foure Worthy and Honourable Peeres of this Kingdome, and some others.—*London.* Printed for *John Thomas*, 1641." Small 4to. pp. 8.—*King's Pamphlets.*

This Frenchman being come into [the] place where these noble peers did sup that night, he privately whispered with the Cook of the Earl of *Leicester*, who also was a Frenchman, and could not speak a word of English, and told him in his own language that if he would undertake to poison the second course that was to be set before these worthy and honourable persons, he would, for his reward and secrecy therein, give him three thousand pound in ready gold. The Cook perceiving this his wicked and bloody intentions told him that if it might gain him a thousand worlds he would not attempt an act so wicked, and withal told him that his treacherous designs he would immediately discover. The Frenchman perceiving it stole out of the doors, for no man present could understand French; And this French Cook understanding no English, whereby to discover this wicked advice of his Countryman, was the reason why he did escape; who, if he had been as greedy of lucre as the other of blood, had despatched out of this world these noble pillars of our Realm.

This was not discovered till after supper, the Cook meeting one of the Earl of *Leicester's* Chaplains which understood French, who told him the manner and form of it as is before related; yet was this French Cook apprehended, and sent for to be examined before the Lords in parliament,[2] and as yet not acquitted.

[2] " Upon information given to this House, ' that there was a design discovered of the killing of some Lords of this House this Night; and that

Not to omit that bloody plot of the Bishops and popish faction, in *January* 1641, spoken on before; how they had privately made seven Articles against Mr. *Pym*, and four other worthy parliament men, wherein they were all arraigned of High Treason. And when they had it obscurely composed, they sent it to be presented to the King's Majesty, and that he would vouchsafe to give his assent thereunto and proclaim them Traitors. Thus we may see their malicious minds, who, when they saw men glorious in the kingdom, and that stood for the safety, peace and prosperity of the Realm, did study to supplant those noble Members, being the next way to supplant the whole Kingdom besides. Thus we may understand their diligence to set the City and Kingdom together by the ears; thus we may see their intents to alienate the Upper House of Parliament from the the Lower House, and the King from both: yet being somewhat frustrated of their expectation of imprisonment of those Members whom they impeached, their malice would not stop there, but it extended farther. Wherein they privately again and obscurely composed Articles against Mr. *Calamy*, Mr. *Burton*, Mr. *Marshall*, and with divers other famous Divines striving to suppress the laborious and painful Ministers of the Word and Gospel, for because they could not bring the parliament into

there was one *Francis Moore*, an *Italian*, that could give a further account of this business,' it is ORDERED, That the said *Francis Moore* shall be sent for to come and attend this House presently."—*Lords' Journals*. Possibly our writer thought that all foreigners were Frenchmen!

dissension, and discord among themselves, they strived to reduce the Church to Heresy, and promiscuous distractions, intending to suspend the chiefest pillars thereof.

After intelligence was given to some joint Confederates with the Rebels, that eighteen were sent to *Newgate*, they amongst themselves appointed a meeting in *Milford Lane*, where they consulted to set the City of *London* on fire, in vindication of their friends, and taking an oath amongst themselves to confirm their resolution. Credible information was given to divers Constables, who summoned a strong watch, and apprehended 36 more of them, who are now committed to safe custody. This was about *February* 1641.

On *Monday* the 21st of *March* : " There was a Bill read in the House of Commons, for the taking away of all Innovations in any Church or Chapel, that hath been set up within these twenty years, As the Altar-Rails before the Communion Table, Pictures, Images, or Crucifixes, and that all Chancels be laid even, and the steps before the Communion Table, or Altar taken away. In this Bill there is a clause for the strict keeping and observing of the Lord's day, And that week day Lectures be set up in all places."[3]

Tuesday the 22nd of *March* in the House of Commons " against Scandalous Ministers, that there shall be Commissioners appointed in every County to enquire after such as within this three years last

[3] *Continuation of the True Diurnall of the Passages*, &c., No. 11.

past as have been Favourers of the late Innovation, any ways scandalous in their lives, or have neglected preaching six weeks together, to be removed from their places, and others put in their room."[4]

"Then there was a conference with the Lords concerning the information lately received from the Governor of *Rotterdam* in *Holland,* of a great fleet prepared in *Denmark* which by means of the Lord *Digby* should have been transported over to *Hull.* To which Declaration, the Lords having declared their assent, appointed three Lords to carry the same to his Majesty, to *York* next morning."[5]

"Then the Lord Admiral sent a message to the Commons, that he had sent a gentleman over on purpose into *France,* to make diligent enquiry what provisions of war there were made, and that he was now returned, and brought him credible information that there are 25 able ships made ready for sea, and five fire ships, being all of them victualled for six months, but whither, or upon what service they are intended is not as yet known."[6]

Saturday, the 26th of *March.*—"The Lords sent a Message to the Commons that there was one Mr. *Cartwright,* had informed them of News from *France,* whereupon the said Mr. *Cartwright* being called into the House of Commons,[7] affirmed that he had lately received very good Intelligence by letters from

---

[4] *Continuation of the True Diurnall of the Passages,* No. 11.
[5] *Continuation of the True Diurnall,* &c.
[6] Ibid. [7] Appendix, Note EEE.

France, from men of great worth and credit; that there is an Army of seven thousand men, ready raised there, which are intended to be transported for *England*, by the 5th of *April* next, but to what intent is not yet known.

"Mr. Speaker also declared that he had lately received letters from *Dover*, That they have received Intelligence thereof, a great Army prepared in *France*, suddenly to come for *England* or *Ireland*." [8]

And the last *Saturday* before,[9] " came news to the House that the French King had sixty sail of men of war at sea, hovering between the Coast of *Devonshire* and *Britain*, manned with many thousand of land soldiers." [10] As likewise of forty thousand Danes to be landed at *Hull*.

In *June* 1642, The papist and malignant party did convocate a council amongst themselves in contriving a destructive way to the state. They at length concluded in a final determination to fire the parliament House, and that they could execute this in the evening. All things were thus determined; many papists and other suspected persons did resort about *Westminster*. But as soon as night approached, the watch was set before their wonted time. But at length there came a vintner's servant, and intimated to some Constables there, that he had once heard certain gentlemen drink with resolute intentions to act something against the parliament

---

[8] *Continuation of True Diurnall*, &c.   [9] *i. e.* March 19th.
[10] *A True Diurnall of the Passages in Parliament.*

house; and one of them did swear that before he went to bed, he hoped to warm his hands at a parliament fire, and with divers other things, all which did intimate some fear and danger, which raised divers of us to stand with our muskets ready charged. Then whereas these malignant parsons' actors perceived the City to take notice thereof, and that their intentions would be prevented, did all depart, and fled, and hid themselves in by places, and by this means escaped.[11]

[1641.] Also a letter sent to the Lord *Burrowes* intimating of a Navy with forty thousand Danes to be landed at *Hull*,[12] but by God's great mercy, when they were within ten leagues of *Hull*, a small company of Dutch ships began the encounter about twelve of the clock on *Monday* the 21st of *March*, continuing fight for the space of two hours very hotly. *Van Trump*, the Dutch Admiral, being then present, behaved himself very valiantly, insomuch that they sunk many of the Danes' ships ere it was two of the clock, when, having spent much powder and shot of either party, they resolved upon parley, which continued for an hour, wherein *Van Trump* desired the perusal of their commission, and to know whither they were bound, the ground of their intents; which being denied, they fell to it again, and continued till it was dark, when, taking the opportunity of the night being very cloudy, they fled, but the wind

---

[11] This paragraph is evidently one of those written according to the space found in the book, and not chronologically.

[12] See *A True Diurnall*, &c.

being contrary, some were driven upon the western coasts of *Dorset* and *Devonshire*.

This Deliverance, (though little regarded by us, yet it) was a very great deliverance in that the Lord did raise the Dutch, and that with so small a number of ships, to destroy so great a Navy; the Lord's Name have all the praise now and for ever.

So there is another Hellish plot against the poor Protestants in *Ireland* and *England*, sent out of *Rome* in *June* 1642, which is too long for me to write.

"There is a great conspiracy discovered in *France*. The Queen and Queen Mother had their hands in it. The Cardinal *Richelieu* should have been made away, with all the prime men of his Council,[13] and a peace concluded between *France* and *Spain*, which done, the Armies should have been turned against the Protestants, and for aid of the Rebels in *Ireland*, if not more. This was bragged at *Vienna* as if done, but his Majesty, having full understanding of the plot, commanded the apprehending of Mons. *le Grand*, and all that in this adhered, and they were put in prison. This is happy News for *England*, and the well affected in *Ireland*; great joy is in *France* for the same." [14]

September the 29th the Earl of *Essex* having gotten possession of the City of *Worcester*, the Town informed him that there was much gunpowder laid

---

[13] See *A Perfect Diurnall*, No. 3.
[14] From *An Extract of severall Letters* . . . *collected and published to prevent False Information*. 1642.

in a vault near his Excellency's lodgings by the Town Hall; and it was confessed by some that were taken prisoners, it was to blow up his Excellency, and to destroy as many of his Forces as they could. This plot was discovered by a worthy gentleman, one Mr. *John Jackson,* an Inhabitant of the said City of *Worcester.*

October the 8th, there was also a discovery made to the Parliament, of a very treacherous Conspiracy against the Earl of *Essex;* That one Captain *Dallison,* a Scotchman, should go to the Army, and he with his Confederates should use means to set the Magazine for the Army on fire, and so to blow up his Excellency with the Army, and that this Conspiracy is fostered by some in the King's Army, who daily expect to hear it.

October the 20th, there was a plot on foot to fire this City of *London,* for the effecting whereof, the Shops and Warehouses that have flax in them, should first have been fired.

November the 12th.[15]—There was a cross petition made by the malignant parties, as those that were monopolists, with their letters patent, and it was contrived in the King's Army. It was a petition for peace without truth, for so some of them did say, "So we have peace, hang up truth." This petition was carried to the House of Lords with some hundreds, and they bid them come in a less number, with seven or eight; but at last the Lords told them they must have the Consent of the Mayor and

---

[15] This date appears to have been December.

Common Council of *London*, before they can grant their petition, but on the [19th] being *Monday*, there was hundreds of those malignants with their weapons, gathered together in *Guildhall*,[16] at such a time when all the chief Council was there. And these Malignants shut the gates upon themselves, and barred them fast with the Tables, intending to cause them to set their hand to their petition, or else to have destroyed the Mayor and Common Council, as afterward did more appear; for four of them took an iron bar, as much as they could carry, to have broke open the door where the Council were, but they could not, for they had set chests and bars against the door. And then the train band came, and two or three pieces of ordnance was fetched, and set against the gates of the Hall, and when they see that, then they opened the gates, and so dispersed; but afterwards some of the Chief Contrivers were sent to prison, as they deserve. Much villany was in this plot, but I yet know not the full of it, and know not whether I set it down right, but it is to the same effect, though it be not in order."[17]

December the 29th, when our Parliament forces had taken *Chichester* in *Sussex*, and the last night the Parliament Commanders being at supper, notice was given that the malignants had plotted, for there were seven barrels of gunpowder in the cellar, with a burning match sticking in one of them, and it was made known by one of their own gunners, that it

---

[16] Gile Hall.   [17] See Appendix, Note FFF.

was to blow them up, and so to have freed their prisoners.[18]

A list was presented to the House of Commons of the Chief Actors in that business, whereupon it was ordered that the Sheriffs of *London* should take a speedy course for the apprehending of them, and commit them to prison to have speedy trial.

[18] See *Rushworth*, part iii. vol. ii. p. 100.

XXVII.

Copy of a Letter from Hull—Sir John Hotham's Speech to the Knights' Meeting at York—The King declareth himself on Howorth Moor—A Letter from York—Heavy and Sad Times with the Poor People of God—God gives Victory to His People.

The Copy of a Letter sent from the Inhabitants of Hull, to the Worshipful the High Sheriff, and the rest of the Gentry in the County of York, now attending his Majesty's pleasure, April 30, 1642.

"Gentlemen,—Now (if ever) stand fast, quit yourselves as Fathers of your Country. Let it appear before God and all the world that truly generous blood runs in your veins; evidence, in God's Name, your heartiest loyalty and dearest affection to his most Sacred Majesty; but while you remember the King, forget not the Kingdom; for the Lord's sake, put not asunder those things which God hath so nearly joined together. Oh consider the honour, the cause of God, the good success of this present parliament; your lives, liberties, your temporal, your spiritual welfare, lie all bleeding this day at your feet, and earnestly supplicate your best assistance; tell us, we beseech you, shall we die, and you live? Can it possibly go well with you, while ill with us? Is it not your own cause and quarrel, nay, God's and the King's, which we maintain? Stand you not as much interested and as deeply engaged to appear, for God and the King's Honour, as we ourselves? Were we disposed to recriminate, we could anathematize [1] before God and man the worthlessness of those unreasonable men, who such [2] the great zealots, not only for the ruin, but the eclipsing of the glory of this blessed parliament. But our intent only is, to beg that at your hands which in Justice you dare not, and in Charity (we are sure) ought not, to deny us, and that's your help and utmost endeavour in this nick of our greatest necessity. Be assured there was never a greater prize in your hands than at this time. In poor *Hull* are embarked two of the richest Jewels in the world, God's truth, and Christendom's peace, each of which in valuation far exceed a King's ransom. We delight not in a needless and superfluous expense of words, and therefore we shall in short tell you what we, or rather God, expects this day at all your hands:—

"That you (and that with instance) petition his most Excellent Majesty to vouchsafe the influence of his Royal favour and gracious presence to his great Council, the High Court of Parliament, the only way, (in human apprehension) to stanch the bleeding wounds of *Ireland* and distracted *England*; that you now help the Lord against the mighty; that with as humble boldness, you manifest your extreme unwillingness to come in a hostile way against us, lest you bring guiltless blood upon

---

[1] Anathomize.   [2] "Suche. To seek? Robson."—*Halliwell*.

your own heads, and kindle such a fire in *England* as will never be quenched. Assure yourselves that, without much caution and greatest circumspection you may raise up such a spirit as will not be conjured down again in haste. Worthies, ponder, we beseech you, our present but sad condition. Set yourselves before God's awful bar; make our case your own. Let your consciences speak. Would you betray so great a trust committed to you, by so great a Council? Would you that we should wound through your sides Heaven and Earth? What shall you attempt against us? Will it in the reflection result upon God the King, the Church, the State, yourselves? Would you to satisfy a good King, set open the gates, and with the same courtesy gratify, a very bad company, who seek nothing less than either the safety of His Majesty's Royal person and posterity, or the security of his Dominions and liege people? Would you have us wash our hands in your dearest blood? In sum, would you have us render you the people of the King's wrath? We are confident you would not. Do then as you would be done unto. Strike in, we beseech you, effectually, whilst you have time. Put not God upon another course of deliverance, lest the honour of *Yorkshire* be laid in the dust for ever. Oh give us in this great strait real testimony of your affections, and you shall for ever have the acknowledgment of the real obligations of all.

"Your affectionate Friends and Humble Servants in the poor Town of *Hull.*"

1642.—The 18th of *May*, there came another letter from the Lord *Fairfax*, Sir *Philip Stapleton*, and other Committees of the Commons House of Parliament residing at *York*, shewing what dangers that poor country lies under, which is too large for me to write of here. And of the protestation of the Freeholders there, *May* 13th, 1642.

About this time there came news that there were many assembled together in a warlike manner in the county of *Yorkshire*, and that there is great preparations for war made in this county, and divers other adjoining counties, which strikes terror to the hearts of all true Protestants, some of the Malignant party saying that the world will never be good till there be some blood of the puritans shed.

Some Part of a Speech made by Sir JOHN HOTHAM, *a Member of the House of Commons, at the Meeting of several Knights and Gentlemen in the said County on the* 23rd *of May.*

" My words at this time shall be confined to these two heads, which indeed are twins, not to be separated. The first is an encouragement to gain perfect honour from your Sovereign. Let loyalty be the rule of all your actions, if you intend to be really honourable, for honour not grounded on loyalty is like friendship without love, lost in a moment, and oft times grows the greatest enemy.

" Next, let your loyalty take its limit from law, otherwise in doing things seemingly good, the end may prove dangerous, and your loyalty prove worse than disloyalty. Therefore the next is obedience to the parliament, that pious and judicious Council whom you in particular, and all the Kingdom in general, have chosen as fit men to discuss and examine all causes that have dependency on his Majesty's safety and the Kingdom's security. Now to disallow of what is by them thought convenient both for his Majesty and the Kingdom's security, is to condemn yourselves of folly that you have chosen men in whom you cannot confide in; but to give you one general reason why the subject being commanded by the parliament ought not to disobey their commands, though by the King commanded the contrary:

"Because the parliament being called and established by the authority of the King and consent of the Kingdom, hath power to command and effect all things that are agreeable to law, tending to the preservation of his Majesty's peace and welfare, and the general good of the subject, they being by King and people entrusted with that weighty and great charge; And if they should foresee an imminent danger threaten his Majesty's person, or the general good, and should not take speedy care to prevent it, they should make a violation of that faith and trust reposed in them. So on the contrary part, if they foreseeing a danger, by their councils and commands endeavour to prevent it, and the persons by them commanded falsify their trust; they are traitors both to their Royal Sovereign, and destroyers of the Kingdom.

"This is the truth; and this is my glory that God has so far enabled me to undergo so great a task, and this is my hope, that all of you will manifest your loyalties to his Majesty, and obedience to the parliament."

Three Letters of Dangerous Consequence read at a Conference of both Houses of Parliament, the two first from Rotterdam, dated July the 1st. The other from Mr. WILMOT *to Mr.* CROFTS *at the Hague, dated July the 22nd, 1642. In which appears a Desperate Design of the Lord* DIGBY, *Capt.* HIDE, *Sir* LEWIS DIVES, *Mr.* JERMIN, *Mr.* PERCY, *and divers Cavaliers, which you may read in the Book at large.*

July the 3rd.—It was informed to the parliament that above one hundred sail of ships of the *Denmarks* are put to sea, with many thousand Foot, and very many Horse; their voyage is pretended to *France* for salt, but it is well known that light Horses do not use to carry salt by sea.

This 3rd of *June* at a Common Hall in *London*, the loan of one hundred thousand pounds was required by the parliament from the city, for the affairs of *England* and *Ireland*, which was granted with so general alacrity and readiness that it being desired all against the loan would hold up their hands, there was not a hand lift up throughout the Hall, except one, who began to speak, as was conceived, against the same; whereupon he was immediately hissed into shame and silence.[3]

[3] See Appendix, Note GGG.

June the 4th, I bought a book of the Oaths of the Kingdom,[4] taken out of the Parliament Roll 1 *He.* 4, N. 17, as likewise a book with letters,[5] one, the Lord *Willoughby* of *Parham*, the King's letter, the Lord of *Warwick's* letter, and the King's declaration in making the Prince Captain of the troop to secure his Majesty at *York* in going against *Hull.*

The 3rd of *June* the King, attended with divers Lords of the House of Peers, and 140 Troopers of Knights and Gentlemen of the County of *York*, and some of the House of Commons, with 800 of the Trained bands as foot guards, appeared this day on *Howorth Moor*, where were between sixty and seventy thousand Freeholders and others. After his Majesty had ridden about the field, he declared that that which he had to say to them, he had put in print, and so dispersed the same through the field. At

---

[4] A small 4to. pamphlet, pp. 8. "Printed at *London* for *T. Bates* and *F. Coules*, June 4th, 1642."—*King's Pamphlets.*

[5] "The Lord *Willoughby* of *Parham* his Letter to an Honourable
Member of the House of Parliament.
His Majestie's Letter to the Lord *Willoughby* of *Parham*.
The Lord *Willoughby* of *Parham* his Letter in answer
to His Majestie's.
With
The *Message* of the Lords to the House of Commons upon
the said Letters.
As also
The Lord of *Warwick's* Letter to his brother the Earle of *Holland*.
And
The Declaration or Resolution of the Officers in the County of *Essex*,
to the Earle of *Warwick*, Lord Lieutenant of that County.
With the Approbation of both Houses concerning the same.
Printed for *Joseph Hunscott* and *John Wright*."
(Printed by Order of the Parliament, June 9, 1642.)—*King's Pamphlets;* 4to. pp. 16.

the delivery thereof, divers of the Cavaliers and others shaked their hats over their heads, and the people cried, "God bless the King, God unite the King and parliament, and God turn the King's heart;" and with this they followed the King from the *Moor* to the City, Sir *John Bourcher*, and the Freeholders, and [he] reading a petition openly in the field, desired the King to comply with his Parliament. The Lord *Saville* having notice thereof, came in a furious manner to Sir *John Bourcher*, saying, "Sirrah, what pamphlet are you reading there?" who answered, No pamphlet, but the thing which he could justify. "What is it? Some seditious petition? I command you to deliver it," which he refusing, the Lord *Saville* was ready to take him by the throat, and laying his hand upon his sword, threatened what he would do to him, if he did not deliver it; whereupon the Freeholders who approved of the same were earnest to lay violent hands on his lordship, but Sir *John Bourcher*, desirous to avoid shedding of blood, delivered the same. But of this you may see more at large in the letter by me.

And in another letter from *York* it is said that these Cavalier rebels, they will go to houses, and take anything they have a mind unto, and say, "Let's see who dares say us nay." They will also familiarly come into a Tavern, or Alehouse cellar, and knock out the bottom of the vessels, and make nothing of it to drink so long as they think good. So likewise if they have occasion for clothes, boots, or any other commodities in the City, they take them without demanding what's to pay, promising when they receive pay or pillage to pay them, which upon the least opposition, they slash them with their swords. And in like manner hath the whole country of *York* undergone the punishment that these Cavaliering Rebels thought fit to inflict on them. As likewise in contempt of all justice, they have abused many honourable personages employed by the parliament in *York*, and other places, swearing bitterly they will be revenged on the puritan parliament, and other adherents [of] the Citizens of *London*. Of this, and of much more misery in other countries you may see in the book or letter that lies by me.

June the 6th.—The Commons received report, that the Queen had pawned the Jewels of the Crown at *Amsterdam*, for two hundred thousand pound, and that a great part of the money is presently to be sent to *York* to the King, and that there is one Mr. *May*, a Merchant in *London*, hath received Bills of Exchange for the present payment of sixteen thousand pounds to his Majesty.

Also, about that time a " letter was presented to the House by one Mr. *Web*, a Merchant, which came from *Amsterdam*, informing him that there is a great storm rising in the north. That the Queen had lately pawned or proffered to pawn a very rich Collar of pearl, and that there is twenty brass pieces of ordnance, and some other pieces, with a hundred barrels of powder, provided there to be sent to his Majesty." [6]

Also about the 12th of *June*, the Lords and Commons received a letter from *Holland*, which the Earl of *Northumberland* read in *Guildhall*, that there is at this time at *Amsterdam* many thousand of carbines and pistols, three thousand great saddles, three hundred barrels of powder, eight pieces of ordnance, making ready to be sent to *England*, for to make war against the parliament, and it is thought to be bought with part of the money borrowed on the Jewels of the Crown. Likewise a Chain of Pearl and other Jewels, sent back, money being denied to be lent on them, by reason of the late order made by the parliament to the contrary.

These and the like assurances of danger caused the Lords and Commons now resident in parliament to publish several propositions in general to all the kingdom. And the Earl of *Northumberland* did declare, at the Hall where the Lord Mayor and Aldermen, with the Common Council of the City were assembled, upon what grounds they did proceed, and their causes of fear, which were these:—

First, because his Majesty, by the persuasions of

[6] From *Diurnall Occurrences*.

"*Die Sabbati*, 11° *Junii*.

"Mr. *Beauchamp*, being called in; was demanded what he knew of the warlike Provisions or Ammunition preparing at *Amsterdam*: He knew no more than what the Letter from his Brother saith.

"He knew the Hand to be his Brother's.

"The Letter speaks of a Storm he fears, from the North, in regard there is great warlike Preparation at *Amsterdam* now in preparing."— *Commons' Journals*, 1642.

the Malignant party, doth endeavour to force a dissolution of parliament, to which end by several persons, and in several countries, he hath endeavoured to raise Arms.

2. That these foreign preparations of Armour, purchased with the Jewels of the Crown, can portend nothing less than such a dangerous design.

3. That these armed Cavaliers at *York*, committing several outrages, on his Majesty's Subjects, giving out several words against the parliament, both dangerous and scandalous, is a free declaration of their intents what they intend to put in act, if they once gain strength by their supposed foreign supplies.

To these they added these Propositions:—

1. Whether it stood not for the better security of the City in general to venture a proportionable stock for the maintenance of Forces to defend and secure the general [stock] from the danger of such intended Stratagems.

2. Whether it were not much better for those that had plate or money to put it into a general stock, the faith of the whole kingdom being engaged for the return of it, than to let such plate or monies be made pillage and prey to the enemies of the kingdom.

To which Propositions they added these Reasons:—

That for such monies or plate so ventured, if the kingdom stood, they were assured to receive the value again with interest, and the rest of their estates secured, but if the contrary, they could neither keep that, nor aught else, their lives and estates running on equal hazard. These Propositions with the reasons were generally liked and condescended unto.

In a letter from *York*, *June* the 17th, on *Monday* at ten o'clock, sixteen soldiers of Sir *Robert Strickland's* Regiment, with divers Cavaliers, came violently and outrageously to Alderman *Vaux*' house, broke all his windows, pulled up his two great posts at his door, carried them away to be burnt in the Court of Guard, saying they were Round Heads. They would have had the Alderman, to have torn him. There was in the house Sir *Philip Stapleton*, Sir *Hugh Charnley*, Commissary *Wilmot*, and a lord besides, the Lord *Howard*; the Sheriffs and Lord Mayor were sent to for help, but none came, after which done, and they all gone, one of the most forward in that rout, and a trooper, falling out in words drew [swords]: The trooper at a blow struck the other's hand off in which his sword was.

Also the Earl of *Newcastle*, Earl of *Newport*, and Captain *Legge*, we hear, are gone to ensure *Newcastle* with a thousand men; also to *Carlisle* is gone Sir *Nich. Byron*; two van loads of arms follows them, and two troops of horses follow them also. At *Hull* they fortify daily at the *North Gate* next the river; an earth wall is built for two rows of musketeers, the gate blocked up with earth. So is *Myton Gate*; they have planted a piece on either side, one in the top of the gate, where in every gate two look us in the face as we go in, and at every gate besides three pieces, one on either side, one aloft.

Yet praised be God there is some good news, for here are letters read in the House of Commons, which came from *Ireland* of the besieging of divers Castles, wherein the Rebels had great strength, and of the slaughtering of a great multitude of Rebels, and finding twenty thousand pound in one of the castles they took from them; and that they had taken an Island which the Rebels had, of almost an invincible strength.

Also about this time there was two ships with the wind were driven into the Harbour of *Southampton*; and they were searched, and found to be laden with great store of powder, for of that kind of provision all their lading did consist of, and being examined where they were to transport that commodity, they boldly answered, That they were sent to supply the Lord *Mountgarret*, and his Forces in *Ireland*, who, they understood, had very much need of it. Upon this confession the shipping was stayed, and the goods seized upon, and the men themselves stayed in *Southampton* until it shall be further determined of them. Thus it pleased God to defeat the intentions of His enemies, and to frustrate the designs against His Children.

This month of *July* divers letters came out of many counties, concerning the papists and malignants, [who] did strive to set the Commission of Array,[7]

[7] See Appendix, Note GGG.

and many Igips [*sic*], derideful words, mocks and scoffs, and reproachful terms by them, were cast upon the Honourable Court of Parliament, with many threats and great preparations to the ruin of them, and this Honourable City of *London*. As also Letters out of *Holland*, from the Queen, and sending of Arms and Ammunition to the same intent, yet God doth keep, and will preserve His Church, so long as they trust in Him.

July the 4th, there were letters read in the House that came from *Amsterdam*,[8] That there were two of the King's ships there which attend the Queen, laden with great store of Ammunition and provisions for war, coming for *England*, and that they have taken in about ninety Cavaliers into the Ships, amongst whom are the Lord *Digby*, Mr. *Percy*, *Jermyn*, and *Daniel O'Neale*; and that they stayed there but for the opportunity of a fair wind; and that the Queen hath pawned, or proffered to pawn, a Jewel valued worth four hundred thousand guilders. There was also a letter read in the house of Commons, which was intercepted from Commissary *Wilmot* to the Cavaliers in *Holland*, informing them of the passages here, and in derision of the parliament.[9]

There were also letters brought to the Commons, from *York*,[10] informing that the King intends to put the Commission of Array in execution there

---

[8] See *A Perfect Diurnall*.
[9] See *Rushworth*, part iii. vol. ii. p. 745.
[10] See *A Perfect Diurnall*.

very suddenly; that there is about a thousand horses with complete arms in *York*, and that there is within eight miles of *York*, about a thousand horse more; that the Lord *Digby* is at *York* with his Majesty, and in great favour. Also there was information given against one Mr. *Elliott* at *York* with the King, of some dangerous words which he should speak against the King and parliament to this effect, that he had thought we should have been altogether by the ears long before now, and that if the King had been as good as his word, the parliament before this time should have had all their throats cut; further adding with a great oath, that the King would stand to nothing.

July the 11th.—" There was also letters read in the Commons, which came from *Hull*, informing that the King is again come to *Beverley*, and hath brought a great company of horse and foot to besiege *Hull*, and [they] have begun to intrench themselves, and to make means to drain the water, which Sir *John Hotham* hath let out to preserve the town, that they have taken twenty-four pieces of ordnance out of the ship which ran ashore there, and placed them in several places to stop the passages by sea and land, and that the King's forces much increase daily." [11]

July the 18th.—" There was in the House of Commons letters read from Sir *John Hotham*, informing that the Cavaliers have made divers attempts by night against *Hull*, intending to burn the same in several places, and that whilst the soldiers should

---

[11] From *A Perfect Diurnall*. See also Appendix, Note III.

be busy in quenching the fire, they would scale the walls, and seize upon the town; but, by God's mercy, this enterprise was prevented by Sir *John Hotham's* vigilance, who so played upon them by his cannon shot that they soon left their enterprise, only they burnt two windmills which belongeth to *Hull*. The Earl of *Newport* being also in this design was, by the waft of a cannon shot, dismounted from his horse, and cast into a deep ditch of water, where, had he not been caught[12] hold of by the hair of the head after once or twice sinking, he had lost his life; which passage being afterwards told to his Majesty, the Archbishop of *York* being present, made answer that it was well his Lordship was not a Roundhead; if he had, he might have been drowned, for that then he would have had little hair on his head to have been holden by.

"Sir *John*, by the same letters, also informeth that he had taken a small pinnace with three great pieces of ordnance, and divers of the Cavaliers with some horse that were going to *Lincolnshire* side to stop the passage on that part to *Hull*."[13]

The Earl of *Warwick*, also, by letters, informed that he had sent some other of his ships to *Hull* who, by his direction, had cleansed the passage by sea, and demolished all the works that were raised by the Cavaliers for the intercepting of the passages to *Hull*.

Also the 6th of this month of *July*, the Earl of *Warwick* by letters informed that Captain *Slingsby*

---

[12] Catched.   [13] From *A Perfect Diurnall*.

and Captain *Wake* stood out, "whereupon," saith he, "I let fly a gun over them, and sent them word I had turned up the glass upon them, if in that space they came not in, they must look for me aboard them. I sent to them my boat, and most of the boats in the fleet. Their answer was so peremptory that my Masters and sailors grew so impatient on them that, although they had no arms in their boats at all, yet God gave them such courage and resolution, that in a moment they entered them, took hold on their shrouds, and seized upon these Captains, being armed with their pistols and swords, and struck their yards and topmasts, and brought them both to me. The like courage and resolution was never seen amongst unarmed men. So, all was ended without effusion of blood, which I must attribute to the great God of heaven and earth only, who, in the moment that I was ready to give fire on them, put such courage into our men to act, and so saved much blood."

But now to go on of this 18th of *July*. "Upon debate of Sir *John Hotham's* letters, it was ordered by both houses that there should be ten thousand pounds sent to Sir *John Hotham* to pay the soldiers and provision of wine, beer, corn, and other victuals for six weeks, and that there should be six small ships sent to remain there, and fitted with ordnance to do service in shallow water of 6 or 7 feet deep, upon all occasions.

"This day also came letters to the Houses from *Ireland* informing of the late death of the Lord

President of *Munster*,[14] whose loss is very much lamented. There was also relation by the said letters of a great battle lately fought in that place with the rebels, besieging of the Lord President's castle, where the Protestants, with a small number, put two thousand of the rebels to flight, and killed about seven hundred of them, and took great booty. Also, in the county of *Limerick*, marching with five hundred musketeers and three troops of horse, they set upon five and twenty hundred of the rebels, drove them out of their quarters, and had killed off near five hundred of the rebels.[15]

"It was also by the said letters informed that divers of the Commanders that came from hence begin to slight the service there, and make means to come for *England* again, giving out what great purchase they could make of their service here at this time."[16]

July the 20th, it is said in a letter from *York* that "divers Commanders out of poor *Ireland*, who left their employment against the rebels to come against us, produce *C. R.* for their warrant.

---

[14] "Our most Noble and never enough to be lamented Sir *William Leger*, President of this Province, is departed this life, dying in his bed, of an infirmity which his Phisitian sayes was occasioned by this restlesse care and study in his charge."—"A True Relation of the late Occurrences in *Ireland*, in two Letters. London. Printed by *A. N.* for *Edw. Blackmore*, July 18, 1642."—*King's Pamphlets.*

[15] See "An Exact Relation of the Victorious Battels Fought by the *English!* Wherein they put to flight 2200, and killed 700 of the Rebels at *Cardoughen* in the Province of *Munster*. London. Printed by *L. N.* and *J. F.* for *E. Husbands*, and *J. Franke*."—Ibid.

[16] From *A Perfect Diurnall.*

It is a sad business; the Lord of His mercy help us!"[17]

"Here are Messrs. *Hide* and *Holborn*, two lawyers that do much mischief; the one makes himself as familiar with the King as if his fellow; hath been seen several times to pull his Majesty by the cloak and, when he talks with him, to play with his Majesty's band-strings; the other will maintain the legality of the Commission of Array."[18]

July the 28th.—There were letters read in the House of Commons from Sir *John Hotham*, informing that the Cavaliers had lately in the night time made another attempt against *Hull*, which he, discovering, soon drove them from their enterprise, after some small skirmish, in which some of the Cavaliers were slain, but the number he could not learn, it being their policy, so soon as any are killed, to carry them away privately, for fear of discouraging the rest; but the paths were seen to be much strewn with blood.

July 30th.—" There was information given at the Bar in the House of Commons against one Mr. *Symmons*, a Minister, for preaching that we are bound to do all that his Majesty commands, and believe all that his Majesty saith, and other like words."

One Colonel *Rose*, a Scot, with a musket ball was shot under the arm . . . it is thought it is mortal, it is reported he went swearing and cursing away,

---

[17] From "Advertisements from *York* and *Beverly*, *July* the 20th, 1642. London. Printed in the yeare 1642." Small 4to. pp. 4.—*King's Pamphlets*.   [18] From ditto. See also Appendix, Note JJJ.

saying had he been so long in *Germany* under the King of *Sweden*, and must he now be slain by Sir *John Hotham*. At *Beverley* they are afraid they shall not be freed of the Cavaliers a long time. . . .

[1642.—"About *August*, in *Ireland*, the Rebels being at one Mr. *Rames'* house, and they taking in all his Father's Books for to burn them, that great God and Lord of Host that sent swarms of flies to plague cruel King *Pharaoh*, that did so oppress His Children of *Israel*; This God did send a swarm of Bees out of a Garden into the house where these cruel Rebels were, that did sting them so bitterly as that they were forced to flee away, and for that time left their mischief undone."[19]

This Finger of God makes me call to mind another great work of God, which I did hear of very credibly, which was in the year 1625, when those wicked cruel Bishops caused that reverend Minister of God, Mr. *Elton*, his Books on the Commandments, to be buried in *Cheapside*. While they were a burning, a man that brought more quires of these books (that he had found out) and laid them on the fire. And that great and mighty God that hath the command of the wind and fire, this God did command His wind to blow one of those sheets of paper out of the fire again, and to lap about this man's face (as he stood to see them burn) and it did so burn his face very much that he was in miserable pain.]

[19] From "Exceeding Happy News from *Ireland*." *London*. Printed for *T. Rider*, 1642.—*King's Pamphlets*.

XXVIII.

PILLAGING AND PLUNDERING — THE SETTING UP OF THE KING'S STANDARD AT NOTTINGHAM — THE MERCY OF THE WICKED IS CRUELTY; WHAT THEN IS THEIR CRUELTY? — GOD'S WONDERFUL PRESERVING SOME HOUSES FROM BURNING — GREAT CRUELTY AND PLUNDERING — THAT MALIGNANT PARTY IS FURTHER STRENGTHENED.

AUGUST the 1st, 1642.—"There were letters brought to the Parliament[1] and read in both Houses, which the Earl of *Warwick* intercepted at sea in a small Cabanet going for *Holland*. One of them was from the King to the Queen, wherein he writeth to her to send him three thousand saddles, three thousand muskets, two hundred firelocks, four pieces of cannon for battery, one cannon, one demi-cannon, two whole culverins, two mortars, four petards, ten field pieces of six pound bullet, mounted, one hundred barrels of powder, round shot, and case proportioned to the several pieces, two thousand pairs of pistols, one thousand of carbines, one thousand pikes."[2]

"Another letter from Mr. *Thomas Elliot*, at *York*, to the Lord *Digby*, where he writeth that things goeth very well at *York*, and that he feareth no-

---
[1] See "Two Letters, the One from the Lord *Digby* to the Queen's Majestie; the other from Mr. *Thomas Elliot* to the Lord *Digby* . . . . Also a Noat of such Armes as were sent for by His Majestie out of *Amsterdam*, under his owne Hand. *London*. Printed by *R. O.* and *G. D.* for *John Bartlet*, 1642. (By Order of the Parliament.)"—*King's Pamphlets*. See also *Some Speciall Passages*, No. 11.

[2] From *A Perfect Diurnall*.

thing, but that the King will hearken to the Parliament for accommodation, but he hopes the Queen will write to his Majesty to hold firm his resolution; and another letter from the Lord *Digby* to the Queen, all of them being sent a good while since."[3]

August the 2nd, in a letter from *York*, wherein is specified how "the country-people complain miserably that they enjoy nothing that they have. That the *Candebed* men, and *Cottingham* men, and *Newland* men, they say, they dare not be seen to read a good book, but he that doth not banish God and good men, he is no company for the Cavaliering rebels. Not to omit the Cavaliers have planted three pieces of ordnance at *Hassel* to hinder any passage by water; and, a keel coming towards us, the principal gunner shot at her, and missed. He swore . . . if he did not sink her the next shot; and the piece brake in pieces, and killed the gunner and some others."[4]

August the 11th.—The Lord Mayor of *London*, for his defaults to the King and kingdom, came to the Lords' House to receive sentence upon his impeachment, the effect whereof was that he should be put from his Mayoralty, never bear office in the city or commonwealth, be incapable of all honour and dignity to be conferred on him by his Majesty, and stand committed prisoner to the Tower during the pleasure of both Houses.[5]

---

[3] From *A Perfect Diurnall*.

[4] From "An Abstract of severall Letters from *Hull, York*, and *Beverley*, of his Majestie's proceedings. *London*. Printed for *Ben. Allen* in *Pope's-Head Alley*. August the second, 1642."—*King's Pamphlets*.

[5] See "The Parliament Censure on Sir *Richard Gurney*, Lord Mayor

August the 12th there came a letter from *Freshford*[6] concerning the Cavaliers that were at *Wells*, how these Cavaliers went from thence to a town called *Shipton Mallet*, and, marching about the town, found out all the honest religious men's houses that were there; those houses they brake into, plundered, and robbed, especially of all arms and ammunition, and made the owners, their wives, and their children, to forsake their houses, and hide themselves for fear of their lives. . . .

August the 17th, "a letter was presented to the Houses from *York*, informing the true state of the King's army, that he hath about four thousand horse and two thousand foot, the greatest part thereof being very desperate, . . . and inconsiderate persons that daily commit great outrage in the country, pillaging and spoiling all that seem any ways well affected to the Parliament, and commit great spoils up and down the country without any

of the Honourable City of *London*, *August* 12, 1642, with the Articles of his Impeachment. *London*. Printed for *John Cave*." Sm. 4to. pp. 8.—*King's Pamphlets*.

[6] This letter, dated from *Freshford*, *August* 7, 1642, and written by *John Aisle*, (M.P.) is entitled, "A Perfect Relation of All the passages and proceedings of the Marquesse *Hartford*, the Lord *Paulet*, and the rest of the Cavelleers that were with them in *Wels*. With the valiant resolution and behaviour of the Trained-bands and other Inhabitants of those parts, for the defence of themselves, the King and *Parliament*. As also what helpe was sent from *Bristoll* to their ayd: with the manner of the Lords and Cavaleers running out of the Towne. And many other things very remarkable. As it was sent in a Letter from the Committee in *Summersetshire* to both houses of *Parliament*. . . 12 *August*, 1642. *London*. Printed for *Joseph Hunscot* and *J. Wright*." Small 4to. pp. 8. Printed by order of the Parliament.—Ibid.

respect of persons, whereby the country is very sorely oppressed by them."[7] They pillaged divers gentlemen's houses about *Hull*. I will relate but one, and that is of one Mr. *Marwood's* house.[8] "It was done in the day-time, and by twenty-four horse, or thereabout; part stayed beyond the river running close by the house, and others kept watch that none should come to hinder their attempt. They threatened Mrs. *Marwood* and her servants with death to discover where her husband was, and swore they would cut him to pieces before her face. . . . They searched all the house, and brake open seventeen locks, they took away all his money, being about a hundred and twenty pounds, and all his plate they could find, and they pretended they had the King's warrant for all their doings, which the King disavows, and is offended to have his name so abused. And, though it be Mr. *Marwood's* lot to suffer first, yet the loose people threaten to pillage and destroy all Roundheads, and name some particular persons, under which foolish name Roundhead they comprehend all such as do not go their ways."[9]

August the 22nd, 1642, the King set up his standard at *Nottingham*.[10] "The likeness of this standard is much of the fashion of the city streamers, used

---

[7] From *Some Speciall and Remarkable Passages from both Houses of Parliament.*

[8] At *Nunmunckton*, five miles from *York*.

[9] From "A Full Relation of all the late proceedings of His Majestie's Army in the County of *Yorke*, with the present state and condition of things there." Printed (by order of the Parliament) for *John Wright*.— *King's Pamphlets*.   [10] See *Rushworth*, part iii. vol. i. p. 78.

at the Lord Mayor's show, having about twenty supporters, and is to be carried after the same way; on the top of it hangs a bloody flag, the King's arms quartered with a hand pointing to the crown which stands above with this motto: 'Give Cæsar his due.'"[11] And so, through evil counsel, proclaimed the Earl of *Essex* traitor, and raising war against his liege people and best subjects.[12] This day at *Nottingham*, the Cavaliers, having disarmed all the townsmen that had arms sent from the Parliament, three householders refusing to deliver their arms, which they bought with their own money, were committed close prisoners to *Nottingham* Castle. They plunder all men's houses whom they please to call Roundheads, and bring in cartloads of household stuff, and sell them before the court gate.

August the 22nd.—" As the carrier[13] was going with a waggon of clothes for the soldiers at *Dublin*, which he was to leave at *Westchester*, and ship them for *Dublin*, near *Lichfield*, the Lord *Compton's* troops seized on the waggons and clothes, and disposed of the clothes among the soldiers, and carried away the waggon and horses, to the undoing of the carrier, who told them what great want the poor sol-

---

[11] "It is a long pole like a May-pole, dyed red, on the upper part whereof hangs a large silken flag (in forme of a scutcheon) with a Red Crosse, and two Lyon Passants upon two Crownes."—*A Letter from a Gentleman neere* Nottingham, *to a friend in* London. "London, printed for *T. Underhill,* Sept. 1, 1642." Folio sheet.—*King's Pamphlets.*

[12] From " A true and exact Relation of the manner of his Maiestie's setting up of His Standard at *Nottingham,* on *Monday* the 22nd of *August,* 1642. *London,* printed for *T. Coles.*"—Ibid.

[13] " *William Whitaker* by name."—*Rushworth,* part iii. vol. i. p. 777.

diers were in *Ireland* for clothes, and how this act of theirs would countenance the rebels that can have such friends in *England* to do that for them here, which they would do there if they could; but all would not prevail to have anything restored."[14]

August the 25th.—At *Rotterdam* Mr. *Henry Jermine* is very free in offers both to commanders and common soldiers to come for *England*; two thousand he proposes, four thousand is intended. The pretence is, to conduct them over for *England*, and that he intends to land at *Newcastle*, or *Portsmouth*, [with] the same *O'Neal* that brake out of the Tower of *England* after he was accused of high treason by the Parliament, that went hence with Prince *Rupert*, and with letters from the Queen to the King, who we hear is safely landed with Prince *Rupert* at *Newcastle*.

From *Rome*, *August* 30th. — " Here is great thirsting after news out of *England*. One friar *John*, Secretary to one of the Cardinals, is the only man that engrosseth the English intelligence, and is very diligent in making the same known to the Pope and Cardinals. The Pope is contriving a way to send some money into *England* to help to maintain war against the Parliament, and to relieve the rebels in *Ireland*, for it is conceived that these wars do very highly concern the whole Catholic cause."[15]

September the 27th.—There came letters to the House from *Chester*, informing that the Cavaliers have plundered Sir *William Brewerton's* house, and

---

[14] From *Speciall Passages*, No. 3.   [15] Ibid., No. 7.

divers other gentlemen's, and honest Ministers' in
that county, and have endeavoured to put the
Commission of Array in execution there, in which
business the Lord *Chomley* and the High Sheriff
have been most active, and in levying of soldiers
upon the county, and making war against them,
whereupon they were both voted guilty of high
treason, and ordered that an impeachment should
forthwith be framed against them for the same.

Some part of the Lord PAULET'S *Cruel Speech to his
Soldiers at Sherborne, on Wednesday before the fight,
being the 7th day of September,* 1642.[16]

" Fellow soldiers, our spies are returned, with
news so good as that I can scarce find in my heart
to wish for better, our adversaries being so naked
in a defenceable condition, as that I do as certainly
assure myself of victory as if an angel from heaven
had foretold it."

(This speech is so full of lies that I want patience
to write further of it. But it is also as full of
cruelty:) " For," saith he, " only I shall interest
you to observe these following directions in and
after the victory.

" Give quarter to none that wears the sword, no,
not to the Earl himself; deafen your ears, and
harden your hearts against all cries and prayers for
mercy. But if you meet with any of their clergy,

---

[16] From "The Latest Remarkable Truths from *Worcester, Chester,
Salop, Warwick, Stafford, Somerset, Devon, Yorke,* and *Lincolne*
Counties. Most of which was sent up Poste from judicious men, of
purpose to be printed. *London.* Printed for *T. Vnderhill.* 1642."

reserve them for more exquisite torments and a lingering death. I intend to have them flayed alive, but if any of you can find a more tormenting and weightier punishment, I shall give place unto it. Be favourable to the town and townsmen of *Yeovil*, for they are, most of them, our well-wishers. As for the Roundheads that are among them, they shall be to-morrow singled out for the slaughter. But when you come to the puritanical towns, *Taunton, Crewkerne, Bristol, Dorchester*, and *Exeter*, then let your swords cruel it without difference of age, sex, or degree. Let those three counties of *Somerset, Dorset*, and *Devonshire*, be fattened with the blood and carcases of the inhabitants, that they may not make head against us. I am ravished with delight, when I consider the renowned glory, great plenty, rare pleasure, rich and brave booties that court you. There is not the meanest soldier among you but shall have more wealth than he can overcome, more choice and delicate booties than the great Turk. These things well invite you beyond any eloquence of mine; therefore, dear hearts, comfort your hearts with this, that you are able to look them dead."[17]

Let all the Atheists in the world come and see if there be not a God. Read and consider the wonderful works of God, that God which would not let the fire kindle or burn His three Children when

---

[17] "For this speech I cannot believe the Lord *Paulet* had any such intention, much lesse a tongue to utter it."—*A Perfect Relation, or Summary of fifty Bookes.* London, 1642.—*King's Pamphlets.*

they were cast in the fiery furnace in *Daniel* iii. 23, 24, 27, that very same God you may see here, doth wondrously preserve this His Servant's house from burning. Let the fury of the enemy do what he can; therefore:—I will praise the Lord with my whole heart. I will speak of all thy marvellous works.—*Psalm* ix. 1.

[1642. *September* the 9th, one Mr. *Coltman*, being by God's providence at his Country house at *Fleckney* in *Leicestershire*, having another Farm house in *Gumly* two miles from the said *Fleckney*, one of his servants came unto him like one of *Job's* messengers, with a relation that Prince *Rupert* with his troops were in their fields, and had taken five of his horses, and had burned his houses and barns. But it fell out otherwise, by the power and providence of God, though it was attempted, and earnestly endeavoured, on this wise.

Captain *Sands*, pulling a note out of his pocket, made no stop till he came to the said Mr. *Coltman's* house, then he commanded his servants (or soldiers) to go into the house and fire it; who accordingly went into the house, fetched out fire, raised the thatch, and put the fire in, and kindled it, (the thatch being extraordinary dry and combustible). But so soon as the wretched persons were down, the fire went out, and fell after them upon their heads, and thus they did three several times with the same success as at the first.

The mean time the Captain and other of his soldiers, continued belching out hideous oaths.

Then the Captain assayed to fire it himself on this manner; he went to a poor man's house, from whence he brought a wisp of straw, put fire into it, then put it into the thatch again, the fire flaming. But the Captain no sooner came down from the ladder, but the fire went out, and fell upon his head again. This not taking effect (he) went into the said house, where a woman was brewing, took two great firebrands of fire, went up the ladder, (like a hangman to do execution) again put in the burning brands into the dry thatch, and kindled it with fanning his hat to and fro, till it did burn, as he thought, to consuming, but with the same success as before, this being the fifth time of their ungodly attempt, for the Captain no sooner from the ladder, but the brands fell after him as before.

Then with hideous oaths he commanded the soldiers to shoot their carbines in several places of two haystacks together, one of them being very old hay, yet God would not let it fire. Then they returned only burning and slamming[18] themselves in rage and malice.

One of the neighbours asked why he would burn that house. His answer was, because he was a Roundhead. There were many spectators who were exceedingly astonished at this miraculous preservation, saying they never knew in their lives before but when fire was joined unto dry stubble it would burn to consumption. So this servant of God escaped only with the loss of four horses; but if his

---

[18] Slam; to beat or cuff violently.

house had been burnt, he had lost about six hundred pounds, his barns being full of corn and other things. All praise and Glory be given unto God..

This wonderful work of God I did hear Mr. *Coltman* relate it himself, and that reverend Minister of God's word, Mr. *Pecke,* wrote it from his mouth.]

September the 10*th. From Leicester.*

Here we have been used not like Christians, for in small villages of thirty and forty houses we have had fourscore or an hundred rogues, rascals billeted, and they take our goods, horses and jades,[19] and sell our barley at twelve pence a bushel, and at this rate sell away all our goods, and take what they left, pay nothing, but take all on free hand; and we dare not speak to them, but they threaten Prince *Rupert* will burn all when he comes, if we furnish him not with money. Here be some outlandish Cavaliers of his crime; good Lord, deliver all good English people from such miscreants, who make no more of a man than of a dog. His Majesty said he would have no papists to be of his guard, but there be of his war many papists, nay, some be worse than heathen or any Infidels.

From Oxford, September the 10*th.*

Last *Sabbath* day at night, being the 28th of *August,* between 11 and 12 o'clock, came two hundred and fifty Troopers, or thereabouts, from his Majesty, as they pretend, to assist the university against the parliamenteers; who having

---

[19] "A hired horse; a worthless nag."—*Johnson.*

obtained the Vice-Chancellor and Mayor's hand for their safe conduct, [were] ushered into the Town by such applause by our scholars as made the streets ring. The Roundheads, which were not a few, depart the city for fear. The Innkeepers, many of them, would not stir to give them entertainment, whom since they have threatened to fire their houses about their ears. Divers outrages are daily committed by them against the townsmen and others, which is more fit to be the subject of a History than a letter; their often taking away victuals, arms, poor countrymen's commodities, which they would bring hither to the Market, the robbing of some, breaking of Houses and pillaging the same, and sundry other outrages, as, calling for things and not paying a farthing for it, threatening others with pistols ready cocked at their breasts, that demand what was due for their own.

" The Cavaliers in *Shropshire,* and all other places where they come, disarm all Towns and families well affected to the parliament, plundering their houses most vehemently, carrying away and spoiling all their goods, terrifying the inhabitants extremely, and driving them to fly for their lives, taking many prisoners; and they have lists of the names of all active persons whom they seize upon, and do most mischief unto; Papists' and malignants' houses generally escape their cruelty; if a running army be not raised to run as fast, the whole Kingdom is in great danger suddenly to be run over. Prince *Rupert's* Army most part consists of Papists, who deal most cruelly with all good men, and Ministers, and all that have opposed the Commission of Array." [20]

Namptwich, September 24th. — "The Commissioners of Array in *Cheshire*, met upon *Monday* last, at a house on the forest of *Delamere*, and as we hear, they combined together by an oath of secrecy, to plunder and disarm the town of *Namptwich*, which they have done by the assistance of about fifteen horse which came from *Drayton* to meet them, under the command of the Lord *Grandison*. The inhabitants of the Town, having certain intelligence of what they intended against them, presently assembled in consultation to take a course for securing of themselves, and Mr. *Clutton*, an active Gentleman, was resolved to fight it out, and disarmed the under-sheriff's man, who came from the Cavaliers, who would not hear talk of any parley, but gave express command to the townsmen of his own company to give fire as soon as the Cavaliers shall come within shot, and not to admit of any parley; but other gentlemen of the Town persuaded the contrary, lest it should be fired, whereupon they came to parley. The Lord *Grandison* and the Lord *Cholmondeley* engaged their honours that no man should be hurt, nor any arms or goods taken, but only desired that the arms might be laid up in the Church, or the Town Hall till they heard further from the King; whereupon the town was given up, but they dishonourably broke their engagement, seizing upon their arms, so soon as they entered the town, searching up and

---

[20] *The Latest Remarkable Truths,* &c.

down for arms, and men; threatening many, pursuing them that fled; many took the river to escape them; they stopped the passages of the town, to be revenged of them within it, rid up and down the gardens to find them out, and imprisoned many; then they plundered the town and all the country, which now lies open for a prey to a perfidious enemy, conducted and strengthened by them of the Array, to all such places where they have been most serviceable to King and parliament. If speedy help come not, we shall be utterly desolate. This intelligence is from many eye witnesses." [21]

"The Earl of *Rivers* hath five pieces of ordnance, ten barrels of powder, and sixty bullets landed at *Frodsham, September* 17. The Lord *Strange, September* 19, brought two thousand men and two Troops of Horse to *Warrington*, and are there billeted for 8 days, and hath 11 pieces of ordnance; besides 'tis reported he expects three thousand men out of *Cumberland, Westmoreland,* and *Northumberland.*" [22]

September the 15th.—The Cavaliers have disarmed most of the trainbands in *Leicestershire* and *Derbyshire*, and plundered divers gentlemen's houses of good quality, as Sir *John Curzon's*, Mr. *Millington's* house, Members of the House of Commons, and divers others. The barbarous Cavaliers in a most inhuman manner murdered an honest woman in *Leicester*, by shooting her with a brace of bullets, whereupon she immediately died. They have burnt

---

[21] Abridged from *The Latest Remarkable Truths.*
[22] From *The Latest Remarkable Truths.*

divers honest men's houses, who will not separate the King and parliament. They have plundered Sir *Edward Rode's* house in *Yorkshire*, and then burnt it to the ground. One Mr. *Augustine Harper*, an honest Gentleman, as he was travelling upon the road, was apprehended by the Rebels, dismounted and disarmed, and the Lord *Carnarvon* told him he would try whether he was a Roundhead, and tendered him the Bible, to be sworn upon it, that he would assist the King with his life and fortune, to destroy the parliament; which the Gentleman refusing, was committed. The truth of this is deposed upon oath, as also the King sent his warrant for the plundering of Mistress *Piggot's* house in *Nottingham*.

The King had a muster this last week; there appeared three thousand two hundred foot, one thousand whereof had no arms, about a thousand of Dragoons, and two thousand Horse. The Lord *Dillon* commands in chief over the Irish Rebels and Irish papists, and commanders that are about his Majesty, of which there are a great number, and none in greater favour than they. The Lord Lieutenant of *Ireland* is wearied with his continued pressing of his Majesty that he may go over to his charge; but such is the power of the Irish Rebels and papists at Court that he cannot have his dispatch, after six weeks' stay at *York* and *Nottingham*. How doth this stand with his Majesty's professions to help the Protestants in *Ireland*, and taxing the House of Commons with delay in sending over the lieutenant, as he did in one of his Messages, and yet himself to delay the Earl of *Leicester's* going over? It is for certain the Earl of *Leicester* told his Majesty that it would much reflect upon his Majesty in the opinion of his subjects, if he did fetch away the Horses from *Chester*, which the Parliament had sent thither for the relief of *Ireland*, yet could not prevail; for *Errington* did obey the warrant, and did bring them, who is a papist.

September the 11th.—There is certain intelligence from the Mayor of *Pembroke* that this last week he hath taken divers examinations upon oath of several persons come from *Wexford* and other parts in Ireland, being to this effect: That *O'Neal* is come from *Flanders* into *Ireland* in a Spanish bottom which carrieth 22 pieces of ordnance, and brought in her a great quantity of arms and ammunition, and about 300 soldiers, most of them commanders; that a Hoy of about 40 ton and 2 pieces of ordnance, came along with her, laden with ammunition; that they took 7 or 8 English and Scots ships, some laden with corn, others with salt and coals, and another ship with 5 bags of Bullion, and other good commodities. That the Commander of the ship wherein *O'Neal* came did declare upon his oath in the Deponent's presence, that *O'Neal* had a commission from the King to oppose all English and Scots that opposed him; that *O'Neal* had six ships in the North of *Ireland*, expects six more from *Dunkirk*, four from *Spain*; and another of the witnesses deposed upon Oath that he was lately at *Nantes* in *France*, where there were six ships making ready for *Ireland*, Irishmen commanding them, two of them carrying 12 or 14 pieces of ordnance, the rest 9 or 8 pieces, and great store of ammunition, and one of the soldiers did declare they went to help the Catholics in *Ireland* against the English there, and would be in *England* likewise before long.

September the 13th.—In *Gloucestershire* the Cavaliers burn the corn growing in the field.

This day the Parliament returned an Answer to the King's Message to this effect, That whilst his Majesty sends Messages about a Treaty, oppression, rapine, firing of houses, are committed by the authority of those Commanders [upon those] whom his Majesty holds himself bound in honour and conscience to protect.

September the 21st.—There were letters read in the House of Commons which came from *Ireland*, that the whole Kingdom is in a most lamentable condition, a great part of the Protestant forces dying for want of means, the Rebels having received great supplies by *O'Neal's* going over into *Spain*: Whereby they are so much increased they are above ten for one against our forces; the Rebels are now confident the Kingdom is their own, it being their frequent talk that the Protestant forces are but Rebels and Traitors to his Majesty, and so accounted by him, being sent over there by a puritan faction in *England* against the King's consent, and they are his only subjects, and have commission from his Majesty to rid the Kingdom of all the English and Scotch, and to kill and to destroy them; and for further confirmation of this business it is informed by letters that *O'Neal* the Arch Rebel, with his forces meeting in the field with Colonel *Leslie*, a Commissioner, under the Broad Seal of *England*, and the King's hand to it, to the effect aforesaid; which business hath so much disheartened our forces, considering how the provisions appointed for that service hath been stayed off by his Majesty, that they stand in a maze, not knowing which way to take to preserve their lives, whereby that Kingdom is even at the last gasp.

The Examination of JOSHUA HILL, *taken at Northampton in the presence of the Earl of* ESSEX, *General of the Army, September* 14.

"The King sent a letter to Master Mayor of *Nottingham*, requiring one thousand pound, and particular warrants to divers private men for two hundred pounds a man, and other several sums; if this were not paid, the Cavaliers threaten to plunder.

"After this his Majesty was pleased to send the Lord *Newark* to Mr. Mayor to double the thousand pound.

"Captain *Legg* said, he thought *Nottingham* men were a generation of devils; and said if he knew a Roundhead, he would knock him over the pate.

"The house of one Mistress *Piggot* was plundered by warrant from his Majesty.

"The trainbands of the County of *Nottingham* being summoned in by warrant from the Lord *Newark*, were all disarmed by Cavaliers threatening any one that refused, to pistol him.

"Sergeant *Brown* and Alderman *Toplady* have used all possible endeavour to have taken the life of one Mr. *Hooper*, steward to the Countess of *Clare*, in charging of him with treason for not delivering up the arms of his lady.

"There were in and about *Nottingham* near five hundred Irish Commanders, Irish and papist, and increased daily."[23]

September the last.—" All the Country over within 12 or 14 miles of *Shrewsbury* are full of soldiers; a good part of them are billeted in *Prince* parish; they are of the Lord *Grandison's* Regiment, and such for condition that I think the earth affords no worse. They have plundered divers men's houses in a most woful manner. Your friend and mine hath had in money and goods taken from him to the value of fifty pound. A gentleman of quality was forced to shift for his life, and leave his house, and they have taken possession of it, and live upon the spoil of his provision, corn and cattle, near 20 men, and at least forty horses, and shew no sign of parting as yet, but endeavour the ruin of the house and his goods; and if any fault be found, they threaten to burn it to the ground. They commit many outrages; they pretend quarrels against the Roundheads, but they spare none where they hope of good booties."[24]

[23] From "A Perfect Relation or Summarie of all the Declarations, &c. Printed for *Francis Coles* in his shop in the *Old Bailey*."

[24] From "Some late Occurrences in *Shropshire* and *Devonshire*. Dated *September* the last. *London*. Printed for *H. Blunden*. October 5, 1642."

XXIX.

SKIRMISH AT WORCESTER—GOD'S WONDERFUL PRESERVING THE TOWN OF MANCHESTER—A FEW TO OVERCOME MANY—HEAVY AND SAD TIMES IN PLUNDERING AND PILLAGING.

1642.—SEPTEMBER the 23rd, Prince *Rupert* came about nine or ten of the clock into *Worcester*, as though to fetch away those forces that lay at *Worcester*, much endangered by the Lord General's forces approaching near the City; about ten Troops, under the command of Colonel *Browne*, with about two or three hundred Dragoons drawn from an advantageous plot of ground, where they had pitched safely to prevent the Cavaliers' flight, were fiercely assailed at great disadvantage, with all Prince *Rupert's* forces, supposed to be strong five thousand horse; they valiantly charged against the Cavaliers, and had a cruel and bloody fight till it came to sword's point. Colonel *Fine*[1] himself rode up to their chief Commander, thrust his pistol at him, discharged and slew him outright. Lord *John*[2] is thought to be slain or desperately wounded; Prince *Rupert* is reported to be shot through the thigh. The parliament forces, being far too weak, were forced to retreat. The Lord General's forces being not come in, some of them retreated into *Worcester* with the Cavaliers, and being discovered in the streets of

---

[1] Probably Captain Nathaniel Fiennes.   [2] Sir John Byron.

that City, they had another bitter skirmish in the streets where divers were slain. The Cavaliers came into the City wofully mangled and bloody; some with the flesh of their head, some with their very skulls also hanging down; some with their ears cut off, and their pistols and carbines being hacked away which they held up for the guard of their heads.[3]

[Remember His marvellous works that He hath done: His wonders, and the Judgments of His mouth.—*Psal.* cv. 5.

O Lord, thou art my God, I will exalt thee, I will praise thy Name, for thou hast done wonderful things.—*Isaiah* xxv. 1.

This also cometh from the Lord of Host, which is wonderful in council, and excellent in works.—*Isai.* xxviii. 29.]

[*September* the 24th, being *Saturday*, the Town of *Manchester* in *Lancashire*, having some Malignants in it, and multitudes of papists near unto it, and being reputed a religious and rich town,[4] hath been much envied, and often threatened, by the

---

[3] See "A perfect and trve Relation of the great and bloudy Skirmish Fought before the City of *Worcester*, upon *Friday*, *Septemb.* 23, 1642. *London*, printed for *Jo. Thomas, Octo.* 3, 1642."

[4] "In the parliamentary publications of the day, Manchester is represented as 'a zealous and godly place,' and held out as an example to others. In Lancashire and in Yorkshire, it is said, there are more papists than in all England besides, and yet God hath most admirably shewn his power, by a handful of men in each of his shires, supporting the Gospel, and the growth of the Protestant religion, against the commissioners of array, and their forces. In this warfare, the trainbands of Manchester were the most distinguished."—Baine's *History of the County of Lancaster.*

Popish and Malignant parties. And at this time the difference was betwixt the Lord *Strange* and the Town, and that about giving up of the Arms to him for his Majesty's use; but more particularly it was intended for plundering and oppressing the poor Christian people, which is that which did procure the malice of the blaspheming enemy; but, blessed be God, notwithstanding the cruelty of the enemy, which was barbarous, for all his strength, which was about, as related (three thousand as some say) three hundred horse strong, and eighteen hundred foot, well armed, and seven cannons shot off about fifty or sixty times, with great iron bullets, that [exceeded] all the fire balls that were made, which were many. Nay, though he caused the outside of our town to be burned, which was done, yet God hath delivered us from all his plots, most miraculously, in an unparalleled and unheard of way.

Blessed be the name of our God, for though we were but weak in comparison of our enemy, and though we had our greatest enemies as well within us as without; though we were a divided people and a distracted people, that wanted ammunition, powder, and shot, and that all our passages were stopped up by the enemy, that we could hardly, but with the danger of our lives, get victuals, or intelligence from any other place; though we were worn out by want of sleep for many nights together, and out in wet service in the field against the enemy by day, and keeping our centuries[5] by night;

[5] *i. e.* guard.

yet God miraculously delivered us, and set us at liberty again; and the Lord *Strange* departed from us yesterday, which was *Saturday* in the afternoon; that though he had deprived us of a former *Sabbath*, yet he had not power to deprive us of another, but he hath removed his cannons, and the soldiers, some of whom having disbanded themselves after their captains were slain, as there were three great commanders slain, one was Captain *Standish*, that was captain of foot soldiers; another was a Cornet of the light horse; the third was one that shot off the cannons. And now the Lord *Strange* hath taken away all his forces home, and (for anything we know) he doth intend to keep them about his own house, for the safety of his person and estate; as he is afraid to be carried to the Parliament to answer for what he hath done, and the truth is that there is such terror stricken into the heart of him and his soldiers, as that it is thought he will never be able to lift up his hand in this cause, he hath had so ill a bargain of this; for, as relation is, he hath lost two hundred men, but it is not certainly known, but an hundred and fifty is thought to be the least; for it hath been the sharpest service, that is thought was in *England* for many years; for upon *Monday* last there was hot service in the field for three hours. In which service were many of the Lord *Strange* his men slain, and upon *Tuesday* was as great and desperate service betwixt *Salford*, (where the Lord *Strange's* people was) and *Manchester*, in which service was many slain of the Lord *Strange's* men.

Three of a heap was seen slain together, the next day, and since, until the Lord *Strange's* going away; during the time that he had either powder or shot, there hath been much blood shed on his side; and blessed be God, of a certain truth it is, for all the cannon shot and musket shot, but two of our soldiers hath been slain, and two others; a boy that was shot, standing upon a stile looking about him, and the other was a man that was looking to find a bullet that was shot, was killed by another in the mean time; and these four is all that hath been slain, and one or two more hurt, but not so as to take away life; cannons have been shot over men's heads, and touched their apparel, and yet none hurt by them. And by reason of an office that I had of providing meat for the soldiers, and to bring it to them, I had two cannon bullets shot over my head, and did touch my next fellow's garment, and, blessed be God for ever, none hurt at all. It is an unheard of deliverance, for which we in the Town, and gentlemen of the country, and soldiers, have cause for ever to be thankful to God for so great salvation; for salvation hath been our walls and bulwarks. This day hath been sermons of thanksgiving for our deliverance in three several places of the Town, besides the Churches' performances, and we are to-morrow to have a solemn day of thanksgiving for God's great mercies instead of our last day of our fasting, which, by reason of the occasion we were deprived of.

Much hurt hath been done in the country by

plundering and pillaging, and in *Salford*⁶ by the Lord *Strange's* soldiers; but God we hope, will make all good if the Parliament will not; but there is hope they will, yet however, the cause of God hath prospered as it hath, men are content with their loss, and though we do not fear the Lord *Strange* his coming again much, yet we are resolved to stand upon our strong guard, while the Parliament forces come to us.

Further, the Lord *Strange* did never enter upon any place of the Town, save that he burned one barn of corn, and two or three cottages, and was to give the man forty pound that set them on fire; but he was slain before he returned back, and is dead and buried, (in our custody) before he received his wages. So that the Lord *Strange* had no other composition,⁷ but as he came with a wicked and malicious heart and intention, he is gone away with a tortured conscience burning within him, as he confesseth, and with a shout of defiance he was sent away withal.

Further there was a Gentleman of *Stopleard*, five miles from *Manchester*, one Mr. *Leigh*, that would have brought one hundred and fifty soldiers to have added to the Lord *Strange*, but when the soldiers heard that the design was against *Manchester*, though they were his tenants, they would not come; here God sheweth His mercy to us; so if all these were put together, they would be set forth a mighty

---

⁶ Soutforth.   ⁷ Compensation.

deliverance, blessed be our God for ever.—*Manchester, October* 2nd, 1642.[8]

I did hear that in another letter mention [was made] of a bullet that glided close to the hair of the upper lip of a man, and did him no hurt.

The Lord *Strange's* soldiers, some of them, wept. Others protested great unwillingness to fight against *Manchester*, affirming they were deluded, or else they had not come thither. Thus the Lord hath preserved an unwalled Town from being destroyed by a great Army, consisting, as some say, of four thousand, some say three thousand, seven pieces of ordnance, two hundred dragoons, an hundred horsemen. To God alone be all the praise !]

October the 5th.—There came "information that his Majesty hath drawn all his forces into an entire body about *Shrewsbury*,[9] and intends to put the difference between him and his Parliament to a speedy issue, for that otherwise he cannot keep his forces together, they are in such distress for want of means, their whole subsistence being by plundering and pillaging, which they are licenced to do." [10]

As also there was information that the Earl of *Derby* continues his siege against *Manchester*, with three thousand men, horse and foot, sparing neither man, woman nor child, insomuch that the said Town is in great distress.

There came more letters to the Commons from

---

[8] See Appendix, Note KKK. [9] See Appendix, Note LLL.
[10] From *Perfect Diurnall*, No. 17.

Holland, signifying that the Queen hath now pawned the Jewels of the Crown, and that the Prince of *Orange* hath raised great sums of money for her. And the States have made stop of four ships at the *Brill*; and it is informed in *Holland* that the King of *France* intends to send aid to the King against the Parliament.

"It is certainly informed by a godly Minister not far from *Shrewsbury* that in one great house which the Cavaliers have plundered and pillaged, they did openly profess they had little to live on but what they took from others. And that when they went to bed, (being about sixty of them) divers of them had crucifixes hanging about their necks. In another great house where they were, they drank a health to the good success of Sir *Phelim O'Neal* in *Ireland*; by which we may see how likely these men are to maintain the true Protestant Religion, the laws of the land, and lawful liberties of the subjects, whatsoever they pretend. And though they pretend they search only for armour, yet they break up and take away whatsoever is of worth, or can be carried away, and spoil other things, cutting them to pieces, and taking away many horses from the people."

"At *Stone* is said that the Cavaliers have taken their cattle, and drive them to their quarters, but do sell cheap pennyworths of other men's goods. A Butcher went to make a purchase amongst them, took a sum of money, and bought cattle at an easy rate, making account of a very great gain; but as he returned, another Troop met him, and took his bargain out of his hand, and sent him home by *Weeping Cross*."[11]

October the 11th.—*South Wales.*— There was report made to the house that the Earl of *Doncaster* having got a company of resolute poor decayed gentlemen, they plunder as well those of the King's side as the Parliament's; and about *Malze* they took six light horse from a gentleman, violently out of his stables, and thrust the gentleman, and his household servants out of the house, and took all therein, whose plate and other furniture were valued at two thousand pound.

October the 14th, from *York.*—"Our condition here is miserable; above twenty houses are plundered in this city, because they will not contribute to maintain the Cavaliers in their designs. The lady *Melton*, who sent her goods by water towards *Hull*, had all her goods, money and plate, to the value of a thousand pound, taken by the soldiers as they were putting into the Barque. The Cavaliers threaten our best Ministers, that if they preach not as they will have them, they will kill them."[12]

---

[11] From *Speciall Passages*, No 7. "I find no less than three places so called ... one is between Oxford and Banbury; another very near Stafford ... the third near Shrewsbury. ' To return by *Weeping Cross*,' was a proverbial expression for deeply lamenting an undertaking, and repenting of it; like many other quibbling allusions to local names.

' He that goes out with often losse,
    At last comes home by *Weeping Cross*.'—Howell's *Eng. Prov.*"
—Nares' *Glossary*.

"Children sometimes get a fall, and then they come home by *weeping cross.*"—*Works of T. Brooks* (Nichol's edition), iv. 259.

[12] From *Speciall Passages*, No. 10.

The Lord General, by his letters, informed the Houses that the King's Army consisted of nine thousand Foot, and fifteen hundred Dragoons, and twenty-five hundred Horse.

There was a letter read in the House of Commons from *Ireland*, That the Papists and Jesuits have incensed the Army against the Parliament, telling them that the rebels have the King's hand and seal for what they do; and if they set themselves against the King's authority, they will incense his Majesty above what the Parliament are able to defend them, his Majesty having disclaimed the courses of the Parliament, and resolved to grant pardon to none that hold Arms by the Authority of Parliament, without the King's consent.

October 21st.—" Information was given to the House, That the King of *Denmark* hath above eight thousand men in readiness to be shipped away, but upon what design it is not known as yet; but it is conceived that they are intended for *England*." [13]

October 21st.—Intelligence was that " the King himself is at Sir *Thomas Littleton's*, fourteen miles from *Worcester*, and the soldiers make lamentable sport of all the goods and cattle they can find. They disarm all the trained soldiers everywhere, and if they meet any man riding upon the ways, they bereave them of their swords and horses." [14]

[13] From *Perfect Diurnall*, No. 19. See "The King of DENMARK, the King of *France*, the King of *Spain*, the States of *Venice* Navies on the Seas, intended for ENGLAND. With the Cause of their comming, and their intents. London, printed for *J. Bandon*, 1642."

[14] From *England's Memorable Accidents*.

At a conference of both Houses in the Painted Chamber it was delivered by the House of Commons (punctual proof being for every particular thing there spoken of) that it appears that his Majesty hath let loose the reins of the Papists (whose mercy is cruelty), that by the power derived from his Majesty to the Earl of *Newcastle*, his Lordship hath granted Commissions to divers notorious Papists in *Northumberland*, Bishoprick of *Durham*, and divers others, to be Colonels and Captains to raise men. And likewise that his Majesty hath such a number of Irish Rebels and Papists about him as is not to be believed; And the physician to Prince *Rupert* is a notorious Rebel, and indicted of high treason in *Ireland*, and that the Papist hath such power with his Majesty as to prevail with him to reject the receiving of any petition from the parliament by the Earl of *Essex*. And yet his Majesty by his proclamation did make many of his people believe he would admit no Papist near him, though none so powerful with him as they. And consider how contrary this hath been to his Majesty's protestations and invocations of heaven and earth to witness his affection to the Protestant Religion.

" The Cavaliers about the King brag that they have locked up the King's ears, and tongue, from the lords about him, and that of late he hath learned to keep his counsels from them. They revile and reproach his Excellency and the lords with him, and both the Houses of Parliament.

And they swear that they will neither give nor take quarter." [15]

The Cavaliers had taken three of the Lord General's men, whom they bound fast to a tree, and most inhumanly shot them to death.

October the 27th.—There came to the Parliament by one Captain *Ashley* from *Cork* in *Ireland*, informing that the Lord *Inchquin*, with about sixteen hundred men, set upon sixteen hundred Rebels in their quarters before *Connaught*, when they were feasting and rejoicing at the low estate of the Protestant Forces; killed seven hundred of them, put the rest to flight, took so great a quantity of arms that being not able to bear them out of the fields for want of carriages, they burned at least two or three thousand pikes, took three great pieces of ordnance, and a waggon, which the Rebels had laden with spare arms, with 16 of the Rebels' colours, and took Colonel *Butler*, and one Captain *John Butler* and divers other prisoners; and all this with the loss of only six men on our side, whereof one was the Lord of *Cork's* second son, whose death is much lamented.

As also they have lately received many great overthrows by the Protestant forces, which slew about one thousand of the Rebels, with the loss of not above one hundred men.

And so in *October* the 29th, when the Lord General left about two hundred of his wounded soldiers in *Kineton* to be cured there, who were

---

[15] From *England's Memorable Accidents*, No. 57.

all most inhumanly slain by Count *Rupert* and his Troopers.

Report is that " Taxes, Billeting of Soldiers, and plundering of men's houses, hath quite undone the whole county of *Shropshire*. The Cavaliers take men's horses away violently, and if they refuse to let them go, they have pistols and swords presently at their breasts. The whole County of *Shropshire* is so impoverished with the robbings and ransackings of these Rebels, that the length of an age will scarce recover their losses, and make them reparations." [16]

October the 29th.—An express out of *Derbyshire*, that Sir *Francis Wortley*, a *Yorkshire* Malignant, is come to *Wirskworth*, 8 miles from *Derby*, with two troops of horse, to pillage that country. They seize upon all the horses that come in their way; they pillaged the parson of *Bakewell's* House named Mr. *Rellisonne*; he withstood them as long as he could with his bow and arrow, but being too weak for them, they slew him.

October the 29th.—In *Yorkshire*, Mr. *Benson* of *Leeds*, an Attorney at Common Law, his house was plundered, all his Writings, Bonds, Bills, Books of Account torn in pieces, the wainscot in his house pulled in piece meal, and most of his house pulled to the ground.

The Rebels in *Pomfret* Castle, surprised eight of Sir *John Hotham's* soldiers at *Munckfroiston* in *Yorkshire*, who craved quarter upon their knees, but such was their cruelty, that they with insulting

---

[16] From *England's Memorable Accidents*, No. 57.

language put two of them by degrees to miserable
torture till they were dead, and wounded and shot
the other six, and tied their hands behind them,
and carried them away in that bleeding condition
to *Pomfret*, saying, no death was bad enough for
Roundheads.

October the 31st, by letters from *Banbury*.—That
the Cavaliers have pillaged and plundered the Town,
and utterly undone the greatest part there.

In this month Prince *Rupert* came for *England*,
and landed at *Dover* with two hundred men, and a
hundred thousand pounds which he carried with
him, and other martial ammunition, with six pieces
of ordnance and fourteen horses.

In *November* we did hear that in *Ireland* at
Clankilly, That one English took a Hill and withstood the Rebels, and slew one hundred, being but
two hundred against five thousand. Then news
came to us that the Rebels had set upon our men;
then immediately we marched out to them, and
drew ourselves into Battalia against the Rebels,
being one thousand to five thousand of the Rebels,
and we all shouted and threw up our caps, and shot
off one of our field pieces, and they all ran away.
Our Horsemen pursued them so fast that they took
into an Arm of the Sea, and our Horsemen rode
into the water, and killed an hundred. So all that
we killed that day were six hundred, and all that we
lost were but thirty-four.

November the 2nd.—There was Report made, that
his Majesty have drawn up a Declaration to his

whole Army, charging none of his Cavaliers to plunder and pillage, as formerly they have done, upon pain of death.

Nevertheless, Prince *Rupert*, Commissary *Willmot*, the Lord *Digby*, and the rest of the greater sort, have since done more spoil than heretofore, and go on in such an inhuman manner that it is hardly to believe the like, as, to wit, *Twyford*, or at *Swansly* in *Berkshire*, near *Reading*, where the people were constrained and forced out of their beds in the night, and glad they saved their lives.

The misdemeanours committed by the Earl of *Cumberland* and his northern Cavaliers are of a most insufferable condition, for they do plunder many honest men's houses who stand well affected to the Parliament, and have imprisoned many men of worth, who do refuse to contribute money to maintain them in this unlawful and unnatural war; they spare none, neither will they suffer any to escape their hands who will not lend money to their illegal designs.

"*November* the 5th, 1642, at *Maidenhead*, it is certain that Prince *Rupert* hath plundered the Lord *Say* his house, Master *Fiennes* his house, Mr. *Whitlock's* house,[17] Members of Parliament, and taken away all his cattle, and destroyed his deer, and such as they could not kill, they brake down the Park pales to let them out. And that when the Mayor of *Banbury* shewed Prince *Rupert* the King's hand and seal that the town should not be plundered, for that his Majesty had accepted of

[17] See Appendix, Note MMM.

a composition, Prince *Rupert* threw it away, and said, 'My uncle little knows what belongs to the wars,' and so commanded his men to plunder, which they did to the purpose, and had no respect to persons, for the malignants suffered more than the honest men of the town whom they call Roundheads. But that which startles us most is a warrant under his Majesty's own hand for the plundering of the Lord *Say* his house, and demolishing of it, and invites the people to do it, with a grant unto them of all the materials of the house; we had thought, till this warrant was produced, that the King had not been accessory to these horrible, pilfering courses. There is a *Banbury* man gone up to the Parliament with the warrant, who informs of most wicked and devilish outrages committed by Prince *Rupert* his forces, yet, to put a colour upon the business, it is given out it is against the King and Prince *Rupert's* mind to plunder, they hanged a man but yesterday, and yet they plundered the more. This warrant, under the King's own hand, is an undoubted truth, and fit to be made known to all the kingdom, that they may see what they are like to expect." [18]

November the 8th, information was that Prince *Rupert* at *Henley* hanged a man on a tree near the bowling-alley, for that he was a Roundhead, and had given intelligence to *Henley* of the coming of the Cavaliers. And Prince *Rupert* possesseth him-

---

[18] From *Speciall Passages, &c., informed to both Houses*, No. 13.

self of all horses he can meet withal, takes by force [from] the carriers that come out of the West country all their white clothes they were bringing up to *London*; he commands all malt, oats, and other provisions to be taken upon ticket.[19]

November the 12th, *Saturday*.—And for the King's army, poor *Brentford* is made a miserable spectacle, for they have taken from them all the linen, bedding, furniture, pewter, brass, pots, pans, bread, meal, in a word, all that they have, insomuch that when the Parliament's army came into the town on the Lord's day at night, the innkeepers and others begged of the soldiers a piece of bread. They have taken from divers of the inhabitants, some to the value of four hundred pounds, some three hundred pounds, some more, some less, and from the poorer sort all that ever they had, leaving them not a bed to lie on, nor apparel, but what they have on their backs, nor a pair of sheets, nor a piece of bread, and what beer they drank not, they let run out in their cellars; divers families of repute, with their wives and children, were driven to such extreme poverty thereby, that they have begged ever since; and took divers of the townsmen (who never opposed them) after they had plundered them, putting them in irons, and tying others with ropes, and so led them away like dogs to *Outlands*. Who can read this without a sad heart and a mournful eye?[20]

---

[19] See *Speciall Passages*, No. 14.

[20] "The King and Prince were then on *Hounsloe Heath*, and were marching towards *Brainford*. . . . There was that day apprehended a

At *Brentford* these tyrants took twenty of our men, tied them together, and hurled them into the *Thames*.[21]

November the 13th, there came letters from *Hereford*, informing that the Lord *Herbert,* the Earl of *Worcester's* son, had lately done a most cruel act in those parts; he, coming with some forces to a gentleman's house, a very religious man, and well-willer to the Parliament, he made spoil of his goods, seized upon the gentleman as he was in his bed, and commanded him to be shot, and for no other cause but that he was a Protestant."[22]

November the 23rd, report was made to the Commons from *Buckinghamshire* that the Cavaliers had been in some part of the county, and made great spoil there, and have driven a thousand head of cattle out of that county, and that they lie all along upon the river of *Thames,* and stop all the provisions

---

gentleman clothed in scarlet, and hanged in a *with* upon a tree, as it is conceived for speaking in honour of the Parliament, and no man suffered to cut him down, or cover his face, until he had been made a publicke spectacle to the whole army, which was then marching by. This was done in the way betwixt *Egham* and *Staines*."—*True Relation of two Merchants of London, who were taken prisoners by the Cavaliers.* London, 1642.

Also see " A True and Perfect Relation of the Barbarous and Cruell Passages of the King's Army, at *Old Braineford,* near *London.* Being presented to the House of *Commons,* by a Committee of the same House, who was sent thither, on purpose to examine the Truth of the particular Actions of the said Army. Printed for *E. Husbands* and *J. Frank,* and are to be sold at their shops, in the *Middle Temple,* and next doore to the *King's Head* in *Fleet-street.* 1642."—*King's Pamphlets;* 4to. pp. 12.

[21] See ". A True and Perfect Relation of the Barbarous and Cruell Passages of the King's Army at *Old Braintford.*" Printed and published by order of " *the* Commons *assembled in Parliament,* 24 November, 1642." [22] See *Speciall Passages,* No. 15.

coming to *London*. Information was also given to the Commons that the King's Cavaliers have made great spoil in *Surrey*, and have plundered and pillaged in divers places in that county, carrying away all their corn, cattle, goods, and what they could not, or would not, carry away, they quite spoiled in a very cruel manner. They have also assessed upon the county of *Oxon* to be paid monthly near upon three thousand pounds, and the like upon *Buckinghamshire* and *Berkshire*, and do plunder in the mean time till the counties condescend to the taxation.

They plunder by commission, and execute it without mercy. They apprehend all men they meet that, being demanded from whence they are, answer, " For King and Parliament." Some they presently put to death for such an answer, as a very good housekeeper at *Thistleworth*, Mr. *Arnall's* brother-in-law, there were seven of the Cavaliers shot him to death before his wife's face . . . five of these were Irish, and two English. They killed another man at *Staines*, others they wound, and all they imprison that so answer.

November the 26th.—There were divers letters brought to the Parliament, which were intercepted coming from *Holland*,[23] from the Duke of *Richmond*, Colonel *Goring*, and some others with the Queen,

---

[23] See "The Discovery of a great and wicked Conspiracy against this Kingdom in general, and the City of *London* in particular. Being a Letter sent from the *Hague* in *Holland*, and directed to Secretary *Nicholas*, but intercepted by the way, and read in both Houses of Parliament on *Saturday* the 26 of *November*, 1642." Printed by order of the Parliament, "for *John Wright*." 4to. pp. 8.—*King's Pamphlets.*

directed to Secretary *Nichol*, to acquaint his Majesty withal; by which letters, in short, thus much was informed, that the Prince of *Orange* has raised forty thousand amongst the Papists for the King, and is about to raise fifty thousand more, and ten thousand foot, and ten thousand arms, and a train of artillery, and many guns and other engines of war;[24] that great forces are made ready in *Denmark* to be also sent to *England*, and two ships, men of war, to conduct them, that they would by no means have his Majesty agree to a peace, but hope the King by this time hath taken *London*, that they would before this time have landed in *England* in *Norfolk* or *Suffolk*, but that they were hindered by cross winds, wishing the King to send some troops of horse into *Kent*, to keep that county in awe, and that they shall bring with them great store of monies from *France* and other parts; there were divers other messages in the letters which will be too tedious to relate.

"The malicious, malignant party, the Cavaliers of *Cornwall*, that daily march under the command of the Lord *Mohun*, doth hourly mischief in those parts, without remorse or pity. They will not suffer them to plough their grounds, to sow their grain, but with their horses they destroy it. They go to the barns, and lodge their horses there, and pluck down their stacks of corn to feed their beasts, and throw it about to make fodder of, and when they leave the place, they set them all on fire, swearing no corn shall grow until the wars be done,

---

[24] See *Speciall Passages*, No. 16.

nay, the very churches they make stables of; is not this barbarous and inhuman?

"*November* the 28th, at *Foy* in *Cornwall*, certain Cavaliers coming there to be billeted, the town did kingly entertain them, on this condition, to pay for what they had. The Captains and commanders took their oaths [that] no soldier that marched under their command should be so base but pay for what he had, and so they did, there remaining three days. The fourth they gave the town notice of their departure, and their drums beat for to give notice. And for their welcome, each place where they had lain, did feast them gratis with great thanks. The word being given, they fell to plundering, breaking open trunks, chests, and boxes, took all their plate and money they could find, and told them they did but borrow it, when the wars were done they would pay it back again.

"At *Launceston*, getting in with the like wile, they likewise plundered that, and, like the devil, they cry all is their own, swearing, . . . blaspheming, and cursing that they will up to the King in spite of opposition. And for the city of *London*, they intend there for to keep their *Christmas*, and make the citizens wait upon their trenchers. But for the Roundheads, they will send them pell mell to their father the devil; they swear they will build in every street a cross, to cross those that survive." [25]

[25] From "A True Relation of the present Estate of *Cornwall*. 4to. London. Printed by *T. F.* for *R. G.* December, 1642."—*King's Pamphlets*.

December the 13th.—" From *Marlborough* it is certified that the inhabitants stood manfully upon their defence so long as they were able; but no succour or release coming timely to them, they were forced to yield, and gave them admittance, who have most lamentably plundered them, for they have carried away sixteen loads of their goods, and above a hundred of their men prisoners to *Oxford*, and they have also burnt a great part of that town, and these Cavaliers have used the women with the like cruelty, as the rebels do in *Ireland*. . . . And the prisoners which they carried from thence to *Oxford* are used so cruelly and inhumanly, that they are ready to perish and starve. And two of these Cavaliering rebels are the Lord *Digby* and the Lord *Grandison*, and Commissary *Wilmot*." [26]

These rebels at *Reading* did hang one Mr. *Boyce*, an honest citizen of London.[27]

December the 26th, by letters it was informed from *Northampton* that they fell upon the Puritans at *Wilby*, and plundered them, and they returned to *Wellingborough*, and *Malling*; and the inhabitants with knives, bodkins, shears, and the like, had given to one of our men thirty wounds.

December the 27th.—It is reported that the Earl of *Newcastle* hath imposed ten hundred thousand pound tax upon the County of *York*, and that he hath caused two gentlemen to be shot to death at *Topliff* for refusing to pay their rates accordingly,

---

[26] *England's Memorable Accidents, from the* 12th *of December to the* 19th *of the same*, 1642.   [27] See Appendix, Note NNN.

and that his popish Army is so barbarous that they will give no quarter to any, but slay man, woman, and child.

About *Newcastle* the Papists and Malignants do live only by plundering and pillaging, and most barbarously and inhumanly take all they can get from the poor distressed inhabitants thereabouts.

December the 31st, " Captain *Wingate's* wife, the Lady *Essex*, were called into the house, who lately came from *Oxford*, and can report of a certain of the usage of the Captains that are prisoners there;[28] which said lady affirmed that they are kept close prisoners, not permitted pen, ink, nor paper, nor book to read in, and that they are almost famished for want of food, being allowed but a penny farthing a day to maintain them, and some days have not bread or water to eat or drink. So they are consumed away to death, and eaten of vermin, and no friends, not their own wives, suffered to come near them to give them relief; that they petitioned his Majesty to use them but as favorable as the Turks use Christians, and that they can find no redress."[29]

---

[28] See " A True and most sad Relation of the Hard Usage and extreme cruelty used on Captain *Wingate*, . . . with others of the Parliament Souldiers. . . . Written by one of the same Prisoners in behalf of them all, to a Worthy and eminent Citizen of *London*. Dated 9th of *February* 1642. *London.* Printed by *George Hutton* at the *Turned Style* in *Holborn. February* 13, 1661."—*King's Pamphlets.* See also *Speciall Passages*, No. 27.

[29] From *A Perfect Diurnall*, No. 33.

XXX.

Marlborough's Miseries[1]—Plundering of the Counties of Northampton and Warwick—Bibles and other Good Books Burned at Reading—Prince Rupert's taking of Cirencester.

But to proceed to let you understand a little more of the barbarous cruelty that those English rebels (I mean the Cavaliers) did use to those honest inhabitants at *Marlborough*. For when these rebels had got into the town, they ran through the streets with their drawn swords, cutting and slashing those men they met with, whether soldiers or not. They set their houses on fire; they had four great fires at one time flaming in four several places. A very sad thing to behold, and at the same time their soldiers breaking up of shops and houses, and taking away all sorts of goods, breaking of trunks, chests, boxes, cabinets, bedsteads, cupboards, presses, coffers, and many that were not locked, but yet they would break and dash them all to pieces; and thence rifled and carried away all kinds of wearing apparel, all money or plate they met with, all sorts of shoes[2] and boots, stockings, hats, and woollen and linen cloth of all sorts, sheets, beds, bolster cases, cutting up the cases and scattering the feathers in the streets to be trampled on by horses and

---

[1] See Appendix, Note OOO. [2] Shoones.

men; also searching men's and women's pockets for money, and threatening them with pistols and swords to shoot, or run them through, if that they would not give them money, by which means compelling many men to lead them to the places where they had hid their money.

One of their Commanders came into the house of an honest Gentleman of the Town, and uttered horrible speeches in a most insolent and insulting manner.

The Lord *Digby* or *Grandison* at another time coming into the same man's house, being a wealthy man, but one who had many children, tells the man of the house that he did and would fine him to pay five hundred pounds, which should be made ready and paid within four days. The good gentleman makes him answer that he could not pay one hundred pounds, for his house had been plundered of all he had, and besides he had eighteen children to maintain, and nothing left to keep them. This lord swears their common oath; what did he tell him of eighteen children; why dost thou not tie them two and two together, and throw them into the river, and drown them; and then asked where they were, for if thou wilt not, saith he, I will; (confirming this with the aforesaid oath); but he should pay him so much money, or else he would hang him at his own door.

Another among them would give a man twenty shillings to teach or tell him a new oath, that he had never either heard or sworn. We never heard such a variety of strange and unheard of oaths, and such frequency of them, that not so many words were scarcely heard as oaths and blasphemies; that except hell were broken loose, we could not hear nor see more intolerable wickedness.

Nay, in their plundering they had no regard to rich or poor, to Roundheads (as they call them) and those that were of the like disposition as themselves, for they pillaged even poor men that live on alms of the town, and beg their bread. The very houses that were burning, and consuming by the fire, that themselves had kindled, were not spared from robbing them of the very goods that they preserved from the fury of the flames.

Besides this, the spoil they did among men's goods was as much as their loss, which they carried away, as in letting out whole hogsheads of oil, and vessels full of strong water, vinegar, aqua vitæ, treacle, and spice, and fruit, and all this thrown about the shops, cellars, and houses. Besides the taking away and burning of books, for they took all the greatest books the Booksellers had in their shops, and all the smaller books they burnt; for in one of our Booksellers' houses they maintained a great fire for five hours together, with nothing but books and papers, insomuch that they had like to have set fire of his house with the greatness of the flame, for they burned the mantletree of the chimney. And in five or six other places more [they] adventured the houses by fire also, as the Mayor of the Town his house, and in a man's shop that sells oil, pitch, rosin, hemp, flax, and tar, and such ready things to take fire, they had kindled a fire, and went forth and left it purposely to burn ; but by the care of a neighbour (the man not being at home) prevented through the will of God. And at a woollen draper's shop, under his penthouse, making a great fire near his shop windows, and some two or three other honest men's houses, which I will not stand to relate the manner thereof, and yet none of these men's houses took fire.

But to relate all their rage and cruelty were almost endless, for they brake up the Town-House, and there they brake the chests and coffers that the Records and Court books and Deeds and Leases of the Town land were in, and carried them away; they likewise brake off the seals, and rent the writings in pieces, as also they did to other men's writings ; And the Town's Grand Charter they also carried away, besides two hundred pounds' worth of cheese that was laid in for the market, which they carried away every pennyworth. They brake up our prisons, and set prisoners at liberty that were in on execution, and delivered them ; besides the spoiling all Books of law, Records, and monuments; and thinking yet they could never do mischief enough, they brake glass windows, cut and slashed men's tables, boards, and chairs with their swords; besides the frights they put many women and children to, by setting the points of their swords to their breasts, threatening them to run them through if they will not give them money, &c.

And all the horses and carts that were in the

town, both good and bad, they took away, many of which were country men's horses, which had been stayed here the *Saturday* before, and on these they carried away our goods. Thus that very thing which was intended for our good, proved to our hurt in the event, and also to the country's loss.

Now concerning the poor prisoners they took. So soon as they took any they stripped him of his clothes, especially the upper garments, and then they demanded money of them; and they searched their pockets and took it from them; and after they had brought a great many together, they compelled them to go into the town again, just before their troops, and so put them altogether into a stable amongst horses, and tied their arms with cords one to another, not permitting wives or friends to come to them to yield them supply of money or victuals; and in the same manner they led them away the next day towards *Oxford*, compelling them to go all on foot in the dirty ways, two by two as they were bound, because they should go just before the mouth of their ordnance, not suffering them to go the cleanest way. And when they came to *Oxford*, they were put into a Tower of the Castle, a great height, where they are not allowed any fire or candle, or straw to lie on, but the bare boards and planks of the room; nor any more allowance than one penny and farthing a day, which is a penny in bread, and a farthing can of beer, which is half beer and half water; by which means many are very ill and diseased.

Now for their number; they carried from *Marlborough* between a hundred and a hundred and twenty, but of these but forty *Marlborough* men, some of which are poor silly 'prentice boys, some others day labourers, and poor simple men of very mean condition, who neither ever had or handled arms in their lives; and one among the rest that we think was scarce ever worth five shillings, who sat trembling and quaking for fear, poor man, all the time of the fight; and we verily think would be ready to sink down at the very sight of a drawn sword. Others they took away prisoners, whose houses and goods were consumed by fire, and in arms neither. The rest were country men, and many of them only men that came to the market; some others that came along at their heels when they had got the towns, who came purposely to pilfer and rifle for goods also; some of them we know.

But for the number of houses burnt, there was fifty-three dwelling houses, within which houses did inhabit just fifty-three several families, and the number of persons in them, just an hundred persons, left harbourless, without house or goods, besides barns all full of corn, except one, which had hay in it; and also stables, woodpiles, and outhouses that were not taken notice of, nor cast in this number.

And by this occasion of burning these men's houses, and the necessity our other poor were brought into, the country about us sending in their benevolence towards the relief of the poor among us, there was relieved thereby six hundred families, and near upon two thousand persons, numbered in those families that had need of relief.

The general loss of our Town amounted to fifty thousand pound in goods, money, and wares at the least, as it is conceived; not accounting of those houses that they burned.

One thing I have omitted concerning their taking prisoners, that is, that they carried into *Oxford* two hundred prisoners, for as they pass through the country they take up men they cared not whom, to make up this number, and compelled them to go along prisoners; some from the plough in the fields, some from their doors as they come to look forth upon them as they passed by. Some they pulled out of their houses in the villages where they dwelt, pretending they were Roundheads, for which they must go away prisoners. And in all the villages taking away horses or goods, or whatsoever liked them, setting their horses into men's barns of corn, and making litter of some, and their horses eating the rest. So in *Marlborough*, they would make stables of linen drapers' and other tradesmen's shops, or in the parlours and places of men's dwellings, fetching away their malt, oats and hay by force, to give their horses, yea, and to sell too, for little or nothing, if they found any chapmen; sometimes selling that for two shillings six pence which is worth twenty shillings. As to instance in Bibles; they would take all, either new or old, and sell them for sixpence, or twelvepence, apiece.

And for the number of these that came against

us was about seven thousand, horse and foot, all hungry, gaping thieves; their chief Commanders were these, Commissary *Wilmot,* the Lord *Grandison,* the Lord Viscount *Crambairn,* the Lord *George Digby* (a prime beast), the Lord *Wentworth,* Sir *William Penniman,* and to divers others, which you may see in the book at large.

The number of their slain and wounded men they kept from our sight and knowledge as much as they could, but they had slain, as is conceived, above two hundred men. Many they buried the next day in the Town, and many they buried in several places in the fields about the Town. Some they threw into a very deep well, three furlongs from the Town, and many they carried away in carts, some say four or five loads, and cast in a river in their way; but their own confession is, they say that twenty-seven Commanders fell, and three Cannoneers were slain, and a great many men more they lost. So that it is conceived by the most, that two hundred men at the least were slain, besides a great many that were wounded, of which wounded men they all, or most, died of their wounds. For some were left behind in the Town, and some carried three, or four, or five miles, towards *Oxford,* and there left; whose wounds seemed to be but light to them that saw them, and yet they proved mortal to them all, and thereof since they are dead.

And yet there was neither man, woman, or child killed on our side in all this fight; only two countrymen were killed, very cowardly, as they were running forth of the Town, when they made no resistance, and one of these did report at a gentleman's house within two miles of the Town that he was going to *Marlborough*, and would receive their pay, but intended not to fight.

And one remarkable thing we may note in it, that a certain Townsman who was a servant to the Lord *Seymour*, who was not in the fight at the first entering into the Town, who was a friend of theirs, came out of a house where the Lady *Seymour* [was] to desire quarter for her; but they being in a rage, regarding not his words, cried out, Shoot him, shoot him, Rogue; whereupon he, clapping the door together against them, they shot through the door, and wounded him; who yet lies very ill, not knowing whether he shall recover, or no.

Now this same party, a little before the first coming of the Lord *Digby* against the town, having been in *Wales* with his Master, or with the Lord Marquis of *Hertford*, and with the King's Army also, he uttered this speech, that there was a fearful black cloud coming upon this Town; and also when the town was almost taken, he was heard to say that now the King had begun his harvest.

And with all other, men, women, or children of the town, not so much as [one] shot.

They had some six or seven great guns, and a great many shots with them, for we found eighteen or twenty great bullets that have been taken up in the Town in several places, besides many that were shot over, and so never found. The weight of these bullets we have seen were some 22 pound, some 18 pound, some 15 pound weight, and some we saw two pound shot, as it seems from some drake, but of all these sorts we have seen and can shew them. And for the special mercies of God to us in the midst of so great calamities, is not to be forgotten by us. For of all those houses or barns that were burned, not one of the owners had stood in this noble cause: and of many that did shew themselves actors therein, or setters forward thereof, though some ventures and attempts were made in their houses by fire, yet they had their houses preserved.

Another remarkable thing is, that a few, even a very handful of men, should with such undaunted courage and resolution stand to defend a town against a great company, and yet not lose a man; for all the men that we had to fight in all this time were but one hundred and forty men at the utmost. For one band of men we had under the command of one Captain *Digges*, who were in a convenient place both to defend the Town, and offend the enemy; yet he suffered them not to shoot one shot, but, as we have heard, sent by a message that he would stand neuter. And many others there were who played the cowards, when danger approached, and the rest of our men were set to guard at such part of the town where we had no assault at all given.

Another mercy, that in all these great shots against our houses, not ten shillings in harm done thereby; and many others more we could observe;

as one in their departure from us, and not wintering here, as it seems they had intended, if they had not heard of the approach of some of the Lord General's forces, who were coming for our relief; and also in regard they had so much plundered the town, they thought here would not be support for them.

The first copy of this was intercepted by the Cavaliers.

March the 6th, 1644.—From *Marlborough* we have intelligence that there are four hundred native Irish lately come in thither, whereby the miseries of the inhabitants of that (for a long time) poor and oppressed Town are much increased, for that many of them are constrained to leave their houses and families, and come to *London* from the cruel usage of the enemy. They have also intelligence that there are about two thousand of the same bloody crew come from *Bristol* to join with the *Oxford* Cavaliers, the fittest company and place for that Romish and popish faction to meet together.

The Remarkable Mercy of God unto some Poor Honest Men of Marlborough, further confirmed unto me by Mistress WILSON, *that was then an Inhabitant there.*

When *Marlborough* was set on fire in five several places, and burnt down whole rows of houses, yet, by the great providence of God, the fire did not burn any house down of those that held for the cause of God, but all those that held with the enemies against us had their houses and barns, to the number of fifty and odd houses, burnt down. Although fire was set to an honest man's house, yet it would not take, for the fire-brand went out again, and did no hurt.

It hath pleased Almighty God to spare my life to see the beginning of this year, 1643, and my God gives me heart and time to take notice of His mercies and of His judgements. And I am, as yet, spared to be as one of *Job's* messengers to bring, or write, heavy and sad news concerning the poor Church of God.

This month of *January*, 1643, it is informed out of *Derbyshire* that Mr. *Henry Hastings*, with his pillagers, rob all the carriers that pass to and fro in those parts.

The information is most certain of Prince *Rupert* plundering of the counties of *Northampton* and *Warwick*;[3] he hath seized upon at least twelve hundred horses, taken, most of them, from the plough and cart, as if he wished famine on this kingdom, which hath hitherto fed him with bread. Nay, it is written from those parts, that, after he had got about threescore carts and waggons from country villages, and filled them with pillage, he kept a fair, and sold divers horses, as well as goods, leaving in many villages neither beds to lie on, nor bread to eat, nor horse, cow, nor sheep, and this he did to some of his friends, as well as those he esteemed his enemies. They go on yet in a further degree in these un-

---

[3] See *The Kingdome's Weekly Intelligencer* (Nmb. 5), *sent abroad to prevent mis-information.*

natural courses, for in *Denbighshire*, to instance there one only amongst divers other places of the like example, these rebels there have possessed themselves of Sir *Thomas Middleton's* house, seized upon all his goods, within doors as well as without, to the value of five thousand pounds, at least; turned out all his servants; and these vile robberies they do by a Royal command, as the Commissioners that have seized on the same, affirm.

1643. *January* the 25th.—A great number (if not all) of the Bibles and other good books were burned (at *Reading*) under the gallows in the Market place at Market time. The Inhabitants are thrust out of their dwellings, and papists entertained, and here is mass daily in divers houses.

A Relation of the Taking of Cirencester,[4] *in the County of Gloucester, by seven thousand rebels under the command of Prince* RUPERT, *Prince* MAURICE, *the Earls of* NORTHAMPTON, CARNARVON, DENBIGH, *and* CLEVELAND, *the Lord* DIGBY, *Lord* ANDOVER, *Lord* WENTWORTH, *Lord* TAAFE, *Lord* DILLON, *Lieut. Gen.* WILLMOT, *Sir* JOHN BYRON, *Col.* GERRARD, *Col.* KYRKE, *Col.* DUTTON, *and Captain* LEGGE, *and divers others, to whom I may say,*

---

[4] This account is taken from "A Relation of the taking of *Ciceter* in the Covnty of *Glocester* on *Thursday, February* 2, 1642 . . . Sent to a Friend in London, by one who was present at, and some days after the Taking of it. Published because of the many false reports that were in print concerning that businesse." The concluding note is, "It is ordered this eighteenth day of *February* 1642, by the committee of the House of Commons in Parliament concerning printing, that this booke, intitled a Relation of the taking of *Ciceter*, be printed by *Michael Sparke* senior."

This "booke" is reprinted at length in the *Bibliotheca Gloucestriensis*.

as old father Jacob said to his sons, for their cruelty, Gen. xlix. 5–7 : " *Simeon and Levi, brethren in evil, the instruments of cruelty are in their habitations. Into their secret let not my soul come. Cursed be their wrath, for it was fierce, and their rage, for it was cruel.*"

1643.—*February* the 1st, these enemies renewed their forces with some fresh troops from *Oxford*, and two whole culverins, besides four small brass field pieces, and two mortar pieces, and so this night some of them quartered within a mile of the town, and gave us alarms all that night.[5]

On the next morning, *February* the 2nd, they were discovered some two miles from the town, where, under a hedge, they stayed some two hours, till all their forces drew together into one body from their several quarters in the villages, and so they divided themselves, Prince *Rupert*, and the greatest part of the army, drawing near the town on the west and the south part ; and the Earl of *Carnarvon*, and his troops, and some other forces, on the north part of the town.[6] About nine or ten of the clock they came, some of them within command of our cannon, which played at them two or three hours,

---

[5] " The prince had two eighteen-pounders, and four field-pieces, and a mortar piece to throw granades."— Rudder's *History of Gloucestershire*.

[6] " They drew their bodies of Foot into their severall places neere the towne : viz. the one to *Galley-hill*, which is by the wind-mill, the other to the *Reddicks*, and the third to *Ilston-meadowes*, where the greatest part of their horse were before, and another Body of Foot, (with some Ordnance) that was drawn into the *Abbey-meadow*, which is on the North-side of the town."—*Perfect Passages*, &c., No. 32.

and often caused them on the west side of the town to retreat behind a little hill, and, all that while, divers parties of our musketeers went out under the shelter of hedges and walls, and skirmished with the enemy.

So there continued at *Barton*[7] a very hot fight for some two hours, our men lying under shelter of the wall, notably giving fire on them within less than musket shot, and our cannon being a little more off than musket shot, all the while furiously playing point blank on their whole body, which lay in an open rising field. Here the Welshmen were seen to drop down apace; but still the horsemen behind them cried, "On, on," and drove them forward, till they had gotten quite under the garden wall. But, before that, the enemy had fired some barns, and ricks of corn and hay that lay quite behind those hundred musketeers, so that the enemy being at the wall, and breaking of it down, and the fire so behind them, that it took away all possibility of retreating, if they stayed any longer, and they being so few, our men were forced out of that work after two hour's valiant resistance of that furious charge of the enemy, during all which time we lost but one man, who, after the guard was entered, could not find his way forth through the fire and smoke.

[7] ". . . which great farm belonged to the Abbey of Cirencester, and was granted to Richard Berners, 36 H. 8, and livery of it was granted to Gerard Croker, 15 Eliz. It was vested in Sir Richard Onslow, Speaker of the House of Commons, during part of Queen Anne's reign, who sold it to Allen Bathurst, Esq." [afterwards Earl of Bathurst].—Rudder's *History of Gloucestershire.*

Our men retreating to the second work, which was hard by, being so hotly pursued by the enemy's fire and smoke, which the wind drove directly upon them, they, and the guards of that work, without any resistance made, very disorderly fled into the town, and were furiously pursued by the enemy, who without quarter killed those they met with, or overtook, which so desperately enraged our men that in the market-place, and from windows, they shot at the enemy almost an hour together, purposing to sell their lives and their liberties as dear as they could.

Whilst the enemy was assaulting the town on the west side at the *Barton*, the Earl of *Carnarvon* and his forces, seeing the *Barton* fired, and our men beaten from their works, sought to enter it on the north side, where there was a sore charge valiantly received by our men, with little loss, who yielded not, till the enemy, who had entered the town on the other side, was on their back.

Thus, about four of the clock, the town was wholly won, and shooting was ended on all sides, and then they took prisoners, and fell to plundering that night, all the next day, and on *Saturday*, wherein they shewed all the barbarous insolence of a prevailing enemy; and I am confident the enemy not only acted over, but outdid their former cruelties and spoil of *Brentford* and *Marlborough*; they spared not to plunder their best friends, for I can assure you ☞ some of the most notorious malignants were the most notably plundered of all the town.

"I tremble," saith my author, "to write of their blasphemies, they tauntingly asked some godly people, 'where is now your God? you Roundhead rogues, you prayed to the Lord to deliver you, and you see how He hath delivered you, ye rebels,' &c."

The number that the enemy lost is altogether unknown, by reason none durst go forth to see the slain of the town forces; both townsmen and countrymen there were above twenty, as can be learned. It is much feared they slew a very godly Minister,[8] who was seen taken by them, and yet cannot be heard of. There lay some of our men naked four days after they were killed, near the place where the enemy, after taking the town, kept his utmost guard, and none durst bury them.

The number of prisoners that they took, and carried to *Oxford*, was between eleven and twelve hundred, amongst which there were some gentlemen of eminent estates and affections to their country, two very godly ministers, divers commanders, and others which were very religious, and of good account.[9]

They stripped many of the prisoners, most of them of their utmost garments, they were all turned that night into the Church, and, though

---

[8] "The Cavaliers did murder a very godly Divine lately at *Ciceter*, with his wife and children, in their coole blood."—*A Continuation of certaine Speciall and Remarkable Passages.*

[9] "... one Mr. *Stanfield*, armed back and brest, with sword and pistolls. The other, Mr. *Gregory* of *Cyrencester*."—*A Particular Relation of the Action before Cyrencester* ... "Written by an Eye-witnesse. Printed in the year 1642." Reprinted in *Bibliotheca Gloucestriensis*.

many of them were wounded and weary, yet their friends were not suffered to bring them a cup of water into the Church that night, but what they thrust in at the back of the Church, having broken the windows, and the like cruelty. I here was shewed unto them when they lay in *Witney* Church in their passage to *Oxford*.

They tied all the prisoners, gentlemen, ministers, and all, in ropes, and made them all go afoot through the dirt in the streets and way to *Oxford*, which was up to the knees sometimes, and in this manner they used a very worthy gentleman, who had been very lately High Sheriff of our county, an aged gentleman, of an infirm health, though of an undaunted courage in this cause.

They shamefully abused the two ministers, reproachfully imitating their manner of preaching, &c.

The captain, who took the ministers, upon the earnest solicitations of one of their friends for their releasement, promised them that for fifty or sixty pounds apiece he would release them, which money being procured, and paid them, he scoffingly answered, that they might well pay as much more to him for not killing them, as he might have done; and so, after that, they were more straitly imprisoned and worse used, and one of their friends, that had a free pass promised him into the town with the money, had very much ado to escape killing and imprisoning.

We lost five pieces of cannon, near upon twelve hundred muskets, and other arms, fourteen colours, and some ammunition, for most of our powder. and bullet was sent unto them before they entered the town.

The value of the pillage of the town is uncertain, but very great, to the utter ruin of many hundred families; and besides the burning of some particular men's houses which were purposely set on fire after the town was won, the *Barton* Farm, with very much buildings in it, and all the corn, hay, and other goods and cattle of one gentleman, which amounted to three thousand pounds and upwards, was burnt to the ground.

February the 3rd, they went into the country, and took away all the horses, sheep, oxen, and other cattle of the well affected that inhabiteth near *Cicester*.

February the 4th, they took away cloth, wool, and yarn, besides other goods from the clothiers about *Stroudwater*, to the utter undoing, not only of them and theirs, but of thousands of poor people whose very livelihood depend on that trade.

Some cause of this our ruin hath been the treachery of our malignant Gentry round about us, who constantly gave the enemy intelligence, and entertainment in their houses, made provision for their armies, and some of them appeared in arms before their neighbour town, which they could endure to see both fired and spoiled.

February the 7th.—There came letters this day fully informing the bloody cruelty of the Cavaliers at the taking of *Cicester*, but, by the way, the cruel carriage of Prince *Rupert*,[10] (for justly so his name may be) in plundering *Northampton* and *Warwickshire* was first related to this effect: That he took away in those two counties at least two thousand horses, with which he made his footmen troopers; six hundred head of cattle, and above sixty cart load of plunder, besides the great spoil the common soldiers made, who loaded themselves with all sorts of pillage that was fit for carriage, and took pure *Holland* sheets and folded them up under their saddles. But to go on; when Prince *Rupert* and these Cavaliering Rebels had entered into the town of *Cicester*, they laid about them in that inhuman manner it would grieve a Jew to hear the relation. They spared none, either of men, women, and children, that they met with in the streets, and most cruelly murdered a godly divine and his whole family, and two other ministers, as is most notoriously known. The like cruelty, in all respects, if it were fully related, could not be paralleled by the Irish Rebels.

And upon the first report of their coming to *Oxford* there were at least four thousand of the inhabitants that went out to see them, divers of the Court, and his Majesty, a little way. The poor prisoners were tied to one another with cords and match,[11] though most of them were men of good

---

[10] Rober.

[11] " A rope or cord made of hempen tow, composed of three strands slightly twisted, and again covered with tow, and boiled in the lees of old wine. This, when lighted at one end, retains fire and burns slowly till consumed. It is used in firing artillery, &c."—*The Imperial Dictionary;* London, 1863.

worth and quality, and two of them ministers, trashing [12] through the mire and dirt, and when they came before his Majesty, they were commanded in the open fields to fall down upon their knees in all the mire and dirt, to beg his Majesty's grace and favour, which they were easily entreated to, the poor men upon the first sight of his Majesty being not a little confident that the bowels of princely mercy would be extended towards them; but they received no other answer but this, that they had brought that misery upon themselves; and were presently carried into the town, and imprisoned in two several Churches, and kept there all night, not allowed either firing, bread or water. But a poor woman passing by, and hearing their lamentable cry for water, water, undertook to fetch them some, which one of the Cavaliers perceiving, gave her the bastinado for it, but she being sensible of their misery, said she would fetch them water, though she were hanged for it. Five or six of them with their miserable usage, and the wounds they received at *Cicester*, died that night; and another, distracted with his sufferings, to expiate [13] his present misery, cut his own throat.

---

[12] To trash, to fatigue.—*Halliwell*.

[13] *i.e.* fully complete and end. See—

"Then look I death my days should expiate."
                                Shakespeare, xxii. Sonnet.

See Dyce's edition, London, 1866, vol. v. 462.

XXXI.

A MEMORIAL OF GREAT STORMS OF RAIN, OF THUNDER, AND LIGHTNING—STRANGE SIGHTS IN THE AIR.

[JULY the 19th, 1643.—In *Norwich* they had a terrible storm of thunder and lightning, the thunder sounding distinctly, as if great pieces of ordnance had been shot off, and such a vehement shower of rain, that boats might have floated in the streets; and withal the lightning struck so thick upon the water, that it made some of the watchmen blind for the time; and the tempest was so furious about a mile and a half from *Norwich*, at a place called *Eatonwood*, near a farmer's house, that abundance of rooks and daws sitting upon the trees were stricken dead;[1] insomuch that one hundred and eleven of their carcases were found the next morning by the farmer's servants, which they gathered and laid upon an heap, and have been since viewed by credible persons. Some of these fowl had their necks broken, and others of them had their bones and bodies terribly rent and shattered, and not one drop of blood was to be seen, either upon the ground, the trees, or their carcases. And that which hath made this accident the more observable is, that not

---

[1] See Blomefield's *Norfolk*, iii. 387; London, 1806.

any profitable creature about the farmer's house was so much as touched, or had any harm, by this furious tempest, but that it fell only upon those ravenous and sharking [2] creatures that are hurtful to man. What this may presage is yet unknown to man, but from the inference we may conjecture, that it may mean God's Judgments upon the plundering and pillaging Cavaliering Rebels, who, like rooks and daws live now ravenously by the sweat of honest men's brows. This month of *July*, the 22nd day, here in *London*, we had very great Storms, or Rain.

October the 29th, 1643, being the Lord's day, from nine o'clock at night, till five o'clock the next morning (the moon shining not that night) there was seen by divers great flashes of fire in the sky, north-west, like to the giving of fire of ordnances; and all that night was very light, almost as light as noonday, that many say the like hath not been seen.

Out of *Suffolk* they write that at that time, that evening after sunset was extreme dark, till about eight of the clock, then it began to grow light on the sudden, and was so light that they could plainly see to read a great print, and could easily discern written letters and words; and yet there was no moonshine, for she rose not until about five of the clock the next morning. It was a quiet and calm light round about, and more than usually when the moon is at her full, and that the stars were rather

---

[2] *To shark*: to play the petty thief; to cheat, to trick.—*Johnson.*

dimmer than ordinarily they are. Some clouds appeared in the north and east with some streams of lightsomeness in them. And those that watched all night to see the event, affirmed that it held so light even almost till morning.

At *Norwich* also they saw the very same light; only this some persons of credit that sat up and watched have added, that about three o'clock in the morning they saw a star fall, longer than any star that ever they saw, and it fell leisurely, a long time before it vanished; they had time to discourse together, from the time it began to fall to the time it ceased. What these things portend God only knoweth. In the Scripture, light is always taken in the good part, and signifies prosperity and joy.[3]

And we have heard some affirm that are lately come out of *Surrey*, that at *Mitcham* in that county, they saw that night strange apparitions in those white illuminated clouds towards the north, and amongst the rest a battle, as if it had been between two armies, which no doubt threateneth a continuation of wars amongst us, but will end in a glorious and happy peace, as some authors have written.

1645.—*February* the 20th, it is by credible persons certified from *Hull*; on *Thursday* night, being the 20th of *February*, after the last fast, about ten of the clock in the night, there appeared visibly in the

---

[3] See Appendix, Note PPP.

air two armies of foot soldiers, which charged each other with much fierceness, and then retreated, and after charged afresh. And thus they did two or three times, and continued till almost twelve of the clock, which was at least an hour and a half. This was first seen by the soldiers that were on their guard, and afterward it was seen by great numbers.]

XXXII.

THE WONDERFUL WORK OF GOD IN THE GUIDANCE OF BULLETS—
BATTLE OF EDGE HILL.

[I WILL praise the Lord with my whole heart: I will speak of all His marvellous works.—*Psalm* ix. 1.

[Here follow these passages: Psalm lxvi. 5; Exodus xv. 11; Psalm lxxxix. 5, 8; cxlv. 5; Isaiah xii. 5, 6.]

1642.—*August* the 23rd, being *Tuesday*, at eight o'clock, there was a skirmish for three hours at *Southam* (in *Warwickshire*) between the Army under the conduct of the Lord *Brooks*, the Lord *Grey*, Colonel *Hampden*, Colonel *Hollis*, and Colonel *Cholmley*; and the Army under the command of the Earl of *Northampton*, Lord *Saville*, Lord *Paget*.

The enemy discharged three times their two pieces of ordnance upon the very body of our army, but not a man hurt by God's great mercy. Nay, God's wonderful mark was observed in the guidance of the adverse party's bullets. For one went over the Lord *Brooks* his head, as also another bullet went close to the Lord *Grey*; some went on one side, and some flew clean over their heads, both horse and foot, touching no man, nor doing any harm at all.

And some bullets grazed along, and some bullets fell down flat upon the ground before them, and struck or spattered dirt in some of their faces; but not a man hurt, which shews the protection of God is over them that trust in Him. Which, after command given on our side to discharge one of our pieces of ordnance, which was charged with musket bullets, which with the scattering many of the adverse party were dangerously wounded, a drummer, with two others, was slain, and supposed many others; and five very good horses found dead.

In the month of *July* 1645 at the taking of *Berkeley* Castle, one of Captain *Pureye's* soldiers, having the same day received an half-crown piece from his captain, put it into the collar of his doublet; not long after which a bullet from the Castle hit the half-crown, and battered it, and afterwards the bullet recoiled to his shoulder, and the strength of it being spent, made but a slight wound there. This from one who saw the half-crown battered, and bullet cut out. It is an act of God's providence as of the soldier, who stuck an horse shoe at his girdle, which preserved his life in like kind.

Now to write a few words of that great fight near *Kineton*.

Edge Hill.

1642.—*October* the 23rd, being the Lord's day in the forenoon, both the Armies met in the midway between *Banbury* and *Stratford-upon-Avon*. And they had a very hot skirmish, their ordnance playing very hot from twelve o'clock till three in the afternoon, and made a great slaughter, and then the main forces joined battle, both horse and foot, and had a furious skirmish on both sides, which continued for all that day.

But that which I would take notice of is God's great mercy and providence, which was seen to His poor despised children, that although the enemy came traitorously and suddenly upon them, and unexpectedly, and four of our regiments falling from us, and our soldiers being a company of despised unexperienced youths, and never using to lie in the fields on the cold ground before the enemy, they being strong, old, experienced soldiers. But herein we see God's great mercy, for all that to give us the victory; for, as I hear, that the slaughter in all was five thousand five hundred and seventeen; but ten of the enemies' side were slain to one of ours. And observe God's wonderful works, for those that were slain of our side were most of them run away; but those that stood most valiantly to it, they were most preserved; so that you may see the Lord stands for them that stand for Him.

If I could but relate how admirably the hand of providence ordered our artillery and bullets for the destruction of the enemy, when a piece of ordnance was shot off, what a lane was made in their army; but when the enemy shot their ordnance against us, O how did God guide the bullets (as I wrote afore at *Southam*) that some fell down before them, some grazed along, some bullets went over their heads, and some, one side of them. Oh how seldom or never almost were they hurt that stood valiant to it, by their bullets; you would stand and wonder. Those that rid most gallantly among an hundred thousand bullets, and faced and charged the enemy, were first, his Excellency the Lord *Bedford*, Sir *William Balfour*, Sir *John Meldrum*, Commander of the Lord *Say* his Regiment, Sir *Philip Stapleton*, Sir *Arthur Haslerigg*, Sir *Samuel Luke*, Serjeant Major *Hurny*, Captain *Hunt*, though left all alone; these are some of those that are chiefly spoken of for their valour, which God did assist of His great mercy. And it is a sweet passage of his Excellency, it is worth the noting, that when Mr. *Marshall* was speaking of the success of the battle, his Excellency replied twice together, *That he never saw less of man in anything, nor more of God.*

Again, consider one wonderful work of our God more; which is, that many of our youths that went forth were weakly, and sickly, some with the king's evil, some with agues, and some with the toothache, which their parents and friends were in great care and grief for; yet, when they have lain days and nights in the wet and cold fields, which one should think should make a well body sick, much more to increase their misery and pain that were ill, yet they have testified that their pain hath left them, and never better in all their lives.

This is the Lord's doing, and it is marvellous in my eyes.

I did forget to write this remarkable passage,

how the King's army shot off thirty pieces of ordnance and killed not passing four of our men; and the first time we shot, we made a lane among them cutting off two of their colours.[1]

November the 5th, being *Saturday*, that treacherous, cruel, and bloody fight was at *Brentford*, where the enemy took Captain *Lilburn* away prisoner. But how the great God and Lord of Hosts did preserve us, and gave us at last the victory, that they were glad to steal and run away. But of this I do intend to write more at large in my book, called "The wonderful working God, or, The God-working wonders."

About the latter end of *December*, at *Twyford*, three miles from *Reading*, the Cavaliering Rebels set upon some of the Parliament Army, and they perceiving the wind against our Army, and a water mill being by them, they set that on fire, to the intent that the wind might blow the smoke, and so smother in our Armies, that so they might have the victory over them. But mark the wonderful works of the Lord, which hath the command of the winds; that at the very time when the mill began to smoke, our God commanded the wind and smoke, to turn back in the faces of His and our enemies so that fourscore of our Army beat three troops of their Dragooneers, and two men of us, through God's help, slew sixteen of the rebels, and not one of us, our Army, was killed; no, nor hurt, that I could

[1] See Appendix, Note QQQ.

hear of; but made the rest of our enemies to run away.

This also cometh from the Lord of Hosts which is wonderful in counsel, and excellent in works.—*Isaia.* xxviii. 29.]

XXXIII.

PLUNDERINGS AND PILLAGINGS (*continued*) — CRUELTY USED TO PRISONERS AT OXFORD — IRELAND AND THE IRISH REBELS — MORE SAVAGE CRUELTIES AND EXTREME MISERIES.

1643. *MARCH* the 9th.—" By letters from *Nottinghamshire* it was informed that the Cavaliers, or rebels, in *Newark-upon-Trent* have of late plundered the Countess of *Exeter*, and burnt down her house in *Newark*,[1] although she had the King's hand and seal for her safety not to be touched, which, when it was shown to the Popish Cavaliers, they made answer that his Majesty did not so well understand the conditions and nature of war, and that he was more fitting for his private study, or palace, than for a camp; it is also signified that they have made the like spoil in other places thereabout, and burnt down a stately dwelling completely furnished, where the King and Queen have been often entertained, and that for no other cause but that it belonged to some well affected Protestants that went not in the same rebellious courses as they do."[2]

March the 23rd.—Certain Relation. That the Earl of *Carnarvon* and Prince *Rupert* with other

---

[1] " Colonel *King's* Regiment marched to Countess of *Exeter's* House, and, after a very smart conflict, gained it."—*Rushworth.*

[2] See *Perfect Diurnall*, No. 42.

great ones, marched to *Wendover*, and have plundered all the towns thereabout of all their goods and household stuff; they have taken and driven away all their horses, beasts, and sheep; they have not spared those who are accounted their own friends, they have spoiled and torn in pieces the insides of divers fair houses, and besides the corn they spent upon their horses they spoiled very much upon the ground, and threw it about the fields, and what goods they could not carry away, they cut in pieces, and threw about the fields and highways as they went. They have cut in pieces their horse harnesses, and things belong[ing] to the plough. They swear horrid oaths that we shall have no harvest this year. How miserably did they use some families, in some were a wife with seven children, in others more, that had neither meat, drink, bedding, nor anything left in their houses, but bare walls; persons of good esteem and ability the day before, but by these inhuman crew robbed of all, and left to the charitable relief of others.[3]

March the 30th came letters from *Lancashire*, shewing that the Cavaliering Rebels had entered the town and put all to the sword they met with, both men, women, and children with all barbarous cruelty, firing the town round, and then withdrew for some space.

March the 25th.—In the County of *Lincoln*, Captain *Stiles* and Captain *Cromwell*, Mr. *Stiles*, the Minister of *Croyland*, with about eighty or ninety

[3] See *England's Memorable Accidents*.

men, came to the town of *Spalding*, which at that time was utterly unfurnished of men and arms, whereof they had intelligence the evening before by some of our malignant neighbours. Near break of day they beset the house of Mr. *Ram*, Minister of the town, where they took *T. Harrington*, Esq., and the said Mr. *Ram*, and in a violent and uncivil manner carried them away to *Croyland*, as also one *Edward Home*, a sergeant under our Captain. "So we three were kept together under strong guard, and one Mr. *Slater*, of *Spalding*, a man of sixty-six years of age, was taken and made prisoners with us. Captain *Stiles* one day quarrelled with us for praying together, and threatened to take away the Bible, and by no means would permit us to have pen, ink, or paper, and on *April* the 13th some companies of our friends advanced toward our relief, whereupon we were all carried down to the bulwark, being all of us pinioned and made to stand in an open place when the cannon began to play. Then all five of us (for there was one more) were set upon the top of the breast-work, where we stood by the space of three hours, our friends shouting fiercely at us for a great part of the time before they knew us." A Captain made three shots at his own father, supposing that they had been *Croylanders*. But how the Lord did preserve and wondrously deliver them you may see more at large in my book called "The wonder-working God, or the God-working wonders."

April the 12th.—There came more particular relation by letters out of *Warwickshire* of Prince

Rupert's taking *Birmingham* to this effect : ' That at the enemies taking the town, they lost at least thirty men, and after they came into the town, they spared neither friends nor foes, but those that trusted them least fared best. When they had plundered the town they fired the houses in several parts of the town, and burnt about forty houses, and had it not been God's wonderful mercy in turning the wind the town had been quite consumed,[5] and yet but four of *Birmingham* men were slain. One particular more I cannot pass. There was in *Birmingham* an old bachelor of almost fourscore years of age, he had much gold lay by him, as it was generally spoken; he would never put it to use, nor lend it freely, scrupling the one, and wanting charity for the other. He was a great man for the King, and spent most of his time in arguing against this unnatural war of the subjects against their Prince, as he called it. But when the Prince had taken the town, the first man he called for was this old man, and at the first salute, he told him he was a man most pernicious and adverse to the King's Majesty, and his party. The old man, kneeling upon his knees, answered he was the most forward in the town for the King, and had made it his work to plead his cause. At which words a Cavalier took him by the throat, giving him a small prick on the

[4] See *Perfect Diurnall*, No. 44.
[5] " The wind at first blew the flame and smoke into the faces of our souldiers, to their great annoyance, and endangering of the Town. But God that rides on the wings of the wind did very seasonably turn it, till the rage of the fire was abated."—*Vicars.* See Appendix, Note RRR.

side, saying, "You old dog, you have three thousand pound which we must have, or your throat shall be cut." The old man they dragged along to his lodging, who, for fear of death, opened a place in the wall, and brought them out eight hundred pound; but they were not satisfied with this, nor was his throat ever the further from cutting, but held the knife there and gave another prick, which brought out of another place five hundred pound more; but this was not enough, he had still the knife at his throat. At last he down upon his knees, taking a deep protestation that he had not ten groats more in all the world, and then they let him go with his life.

April the 18th.—It is informed out of *Warwickshire* that Prince *Rupert* sent his horse abroad into the country about *Lichfield*, and drove before them poor countrymen to *Lichfield*, compelling them to go into the van of those soldiers that assaulted the Close there, where they were killed like dogs, a hundred of them falling in a little compass. It is a wonder that such horrid actions as these are of this barbarous Prince, should not make the malignants of this kingdom ashamed to adhere to the actions of this man, so apparently tending to the destruction of this kingdom.

It was also informed that the King's forces have plundered a town called *Auster*, which is five miles beyond *Stratford-upon-Avon*, in the county of *Warwick*, and that they have undone the richest market town of the bigness in all the country, for besides good store of plate and other commodities which they took from gentlemen, they have taken all the shopkeepers' cloth, and other rich wares, to a very great value.

April the 22nd.—" There came letters from *Reading* which informeth for a truth by those that were eye-witnesses thereof that before the Lord *Grey* came thither, Col. *Aston* sallied out on that part of the town, and seized on all, men or women, that he could meet withal, and brought them into the town, and when any breach is made in their works by the Parliament forces, he forceth women and children to make up the breach, or stand in the mouth of the cannon, refusing to let any of them depart the town." [6]

May the 17th.—" From *Buckinghamshire* [it is] informed that the *Oxford* rebels have of late made cruel spoil in that county, robbing and pillaging them of all they have, burnt a town . . . . . and slew divers." [7]

May the 20th.—It is informed out of *Derbyshire* that the Earl of *Newcastle* sent a great force into *Derbyshire* to plunder that shire, which they performed, leaving no place unransacked, but ruining in inhuman and barbarous manner, neither sparing friend nor foe. So that county is not left worth anything, only *Derby* itself, which Sir *John Gell* guarded, and one or two other places; or else the whole shire is wholly despoiled of all they have.

May the 27th.—It is informed from *Oxford* that

[6] From *Perfect Diurnall*, No. 46.   [7] Ibid., No. 49.

the Cavaliers at *Burfort*, they set fire on some hay, which burnt thirty load of hay, much oats in a barn, which [was] near being fired also, and some corn also.

May the 31st.—It is informed that these English Rebels came to a Town called *Ilmington* (which lies in three several shires, *Warwickshire*, *Worcestershire*, and *Gloucestershire*) and they pillaged and plundered the most part of that poor town, and it was indangered by them at least three hundred pound, and no distinction made between either friend or foe.

Cruelty used to Prisoners at Oxford.

Extract of a Letter from a Friend near Oxford, June the 5th, 1643.

"Sir, I suppose by this time, Captain *Wingate* is with you. I doubt not but he will put the business out of controversy, which had so long been questionable, which is, whether the prisoners here are used well or ill. ☞ He will tell you that himself was twenty weeks a prisoner, and had neither pen, ink, paper, nor any printed book; ☞ that he could not be permitted the Bible, nor Testament; that divers have been starved to death, and beaten to death; how men could not have food for their money, but were kept to five farthings a day, and that some had money brought, and it was kept from them; that eleven Captains are dead through cruel usage; that the (Cavaliers or) Rebels to the Parliament prisoners at *Oxford*, have equalled or exceeded them in Queen *Mary's* day's; that all this cruelty does not proceed from Marshall *Smith*, though he be a fit instrument for any Tyrant that ever was, (yea, he might make a slaughter slave for the Cannibals) but from the higher powers.[8]

"By Declaration of the Lords and Commons in Parliament, it is specified that the lamentable condition of *Ireland* is much, for the poor Protestants in some places are forced to kill their Horses to satisfy their Hunger, and very many others have perished by Famine. Set forth *June* the 24th, 1643.

"We the Lords and Commons assembled in Parliament, being by several letters fully informed both from the Lord Justices and Council of *Dublin*, and also from other parts of the Kingdom of *Ireland*, of the extreme condition of the whole Army, and the lamentable estate of the Kingdom in that the most parts of the army, our soldiers, want bread for their bellies, clothes for their backs, and shoes for their feet; and in some parts they have been forced to kill their horses to satisfy their hunger; very many of the poor English in several places have perished by famine, and very many have eaten the very hides of horses to keep them from starving; which have brought very many of them to such a condition of weakness that they appear rather like walking anatomies than fighting men."[9]

[8] Appendix, Note SSS.
[9] This declaration is given at length in *Rushworth*, part iii. vol. ii. p. 539.

As also I did hear of a company of women being together, and in great distress for want of food, did condition to cast lots to eat one the other. And so the lot falling on one woman, the woman did intreat very much to spare her life a little longer; and so it pleased the Lord on a sudden they did hear that six horses were come into the town, which when they were killed, these poor souls did get some part of them, and so the woman's life was spared for that time.

This month of *June*, when Prince *Maurice* his forces were last at *Broadway* in *Worcestershire*, they seized upon a very honest gentleman named Mr. *Stevens*, (who the last summer had his ricks of corn set on fire by the King's forces), whom they would hang up in the midst of the town, to be a terror to those they call Roundheads; and although nothing was laid to his charge, and his wife and children intreated upon their knees to spare his life, yet those hard-hearted wretches would not hear them; but it pleased God to save him out of the mouth of those lions in a wonderful manner. For when they were actually about to put this wicked practice in execution, there came a Colonel of their own, *Tarverfield* by name, which came that way by mere accident (not being in the town, nor having any command of soldiers there) and passing by, seeing them about an inhuman business, he would not suffer them to do it, saying he would complain to his Majesty, if they offered him more violence, by which means he was secured from them.

And in Sir *William Brereton's* letter, dated *June* the 17th, it is to this purpose informed, That there landed [from] two barks many Irish Rebels in *Werrall* in *Cheshire*, which acknowledged in the presence of divers sufficient men, that they had washed their hands in the blood of the English and Scotch in *Ireland*, ☞ and now hoped to wash their hands in the blood of English men in *England:* which Rebels being brought into *Chester* were accused by several of those poor English who fled from *Ireland* to *Chester* for refuge, to be the persons who cut their husbands' throats; and many of these bloody Rebels are now in the Queen's Army with us.

And the examination of *John Dod Clerke* taken by a select Committee of the House of Commons, *July* 8th, 1643, saith, That after he had suffered many miseries in this rebellion of *Ireland*, he repaired to this Kingdom, and some occasions carrying him to *Oxford*, he stayed there seven weeks, and came out of *Oxford*, *June* the 13th, 1643; That during his stay there, he saw a great number of Irish Rebels, whom he very well knew to have had a hand in the most barbarous actions of that Rebellion; among whom was one *Thomas Brady* who at *Turbet* in the county of *Cavan*, in the province of *Ulster* in *Ireland*, within seven miles where this examinat lived ☞ as thirty-six old men, women, and children, not able to flee were passing over a bridge, caused them all to be thrown into the water, where they were all drowned.

But of these cruelties I have books by me which

sheweth them more at large, and what we may look for here, (if God be not the more merciful unto us) when there be so many of these cruel men come over here, and are in the King's Army, and in the Queen's Army, and still more are sent for. And many of these Rebels have testified that their rebellion in *Ireland*, and what they did there, they had both the King's and Queen's consent to it, and had the King's broad seal to shew for it.

The Mercies of the Wicked are Cruel.

"Under two or three witnesses let everything be established."

July the 17th, 1643.—It is informed again how the popish crew do use the poor inhabitants in *Bradford*. After the Earl of *Newcastle* had battered all the chimnies down in the town, that there were scarce six left standing, which forced Sir *Thomas Fairfax*, with about fifteen hundred men, to quit the town, and leave it to the violence of this cruel popish army, where also he was forced to leave his lady, she being wounded with a shot in the shoulder. After his departure hence, the barbarous and merciless popish soldiers entered the town, and slew many of the inhabitants with their wives and children, and most inhumanly they threw one child into the river, and they have not left one man in the town under the age of sixty, but have either slain them, or driven them away.

July the 17th.—It is credibly informed that the

Queen's army, a most filthy, wicked crew, in her march to *Oxford*, made it their care to free the inhabitants of *Burton-upon-Trent*,[10] who are generally well affected to the Parliament, and, therefore, they sent twenty-seven colours of foot, and about sixteen colours of horse, to do execution upon the Parliament forces residing there. They faced it upon *July* the 13th last, first, with their horse by break of day, who were forced to retreat; afterward, about five or six o'clock, they returned with the foot. Then the service began to grow very hot, the town having been twice summoned by a trumpeter to yield, but bravely resolved to fight it out, which they did till near six o'clock at night. But at last our men, being wearied with the whole day's service, and oppressed by an over-daring multitude of the enemy, they were driven from their guards, and then soon left the town. Brave Colonel *Houghton*, his Lieutenant, Colonel *Sanders*, Captain *Watson*, and divers other commanders, all men never enough to be honoured, after quarter demanded, and granted, were grievously wounded and killed. Our foot soldiers, after quarter promised, they put up in the tower of the Church where the bells hanged, and then blew up the tower with gunpowder; the Queen causing the chief master-gunner to be brought before her, and killed, or cut to pieces, before her face. They tied some men back to back, and then threw them into the river *Trent*. The townsmen they wounded many, they killed many, they spoiled

[10] See *Perfect Diurnall*, No. 4.

all, and pillaged the town of all that was worth the carriage away, and then they set the whole town on fire, and so left it.

The forces under Prince *Rupert*, besides *Birmingham*, and some other places, formerly ruined by them, have lately burnt *Shawell*, and, not contenting themselves only with the goods and houses, and utter destruction of all other things in that and other places where they became conquerors, but also thirsting after the precious blood of men, have lately executed and hanged up some well-affected inhabitants of that town, and in some places in *Gloucestershire*,[11] the ministers, for their denial to renounce the solemn covenant which they had lately taken according to the appointment of both Houses of Parliament. So cruel are these miscreants to enforce men contrary to their conscience, and all laws of nature or nations, to renounce their solemn oaths made unto God for the defence of the true Protestant religion.

July the 26th, being the Fastday, the whole town of *Rowley*, in *Staffordshire*, assembled in the church to keep that solemn day of humiliation; in the midst of this their devotion, there came some troopers of the Cavaliers from *Dudley Castle*, about

---

[11] " The progress of the royal forces about this period gave rise to the following rhymes, which are assigned to July 31, 1643 :—

' Bristol taking,
Exeter shaking,
Gloucester quaking.'

—Corry and Evans, *History of Bristol*, i. 414."—*Bibliotheca Gloucestriensis.* Gloucester, 1825.

two miles distant from that town, and violently carried many divers of the well-affected inhabitants of that town out of the Church.

The virgins in *Norwich*, hearing of the Cavaliers' violent outrages committed upon their sex wheresoever they get the victory, are so sensible of their reputations, that they have readily contributed so much money as hath raised and armed a goodly troop of horse for their defence, which is called the Maiden Troop.

It is informed from *Ireland*, that the justice of God is yet more evidently seen in this, that the wicked and cruel Rebels that would not hear the cries, either of young or old, calling unto them for mercy to spare their lives, but used all the Protestants with most barbarous cruelties, killing, murdering and slaying all that come into their powers, and leaving their bodies to be devoured of wolves, hogs, crows and kites, by which means there have not been less than two hundred thousand Protestants, men, women, and children, English and Scottish, massacred in that kingdom since that odious Rebellion brake forth; yet behold the just hand of God upon those Rebels, in the same place or province where they exercised so much cruelty on others; for whereas the English and Scottish soldiers now go into many parts of it, to view the country, and seek provision, coming into some small villages and seeing the houses smoke, enter the houses to know what inhabitants dwell in them, they find in some house one man dead and murdered, and sometimes four, in some houses six, in some eight or ten persons, all feeding upon the dead carcase. And in some places they found the whole household dead, except one or two men, and in others they found all dead, and starved with hunger, as appears by the leanness of their bodies, their bones plainly appearing through their skin, and even those whom they found living seemed like to walking anatomies. So that those that fed hogs with the flesh of Christians, are now forced to devour and eat up one another. The Lord is holy in all His ways, and just in all His works, repaying the wicked according to their deserts.

Some part of a Copy of a Letter from Exeter of the Miseries thereabouts, August the 3rd.

"Sir *John Barkely*, a great Commander of the Cavaliers, hath done very great spoil amongst us, posting to and fro, with an hundred and fifty horse, imposing upon the subject such heavy taxation, that the subject cannot bear, their horses and goods plundered, their persons threatened, and imprisoned; and it is no news to the world, that this country hath had his share of troubles. For since the siege of *Sherborne Castle*, full fourteen months, when first Sir *Ralph Hopton* took his flight in the north part of *Somerset*, we have not been free of soldiers, and no small number, but by thousands, 4, 5, 6, 7, 8, and ten thousand still in pay of our own party, and at length came the rabble of *Cornish*, and they swept the country clean where they went, yea, and forced men to carry arms; but they have done them as little service as they did us at *Modbury*, when they all ran before they came near the place.

1643. *September* the 7th.—There is a letter come out of *Norfolk* which informeth that Colonel *Cromwell* hath battered the town of *Lynn* sorely, from *Old Lynn*, the shot of whose ordnance hath slain divers men, women, and children, and that the lamentable shrieks and cries of women and children are heard a great way out of the town; and yet the townsmen are so cruel and hard-hearted to them that they will not suffer them to depart out of the town.[12]

September the 27th, "Sir *Lewis Dives* came with a party of four hundred horse to *Ampthill*, within five miles of *Bedford*, and surprised divers of the well affected Gentry and Freeholders of that county that were met there as a Committee appointed by the Parliament, and carried them away prisoners to *Abingdon* and *Oxford*, with about a hundred horse."[13]

October the 8th, our sad Informer assures us that his Majesty's forces have lately invaded the town of *Ockingham* in *Berkshire*, and practised all the most barbarous cruelty which malice or fury could invent. For what the sword left untouched, the rage of the flame devoured; there was no moderation observed in the estates of poor or rich, well affected or malignant, they distinguished not twixt friend or foe, but whatsoever goods did come into their hands it was accounted lawful plunder. They have made

[12] Appendix, Note TTT.   [13] From *A Perfect Diurnall*, No. 12.

the inhabitants the unparalleled subjects of distress, and turned their towns into a wilderness.

About this time there came news of the cruel tyranny of those barbarous Cavaliers to the inhabitants of the city of *Exeter*. *Exeter*, that famous city in the west, having for the space of three months defended themselves against the proud enemy, who had so strongly beleaguered the said city of *Exeter*, they, the inhabitants thereof, could neither have relief brought to them by land or water, though many times they sallied forth against their foes, and manfully combated with them, the enemy being at the least eight men for one, having also continual supplies of victuals and ammunition sent them from the Cornish Cavaliers, and divers other places. The Citizens together with the consent of that Noble Commander, the Earl of *Stamford*, being in great distress for want of relief and ammunition, having first made an agreement with Prince *Maurice* upon several Articles, whereby to prevent the resolute Cavaliers from plundering and pillaging their houses. But how little conscience these cruel enemies make of their promises and ways; [it] is too well known in all the western parts, that they which are called Prince *Rupert*, and Prince *Maurice* his Cavaliers, are most of them addicted to such cruelties, that they shew themselves more like tigers, or savage beasts, than humane men, as shall appear in the following discourse, wherein shall be expressed nothing but what the author of the news was an eye-witness of.

The Cavaliers having entered the forenamed city of *Exeter*, used the people most cruelly, and did all the violence they could do to them, only sparing their lives, whereby we may perceive how far they are from keeping their promises which they make. The rude soldiers would not forbear upon the least discontent given to them, to draw their rapiers upon the citizens, and wound them; but especially when they are in their cups, they swagger, roar, swear, and domineer, plundering, pillaging or doing any other kind of wrong; to break shops and houses, they count it as nothing, taking away boots, shoes, stockings, hats, or any other commodities they can lay their hands on, and no justice dares to resist them, and by this means the city is in such a miserable condition that they are even terrified to the death.

The Magistrates of the City are fined at extraordinary rates, and when they have paid what the Cavaliers demand, they will force them, as they do in other places, to repay it again. The better to manifest the inhumanity of these barbarous Cavaliers, *Gloucester* and *Cirencester* by woful experience can testify.

Cirencester in *Gloucestershire* having three several times manfully withstood the furious assaults of these Rebels, was at last taken by them, where they used such tyranny that paguns and heathen would not have done the like in their own countries, for after they had entered the town by force they slew all the men that stood in opposition; and those that kindly laid down their arms to them and yielded, they carried them away into *Oxford* prison, where never men endured more misery. This being done, they plundered the town of gold, silver, brass, household stuff, pewter, and lodging, even all they had; so that from the richest to the poorest they were all undone, insomuch that neither rich nor poor, old or young, friend nor foe, escaped their fury.

Not long after this, they laid strong siege against *Bristol*; and after many battles they sent a messenger into the city, which told them if they would surrender it up by fair means, they should have fair quarter, and that never a man in the city should have one penny worth of wrong, only fifty thousand pound to be given them for composition, and all their soldiers to be new apparelled, which indeed had much need, for there were never so many tatterdemalions[14] seen in *Bristol* before. But having entered the city, the best meat, the choicest wine, and cleanest lodging seemed not good enough to please these tattered Cavaliering Rebels, who before wanted all things.

They went into some cellars where was plenty of wine and beer, drank their fill, and let the rest run about the house. They brake the covenant which was made, in the very first hour that they entered the city, and fell to plundering, pillaging, robbing, stealing, cutting, and slashing, as if they never had been brought up to any other practice. So that now they that gave them entrance into the city do

[14] Tattary mallions.

sorely repent the bargain. I will relate some little part of the misery and slavery that some of the people now remain in, which before used all the means they could to entertain these wild Cavaliering Rebels into the city of *Bristol;* and although the city was surrendered up in *July* the 26th, 1643, yet the relation of their Miseries, (which the inhabitants of this city of *Bristol* endureth) came not forth till towards the midst of this month of *October*, 1643, which here followeth.

But by the way I will speak a few words to the Malignants, which is this ; That amongst the many miseries' and heavy judgments which the Lord doth send among us, this is none of the least, (but one of the greatest) that is, the sin of Infidelity.

That very many men here and in other parts, although rational men of great learning and knowledge, yet they will not believe that God is so just as He is, nor that these cruel wicked blasphemous Cavaliers in the King's Army are so vile as they are.

As if the Lord have sent this heavy sentence unto them as in *Isaiah* the vi. 9, 10, " Go and say unto this people, ye shall hear indeed, but ye shall not understand, ye shall plainly see and not perceive. Make the heart of this people fat ; make their ears heavy, and shut their eyes, lest they see with their eyes, and hear with their ears, and understand with their heart, and convert, and He heal them."

XXXIV.

SAVAGE CRUELTIES IN BRISTOL—OF THE CRUEL PLUNDERING AND FIRING THE TOWN OF OCKINGHAM, IN BERKSHIRE.

A RELATION of the King's Armies since their entering into the City of *Bristol*; of their extreme Plunderings, Murders, and other Villanies committed by them upon the persons and estates of his Majesty's faithfullest subjects, abundantly sufficient to convince the consciences of all men that speak so much in the vindication of them; their carriage being directly contrary to the Articles of agreement for delivering up the said city, between Colonel *Nathaniel Fiennes*, Governor of the said city, on the one part, and Colonel *Charles Garard* and Captain *William Teringham*, for, and on the behalf of Prince *Rupert* on the other part. July 26th, 1643.[1]

The Articles were as followeth :—

1. That the Governor *Nathaniel Fiennes*, together with all the officers, both of Horse and Foot, now within and about the City of *Bristol*, Castle, and forts, may march out to-morrow morning by nine of the clock, with their full arms, horses, bag, and baggage, provided it be their own goods, and that

---

[1] This account is taken from "The Tragedy of the King's Armies' Fidelity since their entering into *Bristol*, together with the too late Repentance of the Inhabitants. *London.* Printed for *C. M.* 1643."

the common foot soldiers march out without arms, and the troopers with their horses and swords, leaving their other arms behind them, with a safe convoy, to *Warminster;* and after, not to be molested in their march by any of the King's forces for the space of three days.

II. That there may be carriages allowed and provided, to carry away their bag and baggage, and sick and hurt soldiers.

III. That the King's Forces march not into the town, till the Parliament Forces are marched out, which is at nine of the clock.

IV. That all prisoners in the city be delivered up, aud that Captain *Eyres*, and Captain *Gookin*, who were taken at the *Devizes*,[2] be released.

V. That Sir *John Homer*, Sir *John Seymour*, Mr. *Edward Stevens*, and all other Knights, Gentlemen, Citizens, and other persons that are now in the city, may, if they please, with their goods, wives, and families, horses, bag, and baggage, have free liberty to return to their own homes, or elsewhere, and there to rest in safety, or ride and travel with the Governor and Forces, and such of them and their families as shall be left behind, by reason of sickness or other cause, may have liberty, so soon as they can conveniently, to depart this

---

[2] "... the enemie had garrisoned an old, but repaired castle at the *Devizes*. And to prevent the spoyle of the country neere *Malmesbury*, Colonell *Devereux* had erected a garrison at *Rounde House* between the *Devizes* and *Malmesbury*."—Corbet's *Historical Relation of the Military Government of Gloucester.* London, 1645.

" ... the word Devises means no more than *border lands*."— Hunter's *South Yorkshire*, i. 174.

town with safety, provided that all the Gentlemen and other persons shall have three days' liberty to reside here, or depart with their goods, which they please.

VI. That all the inhabitants of this city shall be secured in their persons, families, and estates, free from plundering, and all other violence or wrong whatsoever.

VII. That the charters and liberties of this city may be preserved, and that the ancient Government thereof, and present Governors and officers may remain and continue in their former condition, according to his Majesty's charters and pleasure.

VIII. That, for avoiding inconveniences and distractions, the quartering of soldiers be referred, or left, to the Mayor and Governor of the same city for the time being.

IX. That all such as have carried any goods into the Castle may have free liberty to carry the same forth.

X. That the Forces that are to march out, are to leave behind them all cannon and ammunition, with their colours, and such arms as is before expressed.

The True Relation of the King's Army's Fidelity since their entering into Bristol.

So many and sundry infallible relations, and sad, yet certain, stories, have come from divers parts of the kingdom, expressing the inhuman, perfidious, and barbarous carriage of the Cavaliers in their extreme plunderings, murders, and other

villanies committed by them upon the persons
and estates of his Majesty's most faithful subjects,
as that they are abundantly sufficient to convince
the consciences, and stop the mouths of all malignants whatsoever, that speak so much in the vindication of them, were it not that the devil hath
blinded their minds, and poisoned their hearts with
a spirit of malignity and contradiction that they
will believe nothing till they feel it as others do.
And because divers ill-affected persons in *London*
to deceive others do still give out that the citizens of
Bristol are in as happy condition as their hearts can
wish since it was surrendered to the King's Army,
we have thought good to let all people see by this
narration in what happiness that city is since the
Cavaliers came into it, and to this present, that
they may judge of it.

To enter, therefore, upon the Declaration, let the
reader compare the Articles of Agreement with that
which followeth, and see what faith can be expected
to be kept by these vile men.

Whereas the Colonels, officers, and soldiers were
ready to march out of the city according to the 5th
Article, with the Knights, Gentlemen, and many
hundred citizens and other persons of the country,
and thought to march out of town, we were not
only stopped in, but hurried to and fro from one
gate to another, not knowing what way they would
bring us out. In the mean time the Cavaliers came
rushing into the city, contrary to the 3rd Article,
who were not to come in till we were marched

forth. At last we were brought without *Temple-gate*, and there stopped till the bridge was laid. In the mean while the Cavaliers fell upon us in a most furious and barbarous manner, plundering and rifling all sorts of persons, mentioned in the said Articles, sparing neither age nor sex, but took away our horses, cloaks, bags, monies, and stripped divers of their clothes, throwing men, women, and children off their horses that rode double, searching the women in an uncivil manner for money, presenting their swords and pistols at such as did in any sort deny them, and when we alleged the terms of agreement, they would not acknowledge any at all; besides other villanies. When they had thus pillaged and rifled us, we were brought without the works, about eight horse and foot. Then we were committed to a convoy of about five troops of horse, and so brought through their army, who fell a railing and reviling at us, and blaspheming God in a most fearful manner, saying it grieved them that they could not butcher us, and bereave us of our lives, and asking, " Where is now your God ? where are your fastings, your prayers and profession, where is your King *JESUS?*" and said, " King *Charles* shall be King, for all King *JESUS*," and that God was now turned Cavalier. This convoy brought us five miles out of *Bristol*, on the way to *Bath*. But the wolf was set to keep the lambs, for they plundered us by the way as we went, of those things that the others had left us, and in our march would not suffer many to drink a little water, being extremely thirsty, by going on so fast in the heat; if any slipped aside to get a little water to drink, the Cavaliers would presently plunder and strip them. This convoy surrounded us with their horse, with their swords drawn, and commanded us to throw away our staves, and to deliver up our knives, and constrained Colonel *Fiennes* to give them a hundred and fifty pound of the money he had to pay the soldiers. They said that they would shortly come to *London*, where they knew they should find us, and then they would conduct us to hell. It seems these wretches are so well acquainted with the way thither, that they will take upon them to conduct others, yea, and thither they themselves must go, if God hear their frequent prayers. . . . .

As they violated the third Article in entering the city before their time, so when they came in, they ran into men's houses like a company of savage wolves, and fell a plundering of all sorts, without distinction, as well malignants as others. But at last by some beggarly and ill-affected persons, they were directed in special to fall upon such as were well-affected to the Parliament, especially the *High Street* and the *Bridge*; the only and chief place of tradesmen, for mercers, silkmen, and linendrapers, in which places they plundered whole shops of wares, whereby many that lived well, and had good estates, are now undone; entering houses with their swords drawn, and setting them to men's breasts, taking women by the throat, thereby forcing them to open their closets, and to bring forth their money and plate, after which they rob them of the best of their goods, and sold them before their faces to the Welsh people for trifles. And when they sold divers commodities to the country people, the soldiers would meet with them going home, and plunder them of the same again. Some men had given money for protection, and yet were plundered. Others paid fines for their goods taken away, and, having regained them, they were plundered of the same goods again.

Together with their plundering, they committed many other barbarous actions, namely, the murdering of a woman . . . . who, it seems, resisted them when they came into the house to plunder, whom they slew with a pole-axe, yet the woman was no enemy unto them, but one that longed for their coming in.

Also, they slew an ancient man, although the man was one that wished them well, yet, because he did not give them his horse so soon as they demanded, a Cavalier shot him to death presently wish his pistol. . . . .

And it is credibly reported by a gentleman that was amongst the Cavaliers during the siege before *Bristol*, that he saw divers of the Irish rebels whom he knew who were not in service, but only followed the army to rob and steal; as also certain Frenchmen who did rob and pillage divers houses near *Bristol*, and slew many of their lean cattle and sheep, out of a mischievous mind, though they made no use of them, yea, slew divers persons also with their swords and pistols.

When they had done plundering, then they quartered soldiers upon all sorts, as well Malignants as others, and all upon free quarter, placing twenty or thirty soldiers in a house upon men of but reasonable estates, which puts them to an intolerable charge, and the more, because divers of the Cavaliers will not be content to feed upon good beef, but must have mutton, and veal, and chickens, with wine and tobacco each meal, and much ado to please them at all; causing, also, men, women, and children to lie upon boards, while these Cavaliers possess their beds, which they fill with vermin. Besides, they fill the ears of the inhabitants with their blasphemous, filthy, and wicked language, which no chaste ear, nor honest heart, can endure; yea, so desperately wicked are they, that those that billet them dare not perform any act of religion, neither to give thanks at meals, nor yet to pray, read, or sing Psalms; but, instead thereof, they fill their houses with swearing and cursings, insomuch that they corrupt men's servants and children, that those who were formerly civil have now learned to curse and swear almost as bad as they. And on the Lord's day these beasts spend their time in dicing, drinking, and carding, and other such abominations. And, whereas the chaplains that go with them should teach them better, some of them swear as bad as any of the soldiers. As, namely, one of the prince's chaplains swore by the flesh of God . . . with many other horrible oaths. And in a tavern the *Friday* after they came into the city, a lord's chaplain wished the devil might roast his soul in hell, if he did not preach such a sermon next Sunday as was never preached at *Bristol*, some part of which sermon was railing at the doctrine of predestination, calling it damnable doctrine of the Roundheads, and in his very sermon in the pulpit burst out into a fearful oath.

We may add further some other blasphemies of the Cavaliers when they entered the town, for they had certain fiddlers who sang blasphemous songs not fit to be mentioned, calling them the 4th and 12th Psalms, and standing in the streets, and praying in a mocking manner, saying, "O Lord, Thou wast with us at *Edgehill* and *Brainford*; but where wast Thou at *Runaway Hill?* and where art Thou now, O Lord?" speaking through their noses, and looking up to heaven. And when their fellow-Cavaliers were beaten and killed before *Gloucester*, those in *Bristol* swore now God was turned Roundhead.

To all this is added a grievous burden, the levying of vast sums of money which are paid to his Majesty and Prince *Rupert*, which are laid upon all sorts, as well malignant as others, besides a weekly tax of about five or six hundred pound a week on the city, for which they are justly served. For had they advanced but the third part so much, of what they now part with for Sir *William Waller*, he might have had by God's blessing an Army sufficient to have secured that city, and all the western parts. They fine such men with great sums of money, whose estate they have totally plundered;

some of whom for non-payment of the said sums they committed to prison, and laid in irons. Many other great miseries the inhabitants there endure, besides a grievous oath they impose upon their consciences.

Having thus heard of the sins of the place, now observe the remarkable judgment of God upon it. It was the endeavour of the Malignants of that city a long time, to get the Cavaliers into it, and to that purpose solicited the court to have an Army to come down to take it. Whereupon Prince *Rupert* came with an Army, but God defeated him, yet they gave not over desiring, till now at last they had their wish, which was to see the King's Army enter, and the Roundheads punished, and expelled out of the city. And when it pleased God the city was delivered up, and the Parliament's garrison for the greatest part expelled, with all the godly Ministers, and many hundred godly people, that were strangers, that came there for shelter, within a few days after they were gone, the hand of God broke in upon them, and hath smitten them with a very contagious and mortal disease, that sweeps away about an hundred and forty in a week, and sometimes many more, which hath continued hitherto. But the use that many make of it, is only a-railing at the Roundheads, saying that they sowed the plague there, and now they reap it; whereas it has pleased God to give us much health, before this cursed crew came in as ever that city did enjoy; but now, (as is credibly reported by such as come from thence) there are few houses where there is not some either sick or dead; wherein you may see how the Lord turneth a fruitful city into barrenness, for the wickedness of them that dwell in it.

October the 9th.—" It is informed that the Town of *Ockingham* hath been lately thrice plundered by the King's forces, where there, and at *Twyford*, they carried away near a hundred cartload of goods; and these imps of their father the devil hath set the said Town of *Ockingham* on fire, in five or six places at once, and have burnt the said Town to the ground, together with all the barns of corn, oats, hay, and other provision, which the Townsmen had laid up in store for winter, murdering and slaying all the men that they found there; insomuch that the inhabitants, men, women, and children there, were forced to fly away from their houses to other places, for refuge and succour, that so they might be freed from their barbarism and inhumanity. It was also further certified, That when they were desired by the inhabitants to have spared their houses and barns of corn, and offered them large compositions, the soldiers made answer that neither Officer nor Soldier dared upon pain of death to omit the execution of any part of their ☞ Commission, which (as they said) strictly commanded them to do what they did."[3]

And thus they ever shew themselves (not men) but worse than savage beasts; for indeed all their

---

[3] From *Mercurius Civicus, London Intelligencer*, No. 22, from *Thursday*, Oct. 19, to *Thursday*, Oct. 26, 1642.

victories that they so much gloried in, have been where they have had no resistance; as this here at *Ockingham* and *Twyford*, a poor, naked, innocent, harmless people, whom they first plundered of all they had, and then burnt their houses to the ground, as you have heard.⁴

A Cessation of Arms with the Rebels in Ireland.

And now, if this were not cruel and vile enough, and as if there were not enough of them, there is (through the prevalency of an evil and wicked Council) a Cessation of Arms with those cruel bloody Rebels in *Ireland*, now agreed on with his Majesty's assent, and was to begin *September* the 15th, 1643, and continue for one whole year, as was certified the Parliament this day (*October* the 17th) with a Copy of the said Articles of the said Cessation,⁵ and will be published in print, that the whole world may see what favour those Rebels of *Ireland* ☞ that have been the death of above an hundred thousand souls, for no other cause but that they were Protestants, have found at Court, not only by the Agreement of the said Cessation of Arms, but throughout all the Articles of the said Cessation, to be styled by his Majesty "Our Roman Catholic Subjects," (not the least mention of Rebels or Traitors, whereas the Parliament, and well affected party of this kingdom, taking up arms for the just

---

⁴ See *Perfect Diurnall*, No. 15.
⁵ These Articles are printed at length in Rushworth's *Historical Collections*, part iii. vol. ii. p. 448 *et seq*.

defence of his Majesty's person, Religion, laws, and liberty of the subject, have been by a hundred proclamations, one after another, declared Rebels and Traitors.)

Whence consider, First, the contradiction; for if the Rebels be Roman Catholics, (as no man doubt it) then they are not the King's true subjects, because they only acknowledge the Pope to be the Supreme Governor on earth, and he is a foreign potentate to whose obedience they are strictly sworn.

Secondly, note, that this Cessation tendeth to the weakening of the Protestants in *Ireland*, and the strengthening of the Rebels there, who, being almost consumed by the late wars, (which was wisely perceived at *Oxford*,) they will now take breath and recover themselves again, to cut a hundred thousand Protestant throats more.

Thirdly, note, that this Cessation is for a year, and then we must hope and believe that they shall be called Rebels and Traitors again. And why but for a year? because the Cavaliers persuade themselves that the Rebels and some of the Protestants will come over, and subdue this kingdom before that time be expired; that this is the main intent of this plot, nothing can be more evident.

And now what we did imagine is coming to pass, if our God, of His great and wonderful mercy, circumvent them not. For *October* the 30th, by letters from *Bridgewater* in *Somersetshire*, it is certainly informed that above a thousand of the Irish Rebels landed lately at *Minehead*, (within a few miles of the said town) whereupon some of the Garrison soldiers in *Bridgewater* began to mutiny, declaring that they would not fight any longer for his Majesty, since he admitted the Popish Irish Rebels to come over in this kingdom, which they would not believe was to establish the Protestant Religion; insomuch that Captain *Windham* made a large speech to pacify and appease his soldiers; the effect was, That these Irish, with about eight thousand more which were shortly to come over hither, were not Rebels no more than ☞ himself, or any of them. Notwithstanding which speech of the said Captain, many of his soldiers have deserted the service, detesting to take part with those Irish Rebels, to ruin their own native country, and to extirpate the true Protestant Religion.

It is also further certified[6] that a thousand Irish Rebels more are landed at *Bristol*.

[6] Sartisfied.

XXXV.

NOTES—OF OPENLY PROFANING THE LORD'S DAY BY PRINCE RUPERT AND THE CAVALIERS.

1643. "*NOVEMBER* the 6th.—It is credibly informed that one of the Cavalier Captains told the inhabitants at his entering the town (of *Ockingham*) that he came to do a wicked thing, which was to fire the town, and that he durst not omit the doing of it for fear of his life. And when the poor amazed inhabitants asked him whether he had a commission to warrant his act, he put his hand in his pocket, pulled out his commission, and gave it them to read, where they found their doom signed *C. R.*[1] Thus the King's name and power are still wrested and abused to countenance such enormous acts, as are highly displeasing to Almighty God, contrary to the known laws of the land (which the King hath sworn and sundry times protested to maintain and keep) and to the utter ruin of poor people, which now have not a hole to put their heads in. Here those cruel Cavaliers had no colour to blemish this town with the odious name of rebellion, for they never took up arms against them.

"*November* the 7th.—Out of *Derbyshire* it is informed that the Cavaliers, which had long infested

---

[1] The word "*Note*" appears against this in the margin of the MS.

the town of *Nottingham* by seizing upon the Bridge and fortifying it, and stopping the road into the town, are at length driven from thence by Sir *John Gell* and his *Derby* forces; but, before they left their works and fortifications, they most barbarously fired all the houses near unto it, and committed all the rapine they could devise in the adjacent parts, whereby it appeareth that the Cavaliers generally through *England* have power given them to burn, destroy, and waste, all places wheresoever they come, as if it were a foreign enemy's country. Such is the Popish hatred against all Protestants whatsoever, and herein they exactly imitate their accursed brethren, the Irish Rebels."[2]

" *November* the 3rd.—From *Oxford* it is informed that on the Lord's day last was fortnight, toward the evening of that day, Prince *Rupert* accompanied with some lords, and other Cavaliers, danced through the streets openly with music before them, to one of the Colleges where, after they had stayed about half an hour, they returned back again dancing, with the same music before them, and immediately there followed them a pack of women, or courtezans it may be supposed, for they were hooded and could not be known. And this the party that related it, affirmeth he saw with his eyes.

Whence note, first, their despite done to God and

---

[2] Taken from " Certaine Informations from severall parts of the Kingdome, and from other places beyond the Seas, for the better satisfaction of all such who desire to be truly Informed of every weeke's Passage. No. 43. From the 6th of *November*, to the 13th of *November*, 1643."

His commandments. Secondly, their profaneness in violating that day God hath set part for His worship. Thirdly, note their insensibility of God's heavy judgements of war upon this kingdom. Fourthly, note what pleasure they take in their wicked courses of plundering, and robbing, and shedding of blood. Fifthly, . . . Sixthly, note that to maintain their sensual pleasures is one of the chief things they fight for. Seventhly, note that they are so hardened in their evil ways that there is small hope of reclaiming them."[3] Thus you see what kind of beasts these be that pretend that they do fight for the true Protestant religion.

[3] From *Certaine Informations*, &c., No. 42.

XXXVI.

THE MISERIES OF IRELAND SINCE THE CESSATION — IRELAND AND THE IRISH REBELS — IRELAND'S LAMENTATION FOR THE LATE CESSATION.

A Copy of some Part of a Letter concerning the Most Sad Condition of Ireland since the Cessation.

THIS letter was sent from *Dublin*, received *November* the 16th, 1643:—

"Loving brother, Every commodity here is very dear, and yet money is exceeding scarce amongst us, poor forlorn Protestants, for we are as dead men out of mind, moneyless, friendless, and comfortless; enemies we have both at home and abroad. Our enemies at home are such as we greatly pity, for they are such as have fought for us, and necessity compels them to rob and spoil us daily. And yet we are loth to part with them, because of the grand enemy abroad that waits their going away to have their will of us, and to maintain them any longer here we cannot. I have twenty soldiers on me weekly, to pay them twenty shillings to buy bread, besides those lodged in my house. I am afraid I shall not have shortly bread for my own family. Besides the charge at home, we lose daily in the streets; the open violence every day done by the soldiers in the streets without controlment, to write, you would not believe; the great men are not free, and yet if we had but to feed them here, they would endure much want of apparel, before they would leave us.

"Our present misery consists as much in the fear of the going away of our soldiers, as the want we are exposed unto here, for we cannot understand the mystery of the times; the policy of estates is beyond our reach. What I have ever feared hath hitherto come to pass, therefore I cannot but make my fears known, which may be removed by a supply sent us of money and provision for an army; they will not be so soon sent hither again, if occasion should require, and if our enemies intended us any good, or peace with us, other than for their own end. I marvel why they sent so many arms hither, since they knew the cessation was on their side, to accept of it, or to refuse the same; but all is not well, the honestest heart is soonest deceived.

"If a supply had been sent betimes, the cessation had not been, and now they detain their monies from us, we fall together by the ears amongst ourselves, and it is to be feared we shall have a necessitated peace with them.

"I am sorry for the loss of the ship that victualled *Dungannon*, and was to bring the rest hither for our store, which is very empty, but was cast away near *Waterford*. So every way we are left destitute of help, and so are left to the cruel hand of merciless enemies, who, whiles we were at peace with them, proved cruel tyrants, so much more must we expect, being now their enemies, into whose hands we are falling; for corn is rising daily, we can expect none from the enemy, and those that should be our friends in *England* will suffer none to come. What case, think you, we are in, for before *February* next, I am persuaded, if not timely prevented, corn will be at forty-eight per quarter. Our monies are gone, that when it comes, we may see it, but not taste of it. For if you should wonder what becomes of our monies, I must inform you. It is carried every day to the enemy for beef and mutton, and other necessaries, and we have nothing to give in exchange but money, for all commodities are with them from foreign parts 50 per cent. better cheap than with us. They have free trade, we no trade; in all things they are advanced, we debased, and we fare the worse, in that our soldiers rob, and spoil, and take away all that should come out of the country unto us. In brief, we are in a very miserable condition, and no hope of amendment, for our kingdom is in our enemies' hands, and we almost at their mercy for our lives and religion. We desire to hear what likelihood of a reconciliation between his Majesty and the Parliament, for therein consists our comfort, our safety. I pray, write me if there be any expectation of relief from *England*, if not, that we may fly for our lives, or else you will be guilty of our blood, to feed us with hopes until we be destroyed. I hope God will punish those that conceal our misery from his Majesty and the Parliament, to persuade either of safety for us, if our soldiers go from us. I marvel any man can think us so secure, and yet what shall they do but dispose us here if no relief come? Famine and the sword are two great judgements upon us at present. If our men and ordnance go from us, how can we that are left behind be in safety? We hear some battle hath been fought in *England;* I am sorry to hear of so much effusion of blood amongst God's people, and the common adversary to escape unpunished, who have shed so much innocent blood. I see we are appointed to destruction. Thus remembering my love to you and to my sister, desiring you to remember my duty to my mother, and love to all my brothers and sisters, I commit you to God, and rest,

" Your very loving Brother.

"*Dublin,* October the 21st, 1643."

November the 18th.—We have certain intelligence that there are twenty-two ships gone from *Bristol,* and those parts, to transport the Irish. There are six regiments already prepared, and ready for their ships, with their commanders and arms; more are preparing, and will shortly follow. And the rebels are to make surrender of all their lands and estates; but for them that will not come on that service, they destroy, except those that fly into *Ulster* to *Munro.* Many castles have been taken from them since the cessation, and many have been slain barbarously, and their cattle and corn taken by violence. Now, let the consideration of this mystery or plot strike amazement in men, that such a rebellion, so bloody, such as have so cruelly slain so many thousands of innocent souls, should be thus easily dealt with, and at that time, when they were not able to continue their war longer, and now to be sent for to finish the work here in *England* in the joining with the bloody Cavaliers here; this is a plain confession that they had their authority to rebel, from *England*, and in obedience to that authority they lay down their arms, and are good Catholic subjects. Oh, hellish plot, to betray two or three kingdoms at one clap!

Landing of Irish Rebels.

December the 13th.—"The House of Commons received intelligence that, since the landing of the former three thousand Irish soldiers at *Chester*, and now there be two thousand of the Irish rebels landed in *Wales*, and three thousand more are suddenly expected."[1]

The Miseries of Arundel.

December the 13th.—"By a letter this day to the Speaker of the House of Commons from Colonel *Morley*, the surrender of *Arundel* Castle[2] was informed to this effect: That a party of *Hopton's* horse entering *Sussex*, made an assault against the Lord *Lumley's* house, and were beaten back by Colonel *Morley* with loss, but, failing in this, they made to *Arundel*, where they entered on *Tuesday* seven-night last, and cruelly plundered the Town,

---

[1] From *Perfect Diurnall*, No. 21.   [2] See Appendix, UUU.

threatening the Castle; the governor, one Captain *Capcot*, being with only fifty-five men, and scarce arms for half of them, or powder, shot, or other provisions. So that the Lord's day following, at which time the Lord *Hopton*, with two thousand horse and foot, in his own person coming to *Arundel*, was compelled to surrender the said Castle upon quarter, to march away with Bag and Baggage."[3]

December the 13th.—We are informed from *Bristol*, that a woman, meeting an Irish rebel in the streets, took hold of his throat, and cried out that he had cut her children's throats in *Ireland*, requesting that he might be apprehended; but instead of committing him to prison, he was rescued from the woman, and freed from any impeachment for that fact.

December the 18th.—There was a letter read in the House of Commons[4] that certifieth that there is about a thousand and a half, or two thousand, more from *Ireland*, lately landed near *Chester*; whereof part of them are of the Protestant forces, and other part of them of the Rebels.

December the 23rd.—There are letters come that speak of a revengeful havoc which the *Newcastle* Army makes in *Derbyshire* and *Nottinghamshire*. Poor people, they were before plundered by pretended friends, and now by cruel enemies. And in a letter from *Derby* dated the 19th of this month informeth that *Derbyshire* is in a miserable con-

---

[3] *Perfect Diurnall*, No. 21.

[4] From Sir William Brereton, at Namptwich. See *Perfect Diurnall*, No. 22.

dition by reason of the pillaging popish army there; which take away all wheresoever they come, and that which they cannot devour they consume with fire. For at *Hollom* pits ☞ they set on a hundred load of coals on fire at once. They have burnt many ricks of hay. Many of the inhabitants of *Ashburn, Wricksworth, Riblcy*, and other towns in the country have been plundered, and are forced to come to *Derby* for fear of being taken by the Commissioners of Array. *Derby* is a town of refuge for many succourless people, for they have above a thousand of the country people come into them. And therefore, our God have all the praise for preserving of *Derby* from those bloody enemies.

1644.—We have intelligence from *Lincoln* that the enemy came to *Waddington*, where some of the Earl of *Manchester's* horse were quartered, and have took two or three troops of our horse. They were surprised by a very great strength, under that Sir *John Byron* that was put in to be lieutenant of the Tower in former times.

January the 19th, we hear there was a letter intercepted[5] written from the supposed Lord *Byron* (the knight commended to be confided in for the keeping of the Tower, not long since) and this letter was written to the Earl of *Newcastle*, wherein with much joy he relates his victory against the *Manchester* men. And because the victory (if we consider his loss) was no great matter of glory, he glories in his savage cruelty, and writes that when some of the

[5] See *Perfect Diurnall*, No. 26.

Lancashire men, routed by him, fled into the Church to save themselves ☞ that he, (though he promised them quarter) put them every one to the sword, and bathed his hands in their blood, saying it was mercy enough to shew any cruelty to the Parliament Rebels.

Some Part of a Copy of a Letter sent from Dublin, concerning the Great Miseries there in Ireland since the late Cessation.

"Sir,—I have written to you several times of our great and prosperous victories against our enemies formerly, but now I must write unto you of the fearful tragedies acted against our poor countrymen by the barbarous Irish since the cessation, our forces being drawn away from hence daily, and our victuals exhausted, through the great and daily concourse of the Irish to this miserable city, we being left as a prey to the enemy, expecting daily and hourly to be massacred and murdered in our beds, through the manifold outrages and slaughters committed upon our poor brethren in their several Castles and Garrisons, as in that of *Catherlow, Marlohon, Racoffie*, and divers other places which the Irish have taken, contrary to their pretended Truce since the bloody cessation, ☞ having cruelly murdered all our men, women, and children that resided in them; they at this present manage all the affairs in the city, the Castle excepted, where our Lords, Justices, and Council, keep themselves close, fearing to be surprised. Our condition is very lamentable;

we are as sheep appointed for the slaughter. Our wives and children [are] swooning in the streets for want of bread, and our woful eyes made spectators of their cruel insolencies, in setting up their Idolatrous Masses in all our Churches whereof they have taken possession, and banished our best Divines, the Lord for our sins having already begun a great famine of the Word amongst us; neither are we suffered to depart the kingdom, but are exposed to the merciless cruelty of hunger, cold, and famine, as also the ending stroke of grizly death, which we hourly expect.

"Oh our miseries are unspeakable, but like to increase if not prevented by sudden and provided death. But our only woe is, that you are like to suffer with us, and that very soon, if some speedy course be not taken for the stopping of the great multitude of Irish papists which daily flock from hence into this kingdom, under pretence to assist his Majesty against the puritans. ☞ I do believe that this shall be the last that ever I shall write unto you, my dear Brother, but in regard of my duty and loyalty which I owe to my country, I will to my best endeavour set down in brief, according to my knowledge, how this plot or misery, contrived and still acted in both kingdoms, hath been aworking these sixteen years, to establish popery both here and in *England*, to the intent that my dear native countrymen may be the more cautious in not falling into their mercies, as we have done.

" About the year 1630 the Earl of *Cork* and the

Lord Chancellor *Loftus*, being Lord Justices of this kingdom, the said Earl being zealous of God's worship, did put in execution the statute against Recusants, which took such effect here that the common sort of Irish came daily to our English Churches for two months and more. In the mean time, the Earl of *Westmeath*, and Sir *Richard Barnwell* of *Crickstow*, are employed as agents to the Queen, in the behalf of all the Irish, and the King's letters of favour are obtained to the Lords Justices, commanding them not to molest his good subjects the Irish in their former liberty of conscience, which was accordingly obeyed. Afterward, the Earl of *Strafford* succeeded in this government, threatened the subversion of popery, (though by him never attempted), and employed *Westmeath* and *Barnwell* the second time to the Queen. These agents fall cunningly to work, and compounded with his Majesty to afford him a mighty sum of money throughout the whole kingdom; if so but they might enjoy their former liberty. Presently they obtained his Majesty's letters again to the Earl of *Strafford*, commanding as they desired; then all things go well with them, but that the money is not gathered. Warrants are issued out, ☞ and none so deeply taxed as the poor protestants, in purchasing the freedom of the papists, who afterwards cut their throats and dashed their children in pieces. Well, the money is collected, the papists take courage, they build abbeys and convents in every corner of the land, the locusts flock in daily to this miserable city, they build their

Mass houses in every street, and increase in three years to the number of fifteen hundred priests, Jesuits, Friars, and Monks, as is here still extant by the computation of *Paul Harris*, one of their own seminary priests. But what is all this to the many insolencies against us, by terming us traitors to the Crown ☞ they having ☞ the King's Commission for their warrant in murdering or destroying an hundred and fifty thousand souls. And great likelihood there is of a strong party, they were assured of in *England*, their Agents, *Nicholas Plunker*, and the rest of his confederates being all that summer before the rebellion with his Majesty at Court, and waiting upon his person to *Scotland*, from whence they posted into *Ireland*, and proclaimed openly the King's authority to handle in that woful manner you often heard.

"You see their cunning tricks in striving to overthrow our Religion. I beseech the Lord to preserve *England* from their tyranny, though I myself never hope to see it, or to escape their cruelty. Hoping to meet you in heaven, I rest,

"Your loving Brother,

"*R. Harrison.*

"*Dublin, January* 2, 1644.

"Sent to Mr. *R. Tuke*, resident in *London*."[6]

[6] The Letter, a small quarto, pp. 5, was "printed in *London* by *G. Dexter*, for *Henry Overton*," in 1643, and was entitled "A True and Exact Relation of the most sad Condition of Ireland since the Cessation, exprest in a Letter from *Dublin*, received the 16th of *Novemb.* 1643. Worthy to be taken notice of by all who have any true Protestant blood running in their Veines."—*King's Pamphlets.*

A Copy of some Part of a Letter from Bristol.

It is informed to this effect, *February* the 10th, 1644 :—

"Loving Friends,—Our news from *Bristol* and the parts of *Somersetshire* thereto adjoining is, that the Lord *Inchquin, Muskerry,* and the great *O'Neal,* the chief actors in the Irish rebellion, are lately arrived at *Bristol,* with a thousand five hundred native Irish Rebels, and have gotten the command of the City and Castle of *Bristol,* most of the former garrison being drawn out thence, ☞ that the bloody-thirsty Rebels might have the chief command of the Town, where they have already set open Mass in five several places, and sent out Warrants to bring in half the provision throughout *Somersetshire,* and the parts of *Gloucester* thereto adjoining, to victual that City, which they intend to keep. ☞ Most of these new arrived Irish are such as have imbrued their hands in the blood of the parents, children, kindred, and neighbours of divers English Protestants, who have fled to *Bristol* for sanctuary ; who now dare not so much as demand justice against these bloody murderers, for fear they should cut their throats there, as they did their kindred's and friends' throats in *Ireland.* Let the world now judge by this fresh remarkable action, what his Majesty's ill counsellors' real intentions are, when the archest native Irish Rebels, who have defiled themselves with the innocent blood of the Protestants in *Ireland,* are made the garrison and commanders of the chiefest city in his actual possession throughout *England*, and his own Protestant soldiers and cavaliers are thrust out from the command and guard of this city, that these Popish Rebels alone may there command at pleasure; and at this very instant, there hath been summoned a new kind of council at *Oxford*, of cashiered Malignant Members of both Houses, and deep protestations made to them of real intentions to maintain and defend the Protestant Religion, Laws, and Liberties of the Subject, which his actions contradict, as all the world and this new convented Council will not only discern, but abhor with great detestation."

February the 15th.—We have information that "Sir *William Brereton* made to the House of Commons this day concerning *Chester* and those parts. In brief [it] is first, concerning the inhumanity of those Irish and other forces with the Lord *Byron* about *Chester*, and the cruel spoil they make in all places where they come, laying all waste before them, and what they cannot devour, they set fire on, or spoil, committing many horrible crimes and insolencies. And further by the examination of sundry prisoners, it is evident there are great forces of native Irish expected daily to land about *Westchester*, and that Prince *Rupert* was also expected in those parts to join with them."[7] As also "by letters from *Gloucester* it is informed to the House of Commons of the intolerable oppressions of this Duke of Plunder-

---

[7] From *Perfect Diurnall*, No. 30.

land (Prince *Rupert*) and his plundering cavalry, lately come into those parts about *Tewkesbury*,[8] and that he sends about his cruel warrants, threatening fire and sword to all those that shall carry, or cause to be conveyed, any victuals or other provision to the garrison at *Gloucester*."[9]

There hath been lately a search made at *Whitehall*, where was found in the Queen's lodgings, and about the chapel there, no less than fifteen hundred rich copes, and about two hundred surplices, which were purposely prepared for massing priests, and their idolatrous services. This is most certain true, though we were persuaded to believe that there were no intentions of setting popery on foot again in this Kingdom.

Ireland's Lamentation for the late Cessation; a few Words of it, taken out of the Writing which Lieutenant-Colonel CHIDLEY COOTE *wrote in February the 16th, 1644.*[10]

[Now I must turn my discourse from the many miseries which] the Protestants of *Ireland* have sustained by those who should have been their best friends. I will speak but a few words of the sudden destruction our too well known enemies would fain bring upon us. The first way they fell upon is, to cut off man, woman, and child at one blow, without distinction of either descent, age, or sex, and

---

[8] *Tewxbury.*   [9] *Perfect Diurnall*, No. 30.

[10] Copied from a 4to. pamphlet, "*Ireland's* Lamentation for the late Destructive Cessation, or, A Trap to Catch Protestants. Written by Leuten.-Colonell *Chidley Coote.* London. Printed by *R. C.* for *H. S* 1644."

not only to kill their bodies, but their souls also, as far as in them lay, ☞ forcing many weak Christians to deny their Redeemer, and then telling them they were in the state of grace, and that they could never die in a better cause, and so hanged them up. As also they inflicted strange kinds of death upon them, as stabbing, drowning, starving the English, and many such horrid deaths as these. And because they did not abound enough in malice as yet to the English Protestants, the Papists in *Ireland* must be enforced to kill their own wives, that they had married of the English, because they had English blood in them, as they said, and all those English allied unto them by their wives. (And of these cruelties you may see more, in a little book called the "Miseries of *Ireland*.") Neither did their rage extend only to the living, but most inhumanly conveyed itself to the dead. They have disinterred the bodies of the innocent Protestants sleeping in their graves, and have exposed them to be a prey either to beasts or birds. Witness their practice in this kind at *Galway*, *Limerick*, and in divers other places.

Again, they revenge themselves on the very English beasts, destined for slaughter. They would not kill them as they did the Irish beasts, but the beasts being alive, [they] cut off great pieces of flesh out of them, skin and flesh together, and so broiling the flesh upon the coals, eat the same, and if the beasts either roar or groan for misery or pain, they would in detestation and mockery of the English, cry out that they understood not their English language.

Trees that the English planted must be cut up, root and branch; all herbs, plants, odoriferous flowers set and planted by the English, and pleasing to them, must therefore no longer grow, but be plucked up. All stately houses, and all manner of costly ornaments and furniture, belonging to the English, must be consumed by fire.

And now, what they see they are not able to do by force, they will strive to do by devilish subtlety and craft.[11] The means to effect this, is by a stratagem, called by the name of a Cessation, which some self-ended counsellors have obtained by their insinuations into his Majesty. Now the Cessation being concluded, and the Rebels having all the estates of the Protestants, and all the food of the Kingdom in their own hands, and suffering none of the food to be sold for any rates whatsoever to the English, of purpose to starve them out of the Kingdom; from all these places following, the Rebels have for the most part starved out the English, since this Cessation, and that merely by stopping provisions and suffering none to be sold unto them. The names of the places are these, and these be the chiefest provinces of the Kingdom, the province of *Leinster*, *Carlow*, *Athy*, the Fort of *Leafe*, *Neafe*, *Trim*, and *Dunkeld*, with many more Castles and Garrisons.

---

[11] The original adds here, "An inherent quality of that Nation."

XXXVII.

A Judgment upon Organs.

[*February* the 8th, 1644.—From *Rotterdam* in *Holland* they write, that there hath been a great pair of organs lately set up in the French Church at the *Hague*, which some priests and others went to play upon during the late frost and snow; but the weather had so congealed the pipes that they could not make them speak without fire in the room; which being neglected, and not removed, or put out, at their departure, the organs took fire, which expanded itself into the Church, and burnt both it and the pipes to the ground. Such ill success have that Romish music had of late in these northern parts of the world, as forerunner of the downfall of popery and prelacy.

Also, it is worth the observation, that a new chapel is building from the ground in the Castle of *Bristol* for the Queen; and the workmen having hoisted up a great beam of timber to set the roof on, the next morning when they came to prosecute their work, they found the beam broken in two, at which they wondered, because nothing had been done to it, or laid upon it when they left it; And that the chief workman fell from an high ladder, and brake his neck. These are not fables, but real truths, and will be verified by the positive oaths of such credible persons as saw it. The application is a stupendous and prodigious omen against popery.

At *Boston* in *Lincolnshire*, Mr. *Cotton* being their former Minister, when he was gone the Bishop desired to have organs set up in the Church, but the parish was unwilling to yield; but, however, the Bishop prevailed to be at the cost to set them up. But they being newly up, (not playing very often with them) a violent storm came in at one window, and blew the organs to another window, and brake both organs and window down, and to this day the window is out of reputation, being boarded and not glazed. Mr. *Warre*, the Minister.

Inquire further of Captain *Cust*, lodging at Mr. *Skelton*, apothecary in the *Old Bailey*.]

XXXVIII.

CRUELTIES AND MISERIES — THE CRUELTY OF THE IRISH SHEWN TO THE INHABITANTS OF BRISTOL—MORE CRUELTIES AND MISERIES.

1644.—*FEBRUARY* the 19th it is certified, "That the Atheistical Marquis, seeing the valiant Scot so resolute, caused part of the suburbs [of *Newcastle*], the *Sandgate*, and two other streets, to be burnt to the ground; wherein at least a thousand families lived, which occasioned a lamentable cry and howling amongst the poor inhabitants. That he also propounded to sink five ships laden with treasure in the harbour. And the Marquis propounded to fire the coal pits, and with a council of war was resolved on it, but was prevented through the mercy of God by the Scots' surprisal of the Boats and Lighters a little before."[1]

February the 24th, it is certified, "that those Irish Rebels that not long since landed with the Lord *Inchquin*, make most cruel spoil in all places where they come: And have lately pillaged the Lady *Drake's* house in *Dorsetshire*, who, after they had carried away what they pleased, they stripped the good Lady, who, almost naked, and without a shoe to her foot (but what she afterwards begged) fled to *Lyme* for safety, and, afterwards these in-

[1] *Perfect Diurnall*, No. 31.

human rogues set fire on her house, and burnt it to the ground."²

February the 25th, we have certain intelligence of a thousand five hundred more Irish landed at *Chester*, all of them bloody Natives, and five hundred mongrels, *Oxford* Protestants. But we must believe they all come to fight for the Protestant religion, as a thief fights for a true man's purse, and so we ought to believe, and therefore we fight against them to keep our religion and our purses from such popish thievish invaders.

The beginning of this month of *March* 1644, it is informed by several credible persons that since the drawing forth of those Irish forces out of *Bristol* to the assistance of the Lord *Hopton*, upon whose departure, there were three other sail of ships, full of Irish, both men, women, and children, designed to come into that city, and were arrived [at] *Crockpill*, whereof the inhabitants hearing, being moved with the insufferable miseries they sustained by entertaining the Irish before, began to mutiny, and declared that they would rather venture their lives and fire their ships, than admit them into the city. Whereupon Alderman *Hook*, (a lukewarm Neuter) called a council together of about sixty of the chief men of the city, who also resolved not to admit them, but sent word unto the Governor of the Castle, that unless some course were taken to send those Irish away, the trained bands of that city would rise in an uproar, which might be a means

² *Perfect Diurnall*, No. 31.

(in regard of the pressures of the common people) of the revolting of that city from his Majesty; upon the receipt of which message the Governor took order that the said ships of Irish should not come in, but appointed them to land at *Upton* in *Somersetshire* near *Bridgewater* which they did. ☞ Those savage Irish, being landed, turned many of the country people out of their houses, took possession both of them and their goods, and cut the throats of divers families within three miles of *Bristol*; which hath forced many others, fearing the like usage, to desert their habitations, to leave all, and fly into other places for succour.

The citizens and inhabitants of *Exeter* and *Salisbury* are now also in much distress, by reason of the compulsion used to enforce many of their inhabitants to take the covenant agreed upon by some desperate Malignants and Cavaliers in counties of *Devonshire* and *Cornwall*, so that many of them, in all ☞ above a hundred families, have deserted their houses, and are come to *London*; who certainly inform, that at *Salisbury*, many of the French cavaliers quartered in that town do commit many insolences upon the inhabitants when they are in their cups, which is usually every day; and sometimes in their drunken fits, in the middle of the night they have cut holes in their hats, wherein they have set candles, and so have run dancing and roaring about the town; and, I tremble to mention, that which I have received from those who were both eye and ear witnesses thereof, that in some of their intoxicating humours ☞ they have drunk healths to the Devil, and to their meeting in fire and brimstone; and committing many horrid and unheard of actions.

In *March* 16th we have true intelligence, that some of the Lord *Capel's* men went against *Hopton* Castle in *Shropshire*, where there were not above thirty men in it, but they made good the Castle, till their ammunition was all spent, then yielded upon fair and honourable quarter, which the enemy so dishonourably broke, and as soon as they entered, laid hold of them, and caused a great pit to be made, into which they cast them, and buried them alive.

April the 15th, "Intelligence was brought that one Captain *Merton*, being captain of the watch in a night, when the enemy came against that place did treacherously surrender up the town of *Wareham* (about four miles from *Poole*) to the enemy, who came against it, with only eleven Troops of Horse; which town was yielded with little or no opposition, there being not above two men lost on both sides. And we are further certified from thence that ☞ when the enemy had entered the town, they most barbarously put many to the sword (and amongst the rest the perfidious Captain)."[3]

The third time of plundering of *Birmingham*. The forces under the command of Prince *Rupert*, Duke of Plunderland, have again lately entered *Birmingham*, and re-plundered it, taking away what-

[3] *Perfect Diurnall*, No. 38.

soever was of any worth or value in the said town, to the utter undoing and impoverishing of the inhabitants.

April the 26th, by one who is come lately from *Oxford*, it is certified that Sir *Arthur Aston*, the Governor of *Oxford*, a grand papist, doth so tyrannize over the inhabitants of *Oxford*, misusing the Mayor and Aldermen, and all the Protestants in the town.

There was a gentleman that was in *Oxford* at a tavern, where he called for a pint of sack, enquiring about some in the town, to whom he came about monies due to him. The vintner asked him from whence he came; he answered from *London*. The said vintner gave notice thereof to Sir *Arthur Aston*, who caused him to be apprehended, and the next day to be racked, and examined upon the rack; he made it appear that his business was about monies due to him, and produced a note, and nothing could be suspected justly by him but fair; yet, nevertheless, such was the Governor's cruelty, that after he had racked him, he caused him the next day to be hanged upon the gallows; but he died cheerfully, only he said it grieved him to part with his wife and two children, whom he left at *London*. And after they had hanged him, they stripped him of his very shirt, and buried him naked.

There was also another hanged because he came from *London*, though nothing proved against him; and Prince *Charles* had got a pardon for the prisoner that was going to execution, and brought the pardon himself for him; and when he heard that the prince was coming with a pardon, Sir *Arthur* with his foot turned the ladder himself, the prisoner being then upon it; and when the pardon came, he was so far gone that he could not be recovered.

There was a poor Brewer at *Oxford* that used to have his drink drunk before his face off his cart; who for putting by a soldier that came with his cane to drink out of a vessel, was so beaten for it that he died.

One *Mary Brook*, servant to Mr. *Church*, an Inn Keeper in *Oxford*, sweeping of the door, said that was the dirt of the papist horses' feet, and wished they were all hanged; at which time Sir *Arthur* himself riding by heard her, and called for her, and caused her to be fettered and manacled with irons, and sent to prison, and from thence to the gallows and hanged. But she having a brother that is page of his Majesty's Buttery, he did petition for her to his Majesty, who called for her, and discharged her; since which she hath made an escape, and is now in *London*, and affirms the same.

[The writer proceeds to relate other cruelties committed in Dorsetshire and Leicestershire.]

May the 24th, the intelligence is, that "the enemy hath Commissioners of Array, who used all the cruelty that possible may be to recruit the *Oxford* Army, and all will not do, for they run away as fast as they press them; of above two thousand that are pressed since they began to recruit, they are all run away except some 300. And they are merely raised by the help of the poor cudgelled countrymen. It would pity any man's heart to see them languish in their blood, for the Cavaliers, they say, do so cut and beat them."[4]

May the 25th, "we have news from *Oxford*, that there is a pardon put for the Irish Rebels, and his Majesty calls those barbarous, infamous, and horrid Rebels of *Ireland* 'Our Roman Catholic subjects.'[5] The Villains are called subjects, and are pardoned, who have imbrued their hands in the Protestant [blood]. They have murdered a hundred thousand souls, and for no other reason but because they were Protestants; and yet these rogues must be pardoned."[6]

June the 3rd, we had news from *Lancashire* of the cruelty that Prince *Rupert* used at *Bolton* in that county; it was thus:

Prince RUPERT's *Bloody Carriage at Bolton*,[7] *expressed in a Letter sent from Mr.* HERRICKE, *a godly Minister at Manchester, to the Lady* HERRICKE, *June* 7, 1644.

"My humble duty remembered, &c. *Lancashire's*

---

[4] *Perfect Occurrences in Parliament*, No. 23.

[5] "It is hard to say whether the *Oxford* Lords, or the Campe Ladies have more enslaved their honours in this Royall Quarrell: shee is no Favourite at Court now that hath not at the least some raggs of popery about her, and his honour must bee clouded that gives such councell as proves fatall to the Irish Rebels."—*Perfect Diurnall*, No. 28.

[6] *Perfect Occurrences in Parliament*, No. 23.

[7] See "An Exact Relation of the bloody and barbarous Massacre at *Bolton in the Moors*, in *Lancashire*, on May 28 [O. S.], by Prince *Rupert*, being penned by an Eye-witness, admirably preserved by the gracious and mighty hand of God in the day of Trouble. *Published according to order.* London. Printed by *R. W.*, for *Christopher Meredith*. August 22nd, 1644."

sad hour of temptation is now upon it. Prince *Rupert*, with twenty thousand at least, is in the heart of the county; he marched with his Army within three miles of *Manchester*, and grievously plundered, taking generally all men with him. ☞ On *Tuesday*, the day before the public Fast, he stormed *Bolton*, the next garrison to *Manchester* for Religion in all the county, unto which many of God's dear servants were fled; in an hour's space he took it, denying quarter to any, whether soldiers or men in the houses, till the sword, drunk with blood, was sheathed. Fifteen hundred, two days after buried, five hundred taken prisoners; the rich in the town asking bread, and none to be had. From thence, with his former cruelty, he marched forward: at this present facing *Warrington*, assaulting *Liverpool*. Our hearts tremble for both; if God give them up, we are the last to be swallowed. Our town is full of soldiers, a complete Regiment of Highlanders sent to us, and Sir *John Meldrum* to command in chief. Our inhabitants are overburdened with billeting, and the rich will become poor. God gives us yet opportunity of praying; two public Fasts in the week, and two or three hours every day praying in the Church. The siege of *York* keeps off all help from us, yet that prospers; they have made their approach within pistol shot, taking the suburbs, raised a royal battery which commands the town. If our sins hinder not, we hope God will suddenly give up that city. They are before the town, with the Earl of *Manchester's* forces, forty thousand. *Lancashire* [is] now the alone desolate oppressed county; pray for us.

"Besides the many honest and godly people that were in this town of *Bolton*, there were also four reverent and learned Ministers to whom they would not grant any quarter, unless they would make public acknowledgment and recantation of their former doctrines, which they absolutely refused, and, like so many zealous martyrs, chose rather to die gloriously for the truth, than to make shipwreck of their consciences. Whereupon they were cruelly hacked to pieces by the furious and inhuman enemy. The names of the Ministers who thus suffered were, Mr. *Haycocks* (who was near an hundred years old, and was a famous preacher in Queen *Elizabeth's* time), Mr. *Tillesby*, Mr. *Harper*, and Mr. *Fogge*."[8]

June the 11th, "out of *Leicestershire* it is certified by letters that the enemy plunders there again with great oppression. In *Ulstrup* and thereabouts they have so plundered that they have drove away all their cattle, sheep, and robbed them of their goods, abused the inhabitants, and left them nothing at all that they could take away from them, and so misused them besides that many of them are sick, and in danger of death thereby."[9]

Colonel *Goring*, after he had thus basely and barbarously plundered *Leicestershire*, and was gone into *Derbyshire*, in his way to *Sheffield*, among many other his wicked acts he came to *Greatrex'* house at

---

[8] From *Perfect Diurnall*, No. 45.
[9] From *Perfect Occurrences*, No. 25.

Brassington, about ten miles from *Derby*, because this *Greatrex* formerly refused to be a Traitor to his Country in conveying a letter from *Goring* to the Queen, when she was in those parts, for which he was offered an hundred pound by *Goring*; he with his own hands set fire of *Greatrex*' house, which he burnt to the ground.

June the 12th, *Liverpool* was taken by Prince *Rupert*, the inhabitants yielding, desiring quarter according to the law of arms; but it was denied them by the inhuman Prince and the Irish Rebels, (his Majesty's good Catholic subjects) who put them all to the sword.[10]

June the 17th.—The King went [to] *Evesham*, where he took the Mayor of the town, and divers of the Aldermen, and carried them prisoners to *Oxford*, and, upon the King's leaving of *Worcester*, the cruel enemy hath burnt down part of the suburbs. The like merciless cruelty they have also shewed to the poor town of *Abingdon* upon his Majesty's coming back to *Oxford*, where they have burnt above sixty dwelling houses to the ground, and all this is for the Protestant religion and liberties of the subject.

[In the beginning of *June* 1644, a great Papist, one Sir *Charles Blunt*, a Colonel in the King's Army, he was pistoled by one Captain *Langston*, one of his own Captains employed under him at *Greenland* house; a just judgment of God on this wretch, for,

---

[10] See Appendix, Note VVV.

in time of peace he murdered a gentleman in his own house. His actions are so notorious that the naming of him is sufficient.]

June the 20th, "we had news from the *Virginia* plantation by letters to some Merchants in *London*, of a late unhappy difference amongst the planters, upon dispute of the divisions betwixt the King and Parliament, and that the faction hereupon increasing very great, they fell to parties, and were putting themselves in arms against each other. But the Indians perceiving this, took the advantage of so fit an opportunity, and came suddenly upon them, and cruelly massacred about fifteen hundred, and have, it is doubted, ere this made a total destruction." [11]

June the 24th, this morning "Information was given to the Parliament, that on the Lord's day last, the King passed through *Hockley in the Hole* toward *Bedford*, and in the way plundered *Leighton*, and sent another party to *Dunstable*, and when the people were at Church, to plunder was not enough, but they cut and wounded many in the Church, and shot a case of pistols at the Minister in the pulpit, but missed him, yet afterwards abused him almost as bad as death." [12]

"*July* the 20th.—This day it was certified that a party of about eighty came from *Dudley* Castle to *Birmingham* Market on *Thursday* last, and did there much mischief, as appears by this ensuing letter.

"Sir, This present *Thursday* the Cavaliers from

---

[11] From *Perfect Diurnall*, No. 47. [12] Ibid., No. 48.

Lichfield, or *Dudley* Castle, about eighty of them, came to *Birmingham;* these Cavaliers came into the town on a sudden, and took nineteen of their horse, and plundered the market of all the beast in the town, about an hundred and forty, and carried away the very calves; but the soldiers got away, and none were of them taken, neither durst the town offer to rise against the Cavaliers, because of the cruelties they should then have exposed themselves to, had they done it."[13]

July the 25th, out of *Wiltshire* it was certified that Sir *Ralph Hopton's* Forces had taken *Woodhouse,* a gentleman's house near *Warminster,* which had a long time held out against them. Upon their taking of it, they first basely and most inhumanly abused all therein, and afterwards hanged up fourteen of the most honest and religious men among them, most of which were clothiers, and worth ten thousand pound a man.[14]

July the 27th, "Colonel *Marrow,* as it was this day certified, hath recruited himself with Irish Rebels from *Chester,* and doth much mischief by plunder in those parts : And it is no wonder that he robs, and

[13] From *Perfect Passages,* &c., No. 31.
[14] " As they desire new waies to blaspheme God, so have they new inventions to revenge their malice on those that bear his Image, as we may see by that sad example lately perpetrated at *Woodhouse,* neere *Warminster,* in *Devonshire,* where, after our Forces had yeelded the house upon quarter, the enemy most inhumanly abused both men, women, and children, and afterwards most wickedly hanged 14 persons, all of them clothiers, men of good estate and quality, which were driven in there for shelter."—*Perfect Diurnall,* No. 52.

steals, and plunders, and all without making any matter of conscience of it; for not long since he affirmed, that if the King bid him to kill his own Father, he would do it. The truth of this is averred by an honourable person, and the Cavaliers being grounded on such principles as these, it is no wonder we hear of such inhuman actions committed by them." [15]

July the 31st, there was a she-spy who was in *Oxford* on the Lord's day last. She relates that on the *Monday* morning, about five of the clock, there were three executed there for spies, without any trial, or so much as council of war being called to pass judgment; namely Mr. *Alcot*, a citizen of London, *Thomas Russell*, and *Francis Tench*, two of Sir *William Waller's* soldiers.

August the 9th, by a letter sent by Colonel *King*, to his friend:—" Noble friend, we are so tormented with this ill conditioned Governor Colonel *Aston*, that we know not what course to take. You know the cruelty that he hath offered from time to time, concerning Master *Martin;* and Sir *William Rane* was plundered upon his death-bed, his ring taken off his finger; the cutting off the Lieutenant's hand at *Towcester*, which is since dead, the beating *Barnardo Davis*, High Constable of *Oxford*, kicking his wife, beating a gentleman of quality that had like to have run him through for his labour, the imprisoning of his fellow Malignant that did not bring

---

[15] From *Perfect Occurrences*, No. 32.

their corn in as they were appointed, had they not been prevented by the Parliament forces. How many poor coachmen have been undone by this Governor *Aston*, they know themselves best; as for *William Bight*, in *Vinegar Yard*, *Richard Beard*, *Henry Richman*, *Robert Harts* in *Fuller's Rents*; some of them kept in prison, some having four horses and a coach taken away from them." [16]

A Copy of a Letter from Derby.

"Sir, Our Carriers are come safe to *Derby*, with the powder which was sent from *London* to us, God be praised. But the enemy had notice of it, and *Hastings* [17] hearing of some carriages which went from *Leicester* (which he supposed to be the ammunition) he sent out a party of Horse from *Ashby-de-la-Zouch*, which Horse marched all night; and the next morning they met an honest poor man, and they asked him from whence he came. He answered, from *Leicester*; and then asked him where the ammunition was that was brought from *London*, and who it was for; to which questions he answered as well as he could; but the villains, one of them discharged a pistol against him, and others cut and hacked him so that the poor man died there most miserably. And when they came to the carriages, they robbed and pillaged all that was worth carrying

---

[16] *A Diary, or an Exact Journal*, No. 12.
[17] "That *Grand Rob-Carrier*, Collonel *Hastings*."—*Continuation of certaine Speciall and Remarkable Passages*, &c., No. 54.

away; but intelligence being brought to the Committee of *Leicester*, they sent a party of Horse, which met with them, whilst they were eating the plums and spice they had robbed the poor man of. They fell upon them, and with little loss they rescued the plunder again from them, and returned it to the Carriers.—*Derby, August* the 15th, 1644."[18]

August 24th.—" It was certified by letters that Sir *Francis Dorrington* (that bloody wolf) met an honest Minister, one Mr. *James*, near *Taunton*, as he rode upon the way, and asked him, ' Who art thou for, priest:' the Minister answered, he was for God and His Gospel; whereupon *Dorrington* shot him to death."[19]

[The writer relates many similar atrocities, that took place in Leicestershire, Derbyshire, Lancashire, Bedfordshire, Dorsetshire, Devonshire, Pembrokeshire, and Warwickshire.]

---

[18] *Perfect Occurrences.*   [19] From the *Weekly Account*, No. 52.

XXXIX.

OF THE CRUELTY OF THE KING'S ARMY IN THE WEST—OF THE SAD AND HEAVY CONDITION OF MANY OF GOD'S CHILDREN IN LINCOLNSHIRE AND LANCASHIRE—OF THE MISERIES IN STAFFORDSHIRE—OF THE GREAT FIRE IN OXFORD—NOTES.

Of the Cruelty of the King's Army in the West.[1]

SEPTEMBER the first, [1644] at least thirty thousand of the King's Army fell upon our Foot, who were not above six thousand, and some few horse; the King's forces encompassing from *Grampound Enedor* and *Foy*, even to *Blazey Bridge*, the King himself being in person, and a great number of the King's forces fell upon four of our Regiments; which, however, they were forced to retreat to our body, yet the foot stood to it against the numerous Army of the Cavaliers, for two who escaped from thirty that the King's forces had slain, and certified to Major-General *Skippon* how the King's forces were resolved to give no quarter. Then Major-General *Skippon* spoke to this effect before the Army :—

"Gentlemen,—You see what a strait we are in, and for the bloody enemy, their cruelty is such that if we yield to them, and cast ourselves upon their mercy, they will put us all to the sword, or to that

---

[1] See *Symond's Diary of the Marches of the Royal Army during the Great Civil War,* pp. 62–67.—*Camden Society.*

which is worse, to be slaves to Tyrants, and therefore let us withstand them, and fight valiantly for His cause, and no doubt He will find a way to deliver us." Hereupon the soldiers were all resolved to stand close to him, and to oppose the enemy with what power they could, and when the King's Army fell on, [they] did very good execution upon them, and slew many; some say our men slew of theirs two for one of ours, Major-General *Skippon* himself fighting like a lion, till he forced the enemy to yield to the propositions of which here followeth.[2]

Articles of Agreement made September the 1, *between Prince* MAURICE, *the Earl of* BRENTFORD, *and* FORTH, *of the one party; and* PHILIP SKIPPON, *Serjeant-Major-General, and* CHRISTOPHER WHITCOT, *Serjeant-Major of the London Brigade, and the rest of the Officers of the Army of his Excellency the Earl of* ESSEX, *who quartered on the West Side of the River of Foy, on the other party.*

I. It is agreed that all the officers and the soldiers, as well horse as foot, under the command of the Earl of *Essex*, being at this time of the conclusion of this Treaty on the west side of the river *Foy*, shall be to-morrow morning, being *September* the 2nd, by eleven of the clock in the morning drawn up in their own quarters, all their cannons, train of artillery, with all carriages, necessaries, and materials thereto belonging, and likewise all the arms, both of horse and foot, and all powder, bullet, match and ammu-

[2] See *Perfect Occurrences*, and *Perfect Diurnall*.

nition whatsoever, [shall be delivered] unto such Officer as the General of his Majesty's Artillery shall appoint to receive the same, except only the swords and pistols of all officers above the degree of corporals, who are by this agreement to wear and carry the same away.

II. It is agreed that immediately after the delivery up of the said Artillery, Arms and Ammunition, That all officers and soldiers, both Horse and Foot of the said Army shall march out of the said quarters to *Leicestheall*[3] with all their Colours, Trumpets, and Drums, and that all officers of foot above the degree of corporals, shall take with them such horse and servants as properly belong unto themselves; and also all Reformado horse and servants, not exceeding the number of fifty, and likewise to take with them all bag and baggage, and waggons of their teams of horse properly belonging to the said officers.

III. It is agreed that they shall have safe convoy of an hundred horse from their quarters, at *Leicestheall*, to *Poole* and *Wareham*, and not touch any garrison by the way.

IV. In case they march from *Poole*, that they shall not bear arms till they come to *Portsmouth* or *Southampton*.

V. That all sick and wounded shall lie at *Foy* till they be cured.

---

[3] Or *Titchfield*, according to *A Diary, or an Exact Journal, faithfully communicating the most remarkable occurrences*, &c.

VI. That they shall have in their march all the money that they can procure from *Plymouth*, and all other accommodations.

VII. That there shall be no moving of soldiers to turn to the King, but such as come voluntarily to his Majesty's service.

September the 7th.—After our great loss and heavy blow which our God hath justly given to us in the west, yet there is mercy with our God that we are not all consumed. But the mercies of the wicked are cruel.

Our scout informs us that the King's party most basely and perfidiously broke conditions, and instead of convoying our men, left them (being unarmed) to the merciless power of the soldiers and heathenish Cornish, who pillaged our foot, yea, and Commanders too, and from Lieut.-Colonels downwards pillaged them, and stripped many to their shirts, and pulled off the boots, shoes, and stockings of Commanders, and made them to go barefoot. Which Major *Skippon* seeing, repaired back to his Majesty, and told him that his generals had broke faith, and that it concerned him in honour to see reparations; but the remedy was worse than the disease. His Majesty made out warrants as if care should be taken, but yet himself broke conditions, by using enticing words to Major *Skippon*, intimating to have him to come to save him. These Cavaliers instead of safe conducting them, not only suffered them to be stripped of clothes, but of three day's provision of victuals they had with them, and to add affliction to affliction, the country would not, or had private directions to the contrary, and durst not, bring any provisions at all. So that they were enforced to march thirty miles without a bit of bread, and in extreme wet weather; and when they came to *Oakhampton*, General *Goring* sent a warrant from the King to the country, to bring in our soldiers provisions; when in all likelihood most of them had been then dead with hunger and cold, with tedious marches, if God had not strengthened them. Which warrant did as good as was intended; nothing to the purpose.

Our scout informs us of one particular more, worth your knowledge; That the sick and maimed soldiers that were left behind by the conditions, the Cornish women came, and stripped their shirts off their backs, and took away their clothes, and left them so lying naked on straw, some under hedges, some in other places. This he was an eye-witness of.

We lost thirty-six piece of ordnance, sixty barrels of powder, six thousand arms.

October the 1st.—The matter and cause of the miscarrying of this Army hath been examined. Treachery plainly appears in the thing. Honest and honourable Major *Skippon* perceived it, but too late to prevent it; therefore smiting himself upon his breast, said, "We are betrayed, we are betrayed." But who the persons are is not yet so clear. Some are known; one is run to the King to secure himself; Colonel *Butler* is sent up by his Excellency, and is committed to the Tower.

This treachery intended against the Lord General was plotting before he went into the west, upon this ground, that divers of the most knowing and active Royalists who live among us would with much confidence say, The Lord General would receive a blow in the west. In particular, a gentleman who is prisoner in the Castle of *Warwick*, namely, Mr. E. *Andrews*, the son of Sir *Ev. Andrews*, who being amongst divers gentlemen at a Tavern in *Warwick*, said before them all, with imperious speeches, that he would be hanged if the Earl of *Essex* came safe back out of the west, and told them they should see the King's Army flourish. This was preparing after the Lord General was gone into the west, when he had a gallant stout Army, such as the King's Army durst not look in the face; for some of the King's Army at the end of *Newbury* battle, said *Essex* will never be beaten, and with fearful oaths swore it. They despairing of any victory, have laboured to compass that by treacherous plots which they could not do by the sword.

1644. *September* the 7th.—We understood of the Earl of *Manchester's* intention to leave *Lincolnshire*, being by the directors general called westward. The suddenness of this call was readily obeyed. It was not to be expressed what sorrow was expressed, when it was understood he was to depart; some crying, " What will become of us within this half-hour after my Lord's forces are gone ? The King's forces will come, cursing and swearing, setting their pistols to our breasts, extorting money at their pleasure, and plundering all others, for," as sad hearts said, "what, will my Lord leave us now, and not first destroy our enemies? What will become of us? All our love and respect to my Lord's army, will now be requited upon us; there are many among us that observe our smiles, which our enemies will turn into tears by blows, and other cruelties; what shall we do? better set fire of all we have and begone, than suffer what we are like to do." These, with many more of like nature, took great impression upon the Army, insomuch that tears fell plenty on both sides.

September the 11th.—" Whereas there hath been such spoil and rapine, and unheard of cruelties lately committed by the enemy within the county of *Lancaster*, insomuch that in some parts the people have hardly anything left them to cover their nakedness, the men taken and carried to prison, the women and children having not bread to eat, which extreme misery being represented unto the Commons assembled in Parliament; It is ordered that upon the 12th day of this instant *September*, being appointed for a solemn fast, the one half of the public collection to be made in all the churches in *London* [and] *Westminster*, and line of communication, shall be employed for the relief of those poor distressed people within the said county of *Lancaster*."[4]

September the 30th, a petition was preferred to the House of Commons, subscribed by four thou-

[4] *Perfect Occurrences.*

sand gentlemen and others of good ability in the County of *Stafford*,⁵ which petition being read, some of it was to this effect of sad complaint. That the pressures, plunderings, taxations, and imprisonments, terror and murders by the enemy are insupportable, who, by reason of the unhappy absence of their Lord General the Earl of *Denbigh*, are preparing to plant themselves in garrisons in those parts for this winter.⁶ And no marvel that the godly people in those parts do so much desire his Lordship's speedy dispatch, for the Cavaliers thereabouts do threaten to suppress all the godly Ministers thereabouts, and have already been at *Welford* in *Warwickshire*, whither a party from *Worcester* came into the Church, and as Mr. *Trapp*, an honest godly man, was going into the pulpit to preach, they pulled him down, and dragged him as if he had been a malefactor, abused him and called him Roundhead, Rogue, puritan, and parliament dog, and carried him away to *Worcester*, leaving the poor people without a Teacher.

[1644.—*October* the 22nd, being the Fast day, this morning the King of the Beggars, (as they call him) was found dead against *Whitehall*, by the Court of Guard there. Of whose death I shall give no other account but what is reported by many that saw him the night before, the Fast night, when all agree that he had been with some Malignants, drinking hard, because it was the Fast day; but he drank so that he was soundly drunk, and the next

---

⁵ See *Perfect Diurnall*, No. 62.   ⁶ Ibid.

morning lay dead in the streets. Whoever pleases to enquire of those that live thereabouts may hear it more at large if they be not satisfied that which I say is truth.

Let all Drunkards and Mockers that jeer at our fasting, and make it their sport, consider well of it; there hath been many examples of this kind; God will not be mocked.]

From *Ireland, October* 24th.—"The House was informed by a gentleman newly come from *Ireland*, That the actions of the Rebels are barbarous; that though they have food enough, yet they eat young children. And no doubt these miscreants would make the same massacre of us, and use us in the same nature, had they power.

"This report was made by a gentleman of credit to the Parliament."[7]

Pulling a Minister out of the Pulpit, and then Dragging him and a Justice of Peace to Prison.

Divers strange and profane cruel actions have been daily performed by the Cavaliers in all parts of the kingdom, where they come, who respect neither time, place, nor person; particularly Captain *Pelham Corbet*, within the hundred of *Cherbery*, in the parish of *Worthen*; hearing that one Mr. *Edward Lewis*, Vicar of the parish of *Cherbery*, a very godly man, did preach twice a day, the Captain *Pelham Corbet* sent a party of Horse out of

[7] *Perfect Occurrences*, No. 14.

his garrison, and commanded them to *Cherbery*, who chose a time when the people were at church on the Lord's day, *October* the 11th, and placed some of the Horse for guards about the churchyard for fear of *Montgomery* Castle, a garrison of ours about two miles off; and the rest rid in the church to the great fright and amazement of the people, men, women, and children; and with their pistols, charged and cocked, went up to the pulpit, and pulled down Mr. *Lewis*, pulling and tugging him in a most unworthy manner. They also went to Mr. *John Newton* of *Heighly*, a Justice of Peace, his pew, pulled out him and his eldest son, Mr. *Peter Newton*, and some other godly people, which they carried away prisoners to *Corbet* their Governor, and so left the people without their pastor; because they would not be content with one sermon a day, now to be without any at all.

[*October* the 8th, 1644, there came news from *Oxford* of the great fire which was thus, as is confirmed by letters from Major-General *Brown*, and divers others, who have had intelligence from some who have been in *Oxford*.

That on the last Lord's Day in the morning, some of the soldiers in the town had appointed a merry meeting, at a fiddler's profane tap-house near the *Red Lion* by the *Fish* Market (going towards *Carfax*) and accordingly they met, with . . . music, drink, and tobacco, one drinking an health to the King, another to the next meeting of Parliament. Other healths they drank to the confusion of them at *Westminster*, and to the destruction of the City of *London*. Thus by drunkenness, music, scurrilous songs, cursing and swearing, profaning God's holy day. About three o'clock in the afternoon the fire began to appear, which by the just hand of God hath burned and consumed in all about three hundred and thirty houses, as the last and truest intelligence says.

Giles or *Carfax* Church is burnt, and so up the town till it came to *Carfax*, the devouring fire consumed all before it.

And here I will set down these observations concerning this fire. First, that when about sixty of the houses were burnt, Major-general *Brown* coming before it, all the soldiers were commanded to the works, and they would not stir unless the townsmen come with them (although many of them before were more industrious at pillaging than quenching the fire) so that there were few besides women and children left to quench it.

Secondly, observe, that the only church that was fired and defaced, though not wholly burnt, was *Carfax*, whereof *Giles Widdows* (the same that boasted that he had cuffed the Devil in his study, and wrought the schismatical puritan) was parson, aud had therein often preached against the observation of the Lord's day: saying, that dancing and playing was as necessary as preaching; so that this part of the town being so well taught, were always the most evident profaners of the Sabbath day by keeping Whitsun Ales, and dancing; amongst whom lame *Giles* himself would put off his gown and dance with them on that day.

Thirdly, observe, that most of the goods which were plundered by the Cavaliers from *Cicester* in *Gloucestershire*, and from *Oxfordshire* and *Berkshire* were here laid up, and most of them either spoiled or burned; God not permitting those ill-gotten goods to prosper, but herein in spoiling, spoiled the spoiler.

Fourthly, observe, that the head-quarters of those who had fired so many towns should now be visited with the most sad and wonderful fire that hath happened these many years in any part of the kingdom.

Fifthly, observe, that this fire was upon the Sabbath day, to shew the just judgment of God, which saith, "But if you will not hear me to sanctify the Sabbath day, and not to bear a burden nor to go through the gates of *Jerusalem* in the Sabbath day, then will I kindle a fire in the gates thereof and it shall devour the palaces of *Jerusalem*, and it shall not be quenched."—*Jeremiah* xvii. 27.

So you see that this sad accident might be a warning unto all profaners of the Lord's day, either at *Oxford* or in any part of the kingdom; it being a sin of so crying a nature, that the Almighty out of just vengeance and judgment upon the committers thereof, hath often punished with fire, as divers places in this kingdom can witness.

With this at *Oxford* the fourth part of the city

is burnt: several brewhouses, twelve bakehouses, nine malt-houses, and very nigh two thousand quarters of malt burned, and spoiled. The loss in all comes to three hundred thousand pounds.]

November the 9th, by letters out of *Pembrokeshire* it was certified that *Gerhard* had extremely plundered the country about *Knighton, Dindon,* and those parts (after he had plundered and robbed divers that lived well before) that many have been starved to death, men, women, and children, and many whom he hath forced to take up arms against their wills, when they had no more to give him, left sick, and lame, and in a most miserable condition. And in the like condition hath he left *Carmarthenshire,* as *Penarth, Trogeren,* and other parts thereabouts." [8]

December the 10th.—"From *Buckinghamshire* it is certified that the King's Horse do extremely annoy them, and that they scout out by forty, fifty, or an hundred together, and go in divers towns, and plunder all that they can make use of, their clothes, beds, bedding, cattle, sheep, poultry, and leave behind them in many places nothing but bare walls, and in some houses nothing but mats to lie on. So that those parts never suffered more than they do now." [9]

December 15th.—It is also certified from *Warwick,* that a great and ancient house of the Earl of *Middlesex,* called *Milcoat* (it is within 3 or 4 miles of *Evesham*) is burnt down to the ground. It is

[8] *Perfect Occurrences.*   [9] Ibid., No. 1.

also reported that *Campden* house, at *Campden*, is burnt and demolished, which, if true, is a great pity, for it was a very stately house, built all with silks, by Sir *Baptist Hicks*, sometime Viscount *Campden*.[10]

December the 25th, (vulgarly called *Christmas Day*) was now kept our Fast-day. This day public information was given in several congregations about *London*, concerning the cruelty of the enemies' forces; who hath driven away many well affected people from their habitation in divers towns near *Plymouth*, and stripped them of all their clothes, inforcing them to *Plymouth* for succour, on purpose to weaken the garrison by wasting provision for their relief. And therefore it was desired that such persons who had any old clothes by them would send them to *Leaden Hall*, from whence they should be sent to *Plymouth* on *Saturday* next. There is an eminent Gospel promise to those that clothe the naked.

Also this day, *December* the 25th, it was certified that the enemy about *Shrewsbury* are very cruel, even to their own friends, as may appear by this ensuing letter.

"Sir,—The King's forces at *Shrewsbury* (to add to their former cruelties) have done a most unchristian action near *Shrewsbury*, where Mr. *Barker*, a gentleman of great estate, lived, and had a very fair house, in which he dwelt within two miles of the town. The said Mr. *Barker* hath always been

[10] Apppendix, Note WWW.

a friend to them, and done much for them from time to time; his son also is in arms in the King's Army at this present. And a while since this Mr. *Barker* died, leaving the said house and goods to some daughters which lived with him, and were in the house, besides the land which he left to his son; and when Mr. *Barker* was dead, there came a warrant from the council of war at *Shrewsbury*, commanding the young gentlewomen to be gone out of the house, and carry away what they had with them to some friends' house where they thought good, or to bring it into *Shrewsbury* and it should be secured there; for they had agreed to fire down the said house, lest the Parliament Forces should come and make a garrison of it. The gentlewomen being much troubled at this sudden message, which was an addition of sorrow to their present grief for their late deceased Father, they begged that it might not be burnt, (for it was a very stately house, few such in those parts,) but could not prevail to have it stand, the Council had ordered it must be burnt. So the gentlewomen, with sad hearts, sent to their tenants to bring in carts to carry away their goods, with which they laded many carts, to the number of about sixteen, intending to have the same carried to some friends of theirs, for they durst not venture it to *Shrewsbury*; but, when the carts were laden, there came a party of Cavaliers from *Shrewsbury*, which forced the carts to *Shrewsbury* with the goods in them, all which they have taken from the gentlewomen, and burnt the house to the ground.

Out of the county of *Buckinghamshire* they also write that the King's forces, under the Earl of *Northampton,* do exceedingly waste and spoil the most fruitful parts of that fertile country. And this is most manifest, that wherever the Cavaliering Rebels come, they totally spoil and lay waste the fruitfullest and most goodly places, and behave themselves as so many boars in a garden, to the infinite damage and prejudice of the poor inhabitants, and with little or no advantage to their own side. The most of their commanders and soldiers may fitly be compared to tigers and bears for cruelty, to boars for waste and destruction, to swine for drunkenness, ... to wolves for greediness.

XL.

Parliament Occurrences — Some Part of the Life and Plots of the Lord Macguire — The Cruel Plundering of the Town of Birmingham — Outrage on a Minister in the Pulpit — Wickedness and Cruelty in our own Armies — Cruelties in Skellum Grenville's Armies.

"Parliament occurrences during these wars are not slightly to be passed over, but deliberately read and seriously considered. Antichrist, popery, and superstition cannot be cast out of the Church but with much bloodshed. What the King and Parliament divided and not laid to heart, can we look to prosper, whilst God is profaned in our armies? Shall we imitate the Cavaliers in their barbarous cruelties? Oh, let all such be speedily cast out of the camp! Oh but whilst commanders of trust are treacherous, ambitious, or covetous, what hope can there be of an end of all these troubles?"[1]

"When will the treaty be?" says one. "Do you think we shall have peace?" says another. "God grant they may agree!" says the third. "If wars last but a year longer, we shall all be undone," saith the fourth. "There is none against peace but such as gets estates by the wars," saith the fifth. "I pray God send the King to *London*,"

[1] From *Perfect Occurrences*, from *Friday*, 27th Dec., to *Friday*, Jan. 3, 1645.

saith a sixth. And at last comes the *faint-hearted*,[2] and saith, "We fight and fight and pay our money, and they tell us we must fight to save that we have, but what do we fight for?"[3]

"Alas, poor wretches, they are many of you that are as blind as beetles! If you were but now in *Cornwall*, where they had greater hopes than ever you had to find favour from the King's party, they had as long promises as any of you, and yet, though they thought thereby to have their estates secured, and an end of their troubles, and thereupon made their agreement with the King's party, yet since that time none in the whole kingdom have suffered more than they. To insert all the particulars whereof would be too tedious, as, particularly, how *Grenville's* soldiers rob, steal, and kill, about *Tavistock* and *Launceston*. How Sir *John Trevanion's* soldiers insult over the country people about *Foy* and *Liskeard*, ravish, rob, and beat the people, their wives and children, and how Sir *William Godolphin's* regiment do drive away the cattle and load away the goods, burn and spoil in cruel manner about *Truro, St. Agnes*, and the furthest part of *Cornwall*. To this I may add the experience of those inhabitants of *Oxford* who are sensible of the misery of the peace of the Cavaliers, insomuch that in that city there are many hundreds that have been exceedingly abused by them, when the Cavaliers in a mad humour have broken open one man's doors, ... cut and wounded others that have crossed

---

[2] "*White-brained Milksop*" in original. [3] *Perfect Occurrences.*

them, plundered, imprisoned, and cruelly handled them, who have been great malignants."[4]

January 4th, 1645.—We had intelligence that a party of the King's horse from *Oxford* were plundering about *Buckland, Hinton,* and those parts, and not only drove away the people's horses and cattle, and took away their cows, and butter, and cheese, but stole away their very poultry.

A great party of the Cavaliers came into *Chipping Norton*, where they quartered, and, at their going thence, to show their impartiality (though there was but one Roundhead in the town) they plundered every house therein of whatsoever was of value, and took two hundred sheep, and above forty pounds from one man.

January 5th.—Complaints are very grievous from the hither parts of *Buckingham* and *Berkshire* against some of the Parliament soldiers, who grew so insolent that when they came to a Parliament man's house to quarter, being told whose house it was, called him a "Parliament dog and rogue;" it is time to reform when such men are employed by the Parliament. And also, common soldiers that will eat nothing but pullen boiled in butter and white wine, and enforce the poor countrymen to do it. But the complaints from the remote parts of these counties where the King's soldiers are quartered,

---

[4] From *Perfect Occurrences*. In the original the following sentence concludes the paragraph:—" It was fitter for a second Book of Martyrs to reckon up a catalogue of all their cruelties in, then so short a toome as this paper can afford."

are such as the like hath not been heard in *Germany*, ... killing men and women most barbarously that were poor inhabitants, and had not left sufficient to relieve the licensed soldier according to his greedy appetite.

January the 11th, we had intelligence from *Oxfordshire* that the enemy, they had plundered *Cullam* most miserably, stripping from women of rank all their clothes, took from Lady *Carey*, an ancient lady sick in her bed, her rings from her fingers, her watch, and whatever they could carry away.

January 16th.—" It was certified that, when the houses in *Gosport* were burnt down, the Cavaliers did much mischief there by cruel plunder, and one of them, a notorious papist, who was chief in firing of the houses, came to a gentleman of the town that had two rings upon several fingers, and this wretched fellow cut off both his fingers for those rings."[5]

January the 22nd.—From *Lincolnshire* it was this day certified by letters that the *Newarkers* have marched out of the town, and done much mischief in the neighbouring villages, not only plunder the country people of all that they are worth, but have taken many of them out of their own houses, and carried them away prisoners into *Newark*, and used them very harshly, especially such as were gentlemen of worth, that so they might redeem themselves with money; a most horrible cruelty.

There is a very little parish, not far from *Win-*

[5] *Perfect Occurrences.*

chester, and all the land that was in it (when times were good) was not worth above four hundred pound, yet this parish was seized by Colonel *Goring* as he passed by, at three hundred pound, which they were commanded presently to bring in, without fail, of which that little parish could not raise any considerable proportion. Whereupon one of the chiefs of the towns was committed, yet a man of small estate, as they are all, and carried to *Winchester*, since which two of the town have been at *Winchester* to certify the King's party that the town can hardly raise eighty pound, and to raise that, all must suffer extremely, and could not possibly raise any more. Whereupon the two countrymen that came to offer the eighty pound were both committed, and remained prisoners in *Winchester* with the other man; and a party from thence was sent out to plunder the town.

January 23rd.—We had more news of the enemies' cruel plundering, as, particularly that the King's *Banbury* forces were got into *Northamptonshire*, and had plundered about *Kilsby*, where they were most inhuman, drove away sixty head of cattle, two hundred sheep, and plundered the townsmen to their very shirts upon the matter, for they left them nothing that was good.

There came also intelligence out of the west that the King's forces have burnt 25 houses in *Gosport*, a village near *Portsmouth*, where were two inns, and some other pretty convenient houses, for a little village town; but such is their cruelty that they do daily burn, rob, and plunder and spoil, and they undo all places where they come.

[*June* the 20, 1642, I did see three of the chief Rebels that came out of *Ireland* were here in *London*, carried to the Tower, viz., the Lord *Macguire*, Captain *Macmahon* (some say he is a Lord, too, both of them Irish men) and Col. *Read*, some say he is a Scotchman, a grave, portable man. I was with the Lord *Macguire* alone, and had some speech with him in the Lieutenant's house concerning my wife's brother, *Zachariah Rampain*, who dwelt in the County of *Fermanagh*, and he said he knew him very well.

And *August* the 11, 1644, being on the Lord's day in the morning, these two great bloody Rebels, the Lord *Macguire*, and Captain *Macmahon*, who have been the cause of the shedding of the blood of so many thousands innocent in *Ireland*, broke forth of the Tower and got away on this manner, they had privately brought them two saws which were made a purpose, [with] which they sawed asunder two very thick doors, and so got out of prison, and climbed over an house, and then slid down, and swam over, or waded through, the tower ditch.]

Many and evil hath the days been of those poor Protestant people in *Ireland*, caused by the cruelty of those barbarous minded men, Lord *Macguire* and *Macmahon*, those Arch grand Irish Rebels; they strove who should exceed others in mischief, their chiefest delights, inventions of cruelty, and daily sights, the tortured souls. The province of *Ulster* did bear a sad part, wherein was slain one hundred fifty four thousands of poor, distressed souls. Oh, how many children have they buried alive! They have fed upon the flesh of innocent Protestants, boasting of their cruelty, saying they never fared better than when they sucked the blood of infants, and fed upon the flesh of Protestants. Here you might see cities, and towns, and castles all on a fire. Such hath been the miseries of our poor brethren of *Ireland* under the barbarous usage of those brace of villains; yet, not contented, they thought to seize upon the Castle of *Dublin*, and to kill, and make away, the Lords and Council that were in the same; but, by God's great mercy, they were disappointed, for meeting with one *O'Neal*, a supposed friend of theirs, to him they disclosed their intent, who misliked the same, revealed the plot, and, being apprehended, and since found guilty, they were sent to the Parliament of *England*, for which kingdom's crown they formerly had cast dice for, before whom their bloody actions being discovered, and found guilty, the one, *Macmahon*, was, *November* the 18th, 1644, at *Tyburn* drawn, hanged, and quartered, and the Lord *Macguire*, *February* the 20th, was also at *Tyburn* drawn, hanged, and quartered, and their heads set on *London* Bridge, and their quarters on the gates of the City.[6]

"*February* the 4th came letters from *Birmingham*,[7] which certify of the Enemies' cruel plunder there, as you may see by this ensuing letter.

[6] See Appendix, Note XXX. [7] *Brimedgham*.

"Sir,—Colonel *Lenson*, the Governor of *Dudley*, a garrison of the King's, six miles from this place, taking the opportunity of Col. *Fox's* absence, he sent out Serjeant-Major *Henningham*, with a party of about four hundred horse and foot, who marched from *Dudley* on *Tuesday* night last, and about eleven o'clock at night they surrounded the town, and, with their horse on the street side, and their foot on the back of the houses, they were placed to keep the people in. And so they fell to plunder very cruelly for the space of four hours, insomuch that the poor women and children did make such a lamentable cry that they might have been heard half a mile off crying 'murther, murther,' and yet could find no pity, but carried away all that they could lay hands on that was worth the carrying away; as—

"*William Waldron*, they broke down his door, and plundered him of all they could lay their hands on.

"*Thomas Gisborne*, they took all his cloth out of his shop, and plundered his house all over.

"*Francis Millard*, they carried away all his iron ware, and plundered his house.

"Widow *Greaves*, a godly poor woman, they took all she had from her, and turned her out in the street in her bare smock, and bare-legged.

"Widow *Weyman*, a godly poor woman, that was gone that night to *Coventry* to be at a fast the next day, they broke open her doors, and plundered her of her iron wares, and took all that was good out of her house.

"*William Allen*, shoemaker, they took from him all the ware in his shop, and all his goods, and stripped his wife and children, and carried away the clothes from their backs.

"Widow *Simmons* they plundered of all she had, pulled her children out of their beds, and carried away their bedding and clothes from under them.

"*Elias Lilley*, with many more, too tedious to set down the particulars, these being the least of their cruelties, some they stripped them, their wives and children, and wounded many, as *Thomas Shew*, his wife, and children and divers others in such a cruel manner, the like was not heard of.

"Dated at *Birmingham, February* the 1st."

In most of the places where the enemies come, they have a thousand women, many of which are Irish, who carry great packs along with them upon some horses for the purpose, in which they plunder and take away whatsoever is of value, wheresoever they come, breaking open doors, chests, and trunks, none daring to resist them.

By letters from *Reading*[s] it is certified that a party of the enemies' horse came to a parish church belonging to a town called *Tilehurst*, on the last Lord's day, when the Minister was in the pulpit preaching unto them, and, to their great disturbance, they went into the Church, and interrupted them, and offered to carry away him, and many other godly men prisoners, if they did not forthwith

[s] Abridged from *Perfect Occurrences*, the 6th Weeke (of 1645).

furnish them with three hundred pounds, of which sum they would not bate one penny, and made them to go presently and fetch it for them, and well they could escape so, too, for the mercies of the wicked is cruelty.

Out of *Worcestershire* it is advertised that a party of the enemies went to the house of one Mr. *Baker*, an active man for the Parliament, at a place called *Hinton upon the Green*, which they totally plundered, and afterwards burnt it down to the ground.

Wickedness and Cruelty committed in our own Armies.

January the 30th.—" The Committee appointed to examine the particulars [were] informed of the several murders and other cruelties committed by our soldiers; it is reported, that two men of Mr. *Hobies*, a Member of the House, were slain by them, and himself called a Parliament dog. It is time to cast out these men that commit these acts, be they never so conformable otherways."[9]

March the 1st.—" Intelligence is that in *Cornwall* and *Devonshire, Skellum Grenville*[10] hath sent out a great press, and by his warrants the men are sent in, who came to him very unwillingly, and are listed, and upon their march, being not used to that service, and his marches are very fast many times, especially when he retreats from *Plymouth*, as he doth often upon our sallying out, and he forceth the foot to retreat with the Horse, and

[9] From *A Perfect Diurnall*, No. 81.   [10] Sir Kenelm Grenville?

those that go not so fast as the rest, they with long sticks which they have gotten for the purpose, with needles put in the end of them, thrust the poor men, as drovers used to do oxen, to force them forward the faster, and thus he useth not only lusty strong men, but little youths, and old grey-headed men, of whom they have pressed divers to serve him. So that *Grenville* now sways those two counties of *Cornwall* and *Devonshire* with much cruelty and tyranny." [11]

[11] Abridged from *Perfect Occurrences*, 10th Weeke.

XLI.

Cruelly Plundering Progress.

MARCH the 1st, intelligence is that a party of Horse from *Newark* marched in to the *Peak* in *Derbyshire*, to a place called *Worsworth*, and there took some honest men of the Committee, a mayor, a captain, and twenty-five dragoons, and plundered the town of some ten horse, besides, robbed them of three hundred pounds in money.

March the 6th "we had intelligence, that two prisoners in *Exeter*, one was a godly Minister, and the other, an honest farmer in *Cornwall*, were both discharged upon exchange, and the discharge under the General's own hand, and yet, when [he] heard of it, he called for them, and offered them the covenant, which they told *Skellum Grenville* was not, they hoped, to be imposed upon them, because they were fully discharged, and others set at liberty for them, and shewed him their General's own hand for it. *Skellum* took the discharge from them, and sent them to another prison, and caused the Covenant to be imposed upon them, which they refused, whereupon, without any trial, and for no other offence but refusing it, and malice together, *Grenville* caused them to be tied together, and sent them both to be hanged, and, accordingly, the yeoman was executed, and, just as the Minister was to be hanged, comes one crying, 'Mercy, mercy,' and so they stayed, and this mercy was to send the Minister back to *Exeter* prison again to be tortured, and almost starved, as he was before."[1]

March the 7th the news is that the Cavaliers "they have robbed *Harborough* in *Leicestershire* from one end of the town to the other, beginning at the sign of the *Ram*, and plundering all along to the *Crown*.

"But none of them exceed *Skellum Grenville*, who hath plundered all *Cornwall* and *Devonshire*, between *Rainhead St. Marywick* from the *Land's end* to the *Temple* and *Cave*."[2]

Also from *Warwick* we have intelligence that the Earl of *Northampton* sent out a party of horse about two hundred, from *Banbury* to wait for the *Gloucestershire* Clothiers, and, when they had intelligence of the Clothiers' coming, they drew out after them, and had a short skirmish, took about fifty prisoners, and all the cloth and horses. (There was seventy-two packs of cloth, which is valued at ten thousand pound.)

1645.—The Parliament hath received intelligence that Prince *Rupert* had executed thirteen English Protestants.[3] The Lords and Commons now in Parliament, being sensible thereof, do declare, That

---

[1] From *Perfect Passages of each Daye's Proceedings in Parliament.*
[2] From *Perfect Occurrences*, the 11th Weeke."
[3] Appendix, Note YYY.

they have just cause so to proceed against those inhuman Irish, whose intentions are absolutely to the dispersion of the crown of *England* from that kingdom, and to the destruction of the Protestants and English there, which is apparent by their setting up the Spanish colours at *Wexford* and *Galloway* in *Ireland*, and have murdered an hundred fifty-four thousand British Protestants in one Province, within four months after the beginning of that rebellion there.

Grenville vexeth *Devonshire* very sore, by forcing the country and laying heavy taxes, and if the weekly assessments be not brought in at the time prefixed by his warrants, he hangs up the constable that is to gather it; having made thirteen examples of this kind.

The Enemy's Cruel Colours.

April the 8th "there came intelligence that Sir *William Waller* had taken one of the enemies' colours, a cornet's colours, which is thought fit to be published, that all men may see how they thirst for the blood of Protestants. There is in the same colours a Protestant's head, with his ears cut off, and the head cut and mangled." [4]

April the 18th we are certified that a brave farm of Sir *William Drake's*, in the parish of *Amersham*,[5]

---

[4] From "*Perfect Occurrences*, the 15th Weeke," where the paragraph ends thus—"(*as if thus they hoped by their Army, to make the conditions of the Protestants in England*), and underneath this Motto: '*Non quadratus*.' They hope to square the Church of *England* to the Church of *Rome*. But God is all-sufficient to defend us, in Him we trust!"

[5] *Admonsham*.

is burnt, with the barns and stables, and, about ten days before, ten or twelve of our disorderly soldiers came to this farm, and demanded quarter, and what not. The master of the house told them he paid for quartering ten men at that time, and had not any for them, upon which they violently entered the house, and forced the man himself to rub their horse heels, not suffering any of his servants to do it. After this, they tied bottles about his neck, forcing him to go to the town, and fetch them sack, who returned with some thirty musketeers, and seized on them; but, upon promise of better deportment let them go, who, in requital, came afterwards, and fired his house.[6]

April the 23rd we hear that *Greenwell* his forces, which are now straitly besieging *Taunton*, are so cruel that they murder and hang up every man, woman, and child that came out of the town, and threaten to give no quarter to any therein.

The condition of the Western parts about *Taunton* is very sad, the enemy's forces before that town have exercised many cruelties upon the inhabitants thereabouts, killing all such as refuse to join with them. They carry away all the women they can find, whose husbands are in *Lyme*, *Taunton*, or other the Parliament's garrisons thereabouts, or whose affection to the Parliament are known, and either knock them and their children on the head with the butt

---

[6] See "*The Weekly Postmaster*, Faithfully Communicating his Intelligence of the Proceedings of Parliament, and many other Memorable Passages, certified by Letters and Advertisements. *Numb.* 2."

end of their muskets, or set them upon the works before *Taunton*, that so they may be shot by the ordnance from the town. They have also their dogs to search out any of the inhabitants, who fly from them to hide themselves in the woods, and no sooner find them but they kill them, with many unheard of cruelties which make one's heart [ache] to mention.'

May the 13th from *Marlborough* it was certified that the enemy's forces had fired divers houses in those parts, took the lead off most of the churches, and afterwards pulled them down.

As also the enemies in *Wiltshire*, that the soldiers belonging to the *Devizes* had burnt down Sir *Edward Baynton's* house near the *Devizes*, being a very stately and magnificent structure; it cost fifteen thousand pounds the building; the iron-work about this house being as near as big as *Whitehall*, cost five thousand pounds. King *James* lay in it, it being a palace fit to entertain a king.

Justice *Drew's* house in the *Devizes Green* is to [be] pulled down.

May the 17th letters certify that the King's forces have burnt down divers houses between *Oxford* and *Bristol*, fearing we would make garrisons of them, as, particularly Serjeant *Glanvill's* house, Sir *William Cawley's* son's house, and Mr. *Band's*, with others, and caused other men to pull down their houses, which, otherwise, they would have fired.

---

⁷ See *Perfect Passages of each Daye's Proceedings in Parliament*, No. 27.

May the 30th there came letters from *Nottingham;* here is some part of a copy :—

Sir,—*Lichfield's* forces, being about three hundred, horse and foot, did lately in the night attempt to plunder near *Nottingham,* entered the town, and fell to plundering, but we beat them back with shame and loss. On this present day *Rupert* and *Maurice,* with about two thousand horse and foot, came into *Burton.* *Rupert* quartered at Mr. *Clark's* house, a clothier, and *Maurice* at John *Appleby's,* a butcher. This day there came a party of horse to *Seckington,* two miles from *Tamworth,* to take up quarter for the King's forces ; the parishioners, and some of the adjacent villages gave the quarter-master, as they agreed, five pounds, that they should not be troubled, neither for quarter [nor] contribution money, nor to be plundered ; yet, so cruel and faithless are their promises, for, no sooner were they quartered at a town near thereto, but warrants were sent, the substance as followeth :—

Nottingham, May 28, 1645.—To the Constables of the parish of *Seckington* there haste post haste ; These are to warn you that you, forthwith upon the sight hereof, send in what provisions your parish will afford to the garrison of *Ashby-de-la-Zouch,* for the use of his Majesty's army, and if you fail herein, you must expect to be exposed to the plunder of the hungry soldier.

May the 31st " was acted the loss of *Leicester,* a great loss indeed, and ill-carried ; it was taken just at the time, and by storming, and entering at the same place, which a gentleman gave notice three weeks before. It may come to light who was in fault. The blood ran down the street, and the Cavaliers were so drunk with wine they found in *Leicester*, as well as with the blood of men, women, and children, that they tumbled up and down the street, many lying along in the streets amongst the dead." [8]

In *May* there were fifty-three of our men surprised in their quarters, and carried prisoners into *Oxford*, and, as they went to prison, the cruel enemy did cut, and hacked, and wounded our men most cruelly, and these fifty-three men Sir *Thomas Fairfax* hath exchanged, and sent up to *London* in carts, and some of them are in the Hospital, and are very honest, religious men, that are *Suffolk* men; (some came from *Sudbury*). It is said it was wrong of their Captain, because he did not draw them off at the time appointed. Such treacherous, careless men there is among us!

May the 31st, *Saturday*.—The enemy in the morning entered the town of *Leicester* in several places, when, for about three hours following, they had a bloody encounter in the market-place, our men betaking themselves to the houses, and did pelt the enemy out of the windows. More were killed in this fight than in the storm. They likewise brought up their cannon to the cross, and did great execution on the enemy. One letter says the channel thereabout ran down with blood, that the enemy

[8] *Perfect Occurrences*, the 25th Weeke.

gave no quarter, but put all to the sword. The number slain is uncertain as yet. The enemy, being masters of the town, fell to plundering unmercifully, making such lamentable devastation that they have not left scarce any in the town either money or victuals, clothes, goods, or moveables, to succour them. The King came into *Leicester* on the *Sunday*, and he hath since sent part of his army into *Derbyshire*. The rest are plundering, and driving away the horses and cattle in *Leicestershire*. Thus briefly for the present I have given you some of *Leicestershire's* miseries.

By another letter, "There were many other bloody outrages committed, the like scarce to be paralleled, that, after they had entered the town, they killed many that begged for quarter, and put divers women very inhumanly to the sword. That, after they had plundered the town, as is before expressed, they turned divers women and children out of their houses into the open streets, almost stark naked, and succourless, and some of them they committed to prison, where they be now in great misery. They hanged Master *Raynor*, an honest, religious gentleman, and another gentleman, a lawyer, in cold blood. At *Wigston* two miles off *Leicester*, after they had plundered the town, they most barbarously murdered Mistress *Burrowes*, and two of her children, her husband, a godly and religious divine being then prisoner at *Leicester*, if not slain. A great part of the plunder of *Leicester*, they have carried into *Newark*. In storming of the town and the fight was (as we hear since, for certain) betwixt two and three hundred slain." [9]

June the 5th "we had the particulars of the taking of *Leicester*, five hundred killed on both sides, of which most were of the enemy's part. The number of those that are wounded are very many. Fifteen hundred prisoners were taken by the enemy in *Leicester*, 19 piece of ordnance, (13 that were of old, and 6 lately sent thither). Three thousand arms taken by the enemy. Two hundred barrels of powder, part of which were of shopkeeper's powder for their sale. Seven hundred horse that were of the soldiers. A thousand and odd horse that country people had brought in, hoping to secure them by being there. Fifty cartload of plunder sent out at one time, and many more afterwards. The prisoners sent, some to *Newark*, and some to *Ashby-de-la-Zouch*, the rest kept in *Leicester*." [10]

It is confirmed that the miseries that the county of *Leicestershire* hath suffered, and the losses, will not be repaired these seven years. In the ruins of *Leicester* you may behold a large map of misery, the townsmen, from the richest to the poorest, being all of them despoiled of their goods. The enemy are about to make them unhabitable, and are pulling down two parts of the town to make the rest impregnable. All the *South-gate Street* is already laid waste, and they are demolishing apace several other streets in the town.

---

[9] *Perfect Diurnall*, No. 97.
[10] *Perfect Occurrences*, the 23rd Weeke.

Cruelties in Ireland.

June the 20th we are informed from *Ireland* " that the rebels are nine thousand; *Inchiquin* not six thousand; and the *Irish* are extremely cruel to the Protestants. In one town they have hanged sixty Protestants, and some they have cut their tongues, others their members, and have massacred men, women, and children in a most bloody and barbarous manner.

" And the King's soldiers in *Ireland* follow them in their bloody actions, as when they look best, they will take men and make them to kneel down upon their knees, and swear by *JESUS* they were for the King, then . . . they would never fight against the King. . . . . And when, out of reverence to the Lord, some durst not so profane the name of God, then they would with their swords hack and cut them on the arms and sides; many of them that have been so used are at *Leicester*, under the surgeon's hands. And is this for the liberty of the subject, think you?"[11]

June the 21st, " there came letters which certify the cruel and barbarous actions of *Gerhard* in *Pembrokeshire* and the adjacent parts, among the rest, that his horse have eaten up all, or most part, of the corn on the ground, and that which they found in barns unthrashed, and could not make use on, they set fire on it, and burnt both corn and barn, and divers other barbarous actions have they committed

---

[11] *Perfect Passages*, No. 35.

in those parts, as hath been certified under the hands of the Committee.

"From *Lincolnshire* it is certified that the *Newarkers* sent out a party of horse, commanded by Capt. *Wright*, to fetch in contribution as far as *Linsey Moor*, and when they came to *Fossedyke*, though the water [was] very high, yet they sware . . . . that they would [go] over. So they passed, and some of them were sunk, and all of them were fain to swim, and when they came to *Linsey Marsh* they sent for the contribution by warrants, upon penalty of plundering them, and carrying away all they had, and otherwise threatening them with fire and sword. The *Newarkers* did so threaten the country people, that they brought in to Capt. *Wright* an hundred pound, which was a great deal of money to raise so suddenly in that place, which he took, they thinking that he had been well satisfied therewith; yet, such was the enemy's cruelty that, after they had received the same monies, they marched up to Sir *Edward Ayscough's* house, and plundered there, and so to divers other houses, in as great cruelties as could be."[12]

July the 10th.—"Out of *Pembrokeshire* it was certified that *Gerhard* hath been most barbarous in those parts, and that particularly about *St. Twinells, Jameston, Penally*, and many parts in *Narberth* hundred, his soldiers not being content with plunder of the country, and carrying away what they could make use of. They have spoiled, not only the corn,

[12] *Perfect Passages*, No. 35.

but the fruit, the people's goods, set fire on their houses .... and put some men and youths to the sword."[13]

July the 25th, we had intelligence that the enemy in *Oxford* have cut down all the trees, both apple trees, and other fruit trees, about *Marston*, and other places near *Oxford*, and have fetched in all the hay they can get about the country, not so much that they want it for their horse, but that we should have none for ours when we come.

August 14, 1645.—Letters from *Plymouth* certify that the *Turkish* pirates, men of war, have landed in *Cornwall*, about *Foy*, and that they have taken away two hundred and forty (of *English* Christians) of the *Cornish* men, women, and children, amongst which, Mr. *John Carew* his daughter, that was cousin to Sir *Alexander Carew* that was beheaded, and some gentlewomen and others of note, and have carried them away; a very sad thing.[14]

Of the King's Forces' cruelly plundering progress through *Lincolnshire*, *Huntingdonshire*, and *Bedfordshire* in a letter is expressed thus :—

"Sir,—It hath pleased God to cast us into a very sad condition; the King's army coming through our country hath seized upon all men they could find, and have taken away my master. He hath been out with them a week, and is now about *Worcester*; they have had six hundred pound of our town, and yet they have taken away seven or eight prisoners,

---

[13] *Perfect Passages*, No. 38.
[14] See *Perfect Occurrences*, the 33rd Weeke.

Ed. Cuthbert, Junior, *Clement Austin*, *Thomas Selby*, Mr. *Francis*, and *Cooper* at the *White Hart*, *Matthew Bowles*, and *Henry Gough*. All those that were too confident of their mercies, now they find by experience to be cruelties. I am persuaded there is not such a generation of hell-hounds in the world as they are, for plundering, . . . and swearing, and drinking, and killing of one another in their drunkenness. For my part, I durst not abide their presence, but went out of the way. The rankest Cavaliers now, both in town and country, say they are like devils, rather than men; all those that were their friends did not hide themselves, nor their horses; but, now they have tasted their barbarous cruelties; they have at least a thousand of our countrymen prisoners with them, and at least three thousand horse out of our county, and *Huntingdonshire*. I believe that, where one that was for the Parliament hath suffered a penny loss by them, their own side hath suffered, some an hundred, some fourscore, some threescore, pounds. There was *Gerhard's* regiment came through the town, but never came within Mr. *Restbury's*, nor Mr. *Nethercoat's*, nor Mr. *Johnson's* houses, nor others for the Parliament, which was a great Providence of God. My master hath paid them down threescore pound upon his own table before they carried away his person, no man knows where, nor what hardship he endures, which is a great grief to us. The King hath enriched himself more than at *Leicester* tenfold; two thousand resolved men would have beat him utterly, his men are so drunken, and so earnest for plundering.

Oundle, August the 30th, it was particularly advertised that his Majesty, the Lord's day before, entered the town of *Huntingdon*, and, with much complimental bowing, saluted all his good friends as he passed through the streets, and was entertained with much expressions of joy and acclamations, as had not been heard there. The Mayor of *Huntingdon*, and two bailiffs of *Godmanchester*, and their brethren, as a further acknowledgment of their delight to see him, taxed the said towns at 5s., 10s., and 15s. a man, (mean men) and others at far higher rates, and presented his Majesty therewith in lump, which Mayor, bailiffs, and forty-three others of his brethren (most Royalists) for their loving expression were carried away prisoners with the army, and many others of that town and other places, known friends to them, carried away and forced to ransom themselves by money.

Presently after the King came in, proclamation was made that, on pain of death, no soldiers should plunder, and that full satisfaction should be made to any who complained of such grievances. No sooner was it made but they fell to plunder, carrying out of divers shops and houses three and four loads of goods, and ware apiece, amongst many, Mr. *Fulwood*, an apothecary, and the two King's Woollen drapers can witness its truth, not leaving them one bit of household stuff in their houses, or wares in their shops. Every house was billetted, though never so poor, some 20 or 30 in a house, who were, by special order, to provide both horse meat and man's meat, and 12*s*. a day to each soldier to spend, which was duly paid, though they were forced to borrow it. In many quarters the soldiers fetched in sheep of other men's, and the landlord pay them four or five shillings apiece for them to dress them for their use, or else swore they would spit their children. Many houses were plundered to nothing, so that tables, stools, bedsteads, and other combustible things lie broken in every room after the bedding, linen, pewter, and portable things [are] carried out. Very many people are not left worth one penny. At their parting they drove away both *Huntingdon* and *Godmanchester* herds of kine about six or seven hundred, and made them pay a mark apiece for every head before they had them again. They left scarce a horse in either town, nor in any other they marched through, so that the country knew not how to get in their corn yet out. The injuries of some particular men are many, and their cruelties inflicted upon some by tying lighted matches between their fingers and burning them, are too many. They knocked off the irons of all the felons, and other prisoners in *Huntingdon* Gaol, which were very many, and condemned men in law for gross robberies and murders, who have all taken up arms for his Majesty.

Colonel *Gerard*, in the presence of many honest men, did openly profess at *Huntingdon* that the Parliament went about to take the crown and kingdom from the King, but they would take such a course before they had done with it, that it should be left scarce worth having; and further wished that the estate which he had in *England* was all of a fire, for things would never be well till it came to that.

The King, to please the country, after many thousand pounds worth of goods sent away without any check, and many men undone, caused lots to be cast between four who had pillaged a poor glover in the town (one *Gumber*) of about five shillings, and one to be hanged therefore, and, at his departure, gave the town and county thanks for their kind entertainment of him. One providence is observable, that divers of the best affected to the Parliament have escaped with the least loss, and many of the King's best friends have suffered most in their persons and estates. Many of the *Huntingdonshire* malignants are convinced of their errors in supposing the King's army saints, but find them more like devils. Some of our *London* malignants are changed in judgement, being at *Huntingdon*, and eye-witnesses of what was performed.

September the 8th, we had confirmation of the Scottish forces their rising from *Hereford*, upon their departure his Majesty came to *Hereford*, his forces fell to their wonted course of plundering the country, and some of the houses where the Scots quartered they pulled down, others they burnt down, but plundered them all. Honest men, that had never so little shewed themselves for the Parliament, were fain to fly, and their wives and children turned out of all.

September the 15th "came letters out of *Shropshire* which certify how the Papists act there for the King against the Protestants, as you may see by the ensuing letter:—

"Sir,—Sir *William Vaughan* by a party from the King received orders to execute much cruelty by fire and sword in these parts, and, accordingly, marched out with them to *Bishop's Castle*, which is a place where are many honest, godly Christians, and there they fired the Church and burnt the pews, and spoiled the place purposely to prevent the people from meeting there to hear those honest, godly, Protestant Ministers that used to preach there. And they also began to set fire of the town, and burnt down four houses, but God kept them from doing so much hurt as they intended at first. And from thence to Captain *More's*, intending to burn down his Manor House. But the Papists of those parts, fearing that, if they went on in this manner to destroy the country by fire and sword, that, after they retreated, they should fare the worse for it, they (for others could not be heard) prayed them to cease, particularly Mr. *Harridge's* wife, and others, who easily prevailed, and so Captain *More's* house was not burnt.

"*September* the 9th, 1645."[15]

September the 15th.—There was a "certain [and brief] relation of the late sufferings of a worthy and honest gentleman in *Northamptonshire* by the enemy;

[15] From *Perfect Occurrences*, the 39th Wecke.

in short, thus: the King's forces at *Banbury* did lastly carry loads of straw into the house of Mr. *Cartwright* at *Ayneho-on-the-Hill*, in *Northamptonshire*, four miles off *Banbury*, and set the straw on fire, and burnt down, not only his own dwelling house, being a very fair, goodly building, wherein the King himself lodged after the battle of *Edgehill*, but also burnt all the barns, stables, and out-houses belonging to it, lest it should be made a garrison by the Parliament, having heretofore plundered him of 940 sheep and great store of rich household stuff, and other goods and rents, to the value of above eight thousand pounds."[16]

[16] *Perfect Diurnall*, No. 112.

XLII.

GORING'S CRUELTY IN DEVONSHIRE—SAD CONDITION OF THE PEOPLE IN CORNWALL—SAD NEWS FROM IRELAND.

WE had intelligence that in this month of *September*, *Goring* marched out from *Tiverton* with six thousand horse and foot, and seven pieces of ordnance, and fell on *Baunton*, the first market-town bordering upon *Devonshire*, in which town was no defence but the inhabitants, who stood in their defence as they were able, but, being overpowered, they were subdued, the town was plundered, and great part of it was burnt. The next morning, the enemy marched to *Minehead*, where were two foot companies of the country, the enemies approaching, the most of them fled, and eleven barks were thrust out to sea, filled with people and goods before the enemy entered, and those were safe, but all else in the town was plundered wholly, and all the ships and barks that were remaining in the harbour were burnt. They killed and wounded many, and, amongst the rest, Captain *Jewell*, to whom they used very much cruelty. From thence they sent a party to plunder *Watchet*.

October the 12th, there came intelligence that *Wallingford's* horse, being out, took six waggons laden with cloth that was coming to *London*, robbed them of all, left them nothing but bare waggons, and their lean oxen, with which they came this day to *London*.

November the 9th, 1645, this sad condition of the people in *Cornwall* was read at our Church *Leonard, Eastcheap*, for a collection for them :—

This doth certify that there are many Cornish families in *Plymouth* who, for their zeal to religion and the Parliament have been three years exiled their habitations, plundered of all their estates, have eaten out their credit in a place of great straits, many parents have rather silently languished under their mortal extremities than suffer their children to beg the streets, the most part have given more bread at their doors in a day than they have now to sustain their families a whole week. There are many poor children fatherless and motherless, many widows friendless, six orphans of one godly Minister, and if God should now be pleased to open a way for the return of these poor exiles, as we trust He will, they have nothing left them, beyond the charities of people, but bare walls, and raked ground to live upon, whose sufferings have been so much the more heavy, and are the more to be pitied by how much their integrities have been more eminent amidst a crooked people, for which they have endured even incredible mischiefs, not only by their bad neighbours, but chiefly by the French and Irish, who, like ravening wolves, still worry in those parts. Many wives have been forced to see the hanging of their husbands, parents of their children, and children of their parents, for not serving the cruel commands of Sir *Richard Greville*, whose tyranny had known no bounds, if the Lord, by a miracle of Providence, had not stayed the execution of forty parties sentenced to the gallows, the sixth that was to be hanged breaking one new halter, and then another, and then two twisted together without any hurt upon him.

January the 28th.—The Letters this day confirm the barbarous cruelty of the Cavaliers at *Marlborough*, where they . . . . . burnt many houses, plundered all, took many honest men prisoners, and amongst the rest the Governor of the *Devizes*, who deserved better.

February 4th.—From the west we had by letters thus: That on *January* the 28th the muskets, pikes, halberts, bullet, powder and match, was loaded out of *Launceston* and the town soundly plundered, the lead that was on the Church and the Town Hall was pulled down and carried away, and all the cheese and other provisions that they could find in the town they plundered for the soldiers.

April the 8th [1646].—We received a letter from *Rutland* of the most barbarous cruel exploits (even worse than that of burying the men alive in *Shropshire*). And that which hath the emphasis, they were our own soldiers. This cruelty was exercised upon certain inhabitants of the town of *Medborn* and for no cause save that they were not willing to have their houses taken from them, about twenty were miserably wounded, hacked and hewed, and divers run through the body .... some both their hands cut off, divers are dead, others dying. After, they went and assaulted the house of the Minister, who hardly escaped with his life. If this be not punished to the full can *England* ever look for a blessing, or that God should ever end her troubles? Hereafter it's like you may see the tragedy at large.

April the 9th.—" We had intelligence of the most cruel and barbarous acts of the enemy, the one in firing *Bridgenorth*, thus certified; That our forces in the town sending a summons to the castle, it was accepted, and a treaty was to follow, but in the interim the Governour sent out warrants to the town to bring a month's provision into the castle, which they being in no capacity to do, ours being quartered in the town, they from the castle presently shot granadoes and fired and burnt down all the upper town except a very few houses.

"The other like cruel and merciless act of the enemy was the burning of *Farrington*, which we had also intelligence of this day that the enemy to prevent our forces sheltering in the town have set it on fire, and have burnt the greater part thereof."[1]

June the 13th, 1646.—We had very sad, disconsolate news from *Ireland*, that about six or seven score of the rebels' horse fell on a dairy of the Earl of *Thomond's*, they brake all the vessels, and drove away about fifty cows, murdered a man and a woman, and burnt several houses.

[1] From *A Perfect Diurnall*, No. 141.

And by letters we are assured of a great defeat that the enemy hath given to the British forces; the manner is thus related:[2]—*June* the 3rd, Major General *Munro* drew out his forces in number of horse and foot about 6000, and marched towards a place called *Benburgh,* near which the enemy lay in number about 9000. The next day, after a long march, he faced the enemy, charged a part of them; they retreated to the woods for advantage, and also ambuscaded the passages, but were beaten off, and were pursued gallantly near to their main body. Night overtaking, *Monrow* seconded a retreat, but providence so ordered that in the night the enemy fell on them unexpectedly, and with great advantage being more in number by many did much hurt to our men, but the alarm being taken the British forces made ready, and there was a very great fight, *Monrow* was routed and forced to fly. . . . . This fight was at a place called *Blackwater,* the Commander of the enemy's forces was *Owen Roe O'Neal.* We lost seven pieces of ordnance, 5000 arms, many of the foot were slain in the fight, many were taken, but presently put to the sword cruelly; 600 horse routed, whereof some were taken and slain. The number slain and lost in all are about 5000, some

---

[2] "One of the first most remarkable Occurrences in *Ireland,* was that grand defeat received by the Scots under Major-General *Monroe,* from *Owen Roe O'Niel* and the Irish at *Benburgh,* and the *Black Water* near *Charlemont,* in the County of *Ardmagh;* touching which the said *Monroe* expresseth himself in a Letter to the Scots Commissioners at *London.*"—*Rushworth.*

Lords were wounded or killed, as Lord *Montgomery*, Lord *Ards*, Lord *Blaney*.

It is an old saying, He that will *England* win, must with *Ireland* first begin; they have already foully done too fair for that kingdom; take timely heed, oh *England!*

XLIII.

Beheading of the King.

☞ *January* the 30th, 1649, about two o'clock, was King *Charles* beheaded on a scaffold at *White Hall*.

Whatever may be unjust with men, God is righteous and just in whatever He doth.

"They took *Adonibezek*, and cut off the thumbs of his hands, and of his feet. And *Adonibezek* said, Seventy Kings having the thumbs of their feet and of their hands cut off, gathered bread under my table; as I have done, God hath rewarded me. So they brought him to *Jerusalem*, and there he died." —*Judges* i. 6, 7.

APPENDIX.

NOTE A.—Vol. I., page 2.

STUKELEY, an *Englishman*, a riotous Prodigall, and vaineglorious fellow, who after he had consumed all his estate, retired into *Ireland*, having lost all hope of getting the Marshallship of *Wexford*, and perceiuing himself to be despised of euery one, and being unable to raise any commotion, after belching vp most vnworthy reproches of his Princesse who had done him many fauors, slipped over into *Italie*, to Pope *Pius* the fifth, and by his flattering tongue, insinuated beyond all credit into the fauour of this pernicious old man, who breathed out the ruine of Queene *Elizabeth*, making great brags, and promising that with three thousand *Italians*, he could drive all the *English* out of *Ireland*, and burne the *English* Fleet; which he afterwards villainously attempted, but to his own ruine.

"This yeere (1578) the *Spaniard*, and Pope *Gregorie* the thirteenth, prouiding for their own profit, under shadow of restoring religion, held secret counsell how at one time to inuade both *Ireland* and *England*, and dispossesse Queene *Elizabeth*, who was the surest defence of the Protestant Religion. Those which know that the principall strength of *England* consists in the Nauie Royall, and in Merchants' Shippes which are built for Warre, thought it were good to fraught the Merchants' Shippes for some long voyage by *Italians* and *Flemmish* Merchants, and whilest they are upon their voyage, this Royall Fleet might be over-whelmed by a greater. At the same time, *Thomas Stukeley* ioyned to his Forces, the Rebels of *Ireland*, by this notable subtiltie. (The Pope) made him Generall of eight thousand *Italians* pay'd by the King of *Spain* for the Warres of *Ireland*. With which Forces, having weighed Anker .... in the end he arrived in *Portugal*—where a greater power by the Diuine Prouidence, puft downe these that threatened *England* and *Ireland*.

"For *Sebastian*, King of *Portugal*, to whom the whole expedition was committed, because, in the heate of his youth and ambition, he had promised the Pope to goe against the Turkes and Protestants, and employ all his power, being drawn into *Africa* by *Mahomet*, Sonne of *Abdalla*, King of *Fesse*, by great promises, treats with *Stukeley* to go before with these *Italians* to *Mauritaine*. And *Stukeley* being easily wonne to that, had consented to it, hoisted saile with *Sebastian*, and by an honest Catastrophe there he ended a dissolute life, in a memorable combate. Wherein dyed three kings, *Sebastian, Mahomet,* and *Abdalemelech.*"—*Annalls: The True and Royall History of the famous Empresse* Elizabeth, *Queene of* England, France, *and* Ireland.—*Translated from the* French *by* Abraham Darcie. 1625.

Note B.—Vol. I., page 3.

" The day that we looked for *Stanley's* arraignment he came not himself, but sent his forerunner, one *Squire*, that had ben an under purvayer of the stable, who, being in *Spaine*, was delt withall by one *Walpoole*, a Jesuite, to poison the Quene and the Erle of *Essex*, and accordingly came prepared into *England*, and went with the Erle in his owne ship the last jorney, and poisoned the armes or handles of the chaire he used to sit in, with a confection he had receved of the Jesuite, as likewise he had don the pommell of the Quene's saddle, not past five dayes before his going to sea; but because nothing succeded of it, the priest thincking he had either changed his purpose or bewraied it, gave *Stanley* instructions to accuse him, thereby to get him more credit, and to be revenged of *Squire* for breaking promise. The fellow confest the whole practise, and, as it seemed, died very penitent."—*Chamberlain's Letters. Camden Society.*

APPENDIX. 283

NOTE C.—Vol. I., page 4.

"This causeless curse to *Queen Elizabeth* [i.e. the Excommunication by Pius V.] was turned into a *blessing;* and as the *Barbarians* looked, when St. *Paul* (having the viper upon his hand) *should have swoln, and falne downe dead,* whilst he shooke it off into the fire, without any hurt, or harm: so *Papists* expected, when the Queen should have miserably expired, stung to the heart with this excommunication, when she, nothing frighted thereat, in silence slighted, and neglected it, without the least dammage to Her power, or person, and no whit the less lov'd of Her subjects, or fear'd of Her enemies."
—Fuller's *Church History.* London, 1655.

NOTE D.—Vol. I., page 5.

"The said Palace, [Westminster] before the Entry thereunto, hath a large Court, and in the same a Tower of Stone, containing a Clock, which striketh every Hour on great Bell, to be heard into the Hall in Sitting Time of the Courts, or otherwise. For the same Clock, in a Calm, will be heard into the City of *London.* King *Henry the Sixth* gave the keeping of this Clock, with the Tower, called *The Clock House,* and the Appurtenances, unto *William Walsby,* Dean of St. *Stephens,* with the Wages of six Pence the Day, out of his *Exchequer.*

"It was first built and furnished with a Clock, out of a Fine which one Justice *Ingham* was fain to pay, being 800 Mark, for erazing a Roll. For that a poor Man being fined in an Act of Debt at 13s. 4d. the said Justice, moved with Pity, caused the Roll to be erazed, and made it 6s. 8d. This Case Justice *Southcote* remembered, when *Catlyn* Chief Justice of the King's Bench in the Reign of Queen *Elizabeth,* would have ordered a Razure of a Roll; *Southcote* being one of the Judges of that Court, utterly denyed to assent to it, and said openly, That *he meant not to build a Clock House.*"—Strype's *Stow's Survey.* London, 1720.

Note E.—Vol. I., page 10.

With regard to the limitations put upon the press, see "A Decree of Star Chamber concerning Printing, made the Eleventh day of *July* last past, 1637," forbidding, under heavy penalties, the printing, or the sale, of any unlicensed books; and specifying the persons who alone were authorized to give licenses; for books of "Divinity, Physick, Philosophy, Poetry," they were the Archbishop of Canterbury, the Bishop of London, or one appointed by them; also the Chancellor and Vice-Chancellor of the two Universities, for the time being. See Rushworth's *Historical Collections*, part ii. vol. ii. pp. 306–315.

The petition in the Litany, "from the tyranny of the Bishop of *Rome*, and all his detestable enormities," was expunged at the revision of the second Prayer-Book of Edward VI., at the accession of Elizabeth. Perhaps it was to this that the writer refers.

Many who were strongly attached to the Church of England took alarm at the innovations at that time creeping in. The following extract from "A Convocation Speech, by Mr. *Thomas Warmstry*, one of the Clerks for the Diocesse of *Worcester*," affords an instance of this:—

"I disrellish neither the Doctrine, nor the Discipline, nor the government of the Church. Not the Doctrine, I embrace it heartily; and I conceive the Church of *England* may be herein the patterne of the world: and that if ever any Church had taken that living water clearly and purely from the fontaine, it is the Church of *England*. Not the Discipline, I entertaine it willingly, so farre as it is established by law: I wish indeed there might bee no private Innovations. I love outward reverence in God's worship, so that it be directed to the right object; not to Altars; not to Images; but to God. I love all Ceremonies that truly tend thereunto, or to decency, or to uniformity, which I acknowledge to be most necessary in religious actions. But I desire that in affectation of reverence, wee breed no contempt; that in contrivances of decency, we bring in no blemishes: That the Church may not seeme to bee infected with the humours of some women in this age, that never think themselves handsomely drest, but when they are in some new and fantasticall fashion : That while we endeavour Vniformity, wee do not multiply division. We may be so busie in drawing the two ends together, that we may break the staffe in the midst. That wee bee not so carefull to preserve Vniformity with others that are without, that wee make dissentions within our owne Church. The truth is, I wish there might be nothing scandalous, nothing frivolous in the Church. Nothing scandalous, not so much as a title. Though I love the sacrifice of Almes, and Praise, and I hope should not refuse me selfe to be a sacrifice unto God, though a burnt one; yet I know no need of any materiall Altar; because I know no materiall Sacrifice, but that Eternall Sacrifice of Christ upon the Crosse. And though it may be urged, that the Primitive Church used the name of Altar for the holy Table, yet that makes it neither necessary nor warrantable for us to doe the like; unless together with the language we could call back the purity, the simplicity of the Primitive times. Now things are ill interpreted, it concernes us to be more cautelous; lest if not now, yet in after ages our language may be urged for the confirmation of Heresie, when it cannot be answered for us, as we may answer for the Primitive times, That the Heresies were not then broacht, and therefore the speech more loose. It is a dangerous thing to give an Heresie the advantage of a Metaphor, which the Devill wants not skill in time to reduce back unto the killing letter. Besides, the language of the Scripture and the Apostles is the most pure and the most ancient language of the Primitive Church; and we read of no Altar there after Christ, but the Altar of the Crosse, or Christ crucified. I desire there may bee nothing scandalous: I wish the true Image of God in Righteousness and true Holinesse may be restored in the spirituall Temples of our soules. But I desire, at least, an abatement in the number, and limitation, for the manner and situation of Images in the materiall Churches, because I doubt they are scandalous to all sorts. . . . .

"And as I desire there may bee nothing scandalous in the Church, so there may be nothing frivolous, or irrationall, that our service may be a reasonable service. I know not why we should have candles in the day time. I wish there may not be so much as an Embleme of a fruitlesse Prelacy, or Clergy in the Church, that only fill the candlestick, but give no light. I love ornaments in the Church, so that they be not toyish or theatricall. I hold it very fit that God, as he is the author of our riches, so he should be served with them. . . . . Yea, an holy congregation is the best furniture of the Church. I wish our speciall care may be for this, and then let the outward adornation, as farre as grave and decent, not be neglected."—" *London, Printed in the Yeare 1641.*"—*King's Pamphlets.*

NOTE F.—Vol. I., page 11.

"Amongst the celestiall comminations or threatenings of God's hand, and imminent scourge, the flaming and fearefull Comets challenge not the last place, for these doe presage both warres and slaughters, with a certaine and almost ever answering event; witnesse that most reported Comet, *rubescens ferali crine*, which appeared above seven weeks, provoking all men to gaze upon it. . . . .

"Touching this ostent of the divine power, namely, the unlookt for apparition, the strange progression or course, the sudden vanishing, and the production of the toyle thereof. What need I speake? . . . .

"Three things onely in this Comet were most wonderfull. 1. The head's circumference or compasse. 2. The beard's prolixity or length. 3. The sublimity or height of the scituation thereof.

"1. The head, or round heape of stars, to the unlearned invisible, was of so vast a compasse, that no man hardly in two moneths, travelling forty miles a day, could run round about it.

"2. The beard is extended in its length to fifty degrees, that is, above halfe a Signe.

"The scituation was not only superlunary, or above the Moone, but also supersolary, or above the Sun.

. . . .

"*The Comet in 1618 was fatall to the Emperor Matthias, and Anne Queene of Brittaine, she departed to the Seats of the blessed Soules, March 2, 1619. March 10, Stilo Angliæ.*"—"The Mathematicall Divine, shewing The present Miseries of *Germany*, *England*, and *Ireland*. Being The Effects portended by the last Comet or blazing Starre, of a dreadfull greatnesse, and in forme of a crooked sword, which was seene with great Admiration in EUROPE. *Anno* 1618. London, 1642."—*King's Pamphlets*.

NOTE G.—Vol. I., page 11.

"Since that last flaming Usher of God's vengeance, that direfull *Comet* of the year 1618, appeared in the heavens, some malignant and angry ill-aspected star hath had the predominance ever since, and by its malign influxes, made strange unusuall impressions upon the humors of subjects, by inciting them to such insurrections, revolts, and tumults; which caused a *Jewish* Rabbi to say lately, that it seems the grand *Turk* thrives extraordinarily in his devotions, it being one of his prime prayers to *Mahomet* that hee should prevaile with God Almighty to *continue discentions still among Christian Princes*. And truly, as the case stands, one may say, that the Christian world is all in pieces. . . . Since you mention that *blazing Starre*, I remember what a noble knight told me some yeeres agoe, That the *Astronomers*, who lay sentinell to watch the motion and aspect of that *Comet*, observed that having pointed at divers Climats, at last it seemed to looke directly on these North-west Islands, in which posture it spent itselfe, and so extinguish'd; as if thereby it meant to tell the world that these *Islands* should be the Stage whereupon the last act of the Tragedie should be play'd. And how many *Scenes* have passed already, both here and in *Ireland*, we know, God wot, by too too wofull experience."—*The Trve Informer;* Oxford, printed by *Leonard Lichfield*, Printer to the Universitie. 1643.—*King's Pamphlets*.

NOTE H.—Vol. I., page 15.

"Now hapned the sad *Vespers*, or *dolfull Evening-song* at *Black Fryers* in *London:* Father *Drury* a Jesuite of excellent Morals, and ingratiating Converse (wanting nothing, saving the embracing of the truth, to make him valuable in himself and acceptable to others) Preached in a great upper-Room in *Black Fryers*, next to the house of the *French Ambassadour*, where some *Three Hundred persons* were assembled. His Text the 18 Chap. of S. *Matthew*, ver. 32, *O thou ungracious servant! I forgave thee all the debt because thou desiredst me, shouldst not thou also have had compassion on thy fellow servant?* &c. In application whereof, he fell upon a bitter invective against the Protestants.

"His Sermon began to incline to the middle, the Day to the end thereof; when on the soddain the Flore fell down whereon they were assembled. It gave no *charitable warning-groan* before-hand, but *crackt*, *brake*, and *fell*, all in an instant. Many were killed, more bruised, all frighted; sad sight to behold the flesh and blood of different persons mingled together, and the brains of one on the head of another. One lackt a *leg*, another an *arm*; a third whole and intire wanted nothing but *breath* stifled in the ruines. Some Protestants coming meerly to *see*, were made to *suffer*, and bare the heavy burden of their own curiosity.

"This accident fell on *Sunday*, the 26 of *October*, which, according to the *new style* observed beyond sea (having the speed of ours by ten daies) fell upon their *fifth* of *November*; a day notoriously known in the Popish Calender."—Fuller's *Church History*.

"The preacher was one *Drury*, a converted Protestant. He inveighed bitterly against *Luther*, *Calvin*, and Doctor *Sutton*, a reverent preacher sometime of St. *Mary Overy's*, in London, who, travelling beyond the seas, was drowned. This preacher said that the sea swallowed him, because he was not worthy the earth should receive him. At which words the house sank."
—*Diary of Walter Yonge, Esq.*, p. 70. *Camden Society*.

"Since the *Sicilian Vespers*, there never was an Even-song more dolorous unto the *French*, nor more lamentable unto the *Scots* and *English*."—*Stow*.

APPENDIX.

NOTE I.—Vol. I., page 24.

"*Martis*, 24° *Nov.* 1640.—One Mr. *Norton*, a Divine, was called in, and examined; and, to divers Questions, demanded of him by Mr. Speaker, answered, that he had a Son at *Cambridge*; and certain Fellows of *Peterhouse* endeavoured to seduce him to Popery; pretending, that Dr. *Cosens* would make him a Fellow of *Peterhouse*, if he would come thither:—Thus much appeared upon Oath:—And he was forced to send for his Son away,—Said, he hath a Copy of the Arguments that passed between them and his Son: That the Questions in *Peterhouse* Chapel are maintained and held, as they are at *Rome*: And instanced several of the Questions.

" Doctor *Coesens' Monita pro Sacello Collegii Sancti Petri Cantibrigia*, were read; and the whole Business, concerning Mr. *Norton*, and those *Monita* and Dr. *Coesens*, were referred to the former Committee for *Smart's* Petition."—*Commons' Journals.*

[The writer seems to have mistaken the name of the Master of this College, for Andrew Perne only held that office to 1589. He built the Library of Peterhouse, which probably brought his name into prominence at the time to which allusion is made. See Le Keux' *Memorials of Cambridge:* Peterhouse College, page 8.]

"In a speech delivered by the vice-chancellor, not many years ago, in a public commencement at *Cambridge*, speaking to the young scholars, and wishing them to take heed of being puritans, he said, What can you get in that way? you shall live poorly, perhaps you may have some three-halfpenny benefice in following them; but come to be children of the church, and then you may be sure of good benefices, you may come to be prebends, to be deans, to be bishops. Thus he persuaded the young scholars to take heed of puritanism. There is mighty strength in this argument upon the hearts of most."—*Burroughs on Hosea*, p. 85. Nichol's edition, Edinburgh, 1863.

NOTE J.—Vol. I., page 28.

For an account of the controversy, " whether the table placed in the room of the altar ought to stand altar-wise," see

Wheatly's *Rational Illustration of the Book of Common Prayer of the Church of England*, p. 263.   Bohn's edition, London, 1848.

NOTE K.—Vol. I., page 30.

"Yea, that cage of most unclean birds, *Sommerset-House*, I mean, in the *Strand*, cleansed in good measure of those *Egyptian* croaking Frogs, the filthy *Capuchin* Fryers and Priests, who lay lurking there too long, like so many muzled Wolves and Tygers."—Vicars' *Jehovah Jireh.*   London, 1644.

"A Chappell at *Somerset-House* was built for the Queen and her Family, with Conveniences thereunto adjoyning for *Capuchin Friers,* who were therein placed, and had permission to walk abroad in their Religious Habits.   Thence forward greater multitudes of *Seminary Priests* and *Jesuites* repaired unto *England* out of Foreign parts."—*Rushworth.*

"It is said that since the Queen came into *England*, the priests do swarm very much in *London.*"—*Diary of Walter Yonge, Esq.*, 1625.   *Camden Society.*

"You heard the last weeke of an Order made by the *Lower House,* for siezing on the Queene's *Capuchines,* and defacing the *Crucifixes* and other *Images* in her Chappell at *Somerset-House;* Master *Martyn* and Sir *Peter Wentworth* being appointed to see it put in execution.   But when the deed was to be done, Master *Langham*, who is Sheriffe for *Middlesex*, pleading that he had the *Posse Comitatus* to assist him, if occasion were, would not admit of the *Militia* of the Citie to be joyned with him, as derogatory to his place and power: and as for the performance of the *Order* required of him, that unlesse a Precedent could be shewed him, wherein an *Order* made by the House of *Commons,* and in a businesse of high nature, had beene executed in the times before, he would desire to be excused from yielding obedience to it now.   Upon which Answer, being so crosse to their desires, they were the more content to hearken to the motion of the *French Agent*, who, upon notice of their purpose, interceded in it, as being contrary to the *Articles* of the marriage, and an apparent breach of peace between the Kingdomes."—*Mercurius Aulicus, March* 20, 1642.

Thursday, March 30, 1643.—"By order of Parliament this day, a Court of Guard was placed upon *Somerset* House for the apprehending of the Popish Priests and Fryers that lye lurking there, and the Queen's Chappell and the Romish Cloysters searched least any provisions or armes should be conveyed thither to assist the Malignants and Popish party in *London*, the Idolatrous pictures and Crucifixes found there were demolished by the Souldiers, and a strict course taken to search all the Vaults in case there should be any provisions or Treasure hid there as is supposed, and the Priests or other Papists found there are kept in safe custody till a further Order of Parliament for the dispose of them."—*Perfect Diurnall.*

Wednesday, April 15.—" The Parliament received letters this weeke from the *French* King, by which he seemeth displeased at the coarse usage of the Capuchin Fryers in Somerset-house, and complaineth that it is a breach of the Articles upon the Marriage of his Sister. Whereupon the Parliament upon consideration of the businesse have againe ordered that the said Fryers and some others of them that lye in *Newgate* should be shipped, and sent away this weeke without any further let for *France* or other forraigne parts. And the Houses also are about to send a letter to the *French* King in full satisfaction to his demands."—Ibid.

NOTE L.—Vol. I., page 31.

A small book entitled "The Femall Glory; or the Life and Death of our Blessed Lady, the holy Virgin MARY, *God's owne immaculate* Mother: To whose sacred Memory the Author dedicates these his humble endeavours. A Treatise worthy the reading, and meditation of all modest women, who live under the Government of Vertue, and are obedient to her Lawes. By *Anth. Stafford*, Gent.—London, printed by *Thomas Harper*, for *John Waterson*, and are to be sold at his Shop in *Paul's* Churchyard, at the signe of the Crowne. 1635." It was illustrated with pictures. The book was severely handled by Mr. Henry Burton, Minister of St. Matthew's, Friday Street, in a Sermon entitled " For God and the King," preached on November 5, 1636, in the following terms:—" Adde wee hereunto another Booke, intitled the *Female Glory*, by *Anthony Stafford*, printed by authority, 1635.

Wherein hee mightily deifies the Virgin *Mary*, calling her *The* [1] *grand white* immaculate *Abbesse of the Snowie Nunneries of those votaries,* to whom *hee* speakes, before whom hee would haue them *to kneele, presenting the All-saving babe in her armes, with due veneration.* Loe heere a change of our God into a Goddesse. And there [2] hee commends *the Sacred Arethmitick in praying on their beades.* And pag. 153 hee commends *Candlemas day for the Lights burning,* and *Masse singing, taken from the Heathen guise, and converted into Christian.* And *That which was performed by Superstitious Idolaters in honour of* Ceres and Proserpine (*Heathen* Goddesses) *may be turned into the prayse and glory of the Virgin Mary.* And pag. 209. *The Assumption of his Lady is set forth with a picture, how shee is taken up into Heaven with Verses.* And pag. 212 Hee seemes to hold the Virgin Mary to have beene without sinne. And pag. 219, 220 Hee boldly beares himself upon the *approbation of the Church of England, in magnifying the Virgin Mary, as considered, not as a meere woman, but as a type and idea of an accomplisht piety.* And page 158 *of Sanctity* its selfe. And pag. 220 *hee preferres the crown of the adoring extreme, before the Puritans* neglecting of her in calling her *Mal, God's mayd, and rejecting Hayle Mary full of grace.* And pag. 223 hee saith, *Of one thing I will assure them, Till they are good Marians, they shall never bee good Christians.* And pag. 235 Of sundry Grandees, hee saith, *All which are canonized for Saints, having erected and dedicated Temples to her memory. Neither have the Princes of this our Ile beene defective in doing her all possible honour, and in Consecrating Chappels and Temples to her memory.* And ibid.: *My arithmeticke will not serve me, to number all those, who have registered their names in the Sodality of the Rosary of this our blessed Lady:* the originall is derived from the battaile of *Naupactum* gained by *John of Austria,* and the Christians, which victory was attributed to the intercession with her Sonne. And pag. 236 hee recites the many holy orders of this Sodality, styling them, Great, worthy and pious people, and concludes thus, For shame, let not us dare deny her that honour and prayse which all the world allowes her. And pag. 274 he Invocates her, saying, O pardon, gratious Princesse, my weake indeavours to summe

---

[1] Pag. 148.   [2] Pag. 157.

up they value, &c. And pag. 248. Thou deservest a Quire of Queens here, and another of Angels, in heaven to sing thy prayses, &c. And I confesse, O my sweetest Lady. And pag. 249. To give thee an estimation answerable to thy merit, is a thing impossible, I must therefore be cōtent to do by thee, as the ancient heathen did by the images of their gods, when by reason of their height they could not place the Crownes, they humbly layd them at their feet: many more passages might be added: as pag. 150, he cals her woman's deerest mistrisse. And pag. 32 *a glorious Empresse.* And pag. 3 *Empresse of this lower world.* And pag. 2 *If Christ was faire above the Sons of men, should not shee bee so above their daughters?* And in his Epistle to his feminine reader, speaking of the Virgin Mary, *This is shee, who was on earth a confirmer of the good, and a reformer of the reprobate. Al her visitants were but so many converts, whose bad affections, and erroneous opinions, the sweetness of her discourse had rectified.* The Leprosy of sinne was her dayly *cure, and they, whom vice had blinded were by her restored to their inward sight, and their prostrate soules adored divine, Majestical vertue, residing in this sacred Temple. The knowledge of her humbled the most proud natures, for the lustre of her merits rendered their owne obscure.* And in his Epistle to the Masculine Reader : *Truly I believe, that the under-valuing of one so great, and deare in Christ's esteeme (as his Mother) cannot but bee displeasing to him, and that the more we ascribe to her (setting invocation apart) the more gracious we appeare in his sight.* And hee concludes it thus : *I will only adde this that since the finishing of this Story, I have read a booke of the now Bishop of Chichester, intituled Apparatus, &c., and I am glad to find that I have not digressed from him in any one particular.* So hee. Loe therefore what a Metamorphosis of our Religion is here. Here is a new goddesse brought in amongst us. The author glorieth, *that hee is the first who hath written* (as hee saith) *in our vulgar tongue, on this our blessed Virgin.* And God grant he be the last. But he beares himself in all this upon the Church of *England,* where, I pray you ? At last I perceive this Church of England is the now Bishop of Chichester in his Apparatus, &c. From whom he *hath not digressed in any particular.* And surely it were strange that such a mystery of iniquity could bee found, but in a Prelate, and in this one by name for a tryed Champion of *Rome*, and so a devout votary to his Queene of Heaven."

Prynne, in his *Canterburie's Doom* (London, printed by *John Macock*, for *Michael Spark* senior, at the sign of the *Blue Bible* in *Green Arbour*, 1646), thus refers to the Book and to the Sermon upon it:—

"This booke of *Stafford's* giving very great scandall to Protestants, and encouragement to Papists, Mr. *Henry Burton*, in his Sermon intituled *For God and the King*, pages 123, 124, 125, discovered, censured these extravagant Popish Passages in it, advising the people to beware of it. For which among other things, he was brought into the Star Chamber and there censured. But on the contrary, this Popish Booke of *Stafford's* with the forementioned scandalous passages in it, were by the Archbishop's speciall direction professedly justified, both by Doctor *Heylin* in his *Moderate Answer to Mr. Burton*, (licensed by the Arch-bishop's owne Chaplaine, and written by his command) *pag.* 123, 124, and by *Christopher Dow*, in this *Innovations unjustly charged, page* 51, 54, and this Booke neither called in nor corrected, so audatiously Popish was he growne, in this particular, among many others."

In *Robert Baillie's Letters and Journals* (printed for the Bannatyne Club, 1841), a reference occurs to the same book. "Search who is about the Prince, if they be orthodoxe, and if any of the chaplains be honest; . . . . . . if *Stafford's* Female Glorie was never burnt."—*Instruction to Mr. Alexander Cunninghame*, vol. i. p. 227.

NOTE M.—Vol. I., page 50.

"Famous and memorable also is that example which happened at *London* in the yeare 1583 at Paris Garden, where, vpon the Sabbath day, were gathered together (as accustomably they vsed) great multitudes of prophane people to behold the sport of *Beare-baiting*, without respect of the Lord's day, or any exercise of Religion required therein: which prophane impietie, the Lord that he might chasten in some sort, and shew his dislike thereof, he caused the scaffolds suddenly to breake, and the beholders to tumble headlong downe; so that to the number of eight persons, men and women, were slaine therewith, besides many others which were sore hurt and bruised, to the shortening of their days."—*The Theatre of God's Jvdgements.*—By the first Author thereof, THO. BEARD, Doctor of Diuinitie, and Preacher of the Word of God in the Towne of *Huntingdon.* London, 1632.

NOTE N.—Vol. I., page 52.

This fire " began in a Malt house, by negligence of a mayde," as we read in *Stowe's Annales.* The Rev. William Whately, the "painful Preacher of Banbury," was the Vicar at the time, and he held a Special Service on the occasion, at which he preached for two hours. He subsequently published his Sermon, entitled "Sinne no more, or a Sermon preached in the Parish Church of *Banbury* on *Tuesday* the fourth of *March* last past, vpon occasion of a most Terrible Fire that happened there on the Sabbath day immediately precedent. London, 1638."

We subjoin an extract, which reminds us of the clear and vigorous style of the late Archbishop of Dublin, his kinsman.

"Carelessnesse and negligence of any person could not haue produced so lamentable a losse, if God's providence had not so disposed, that such negligence should haue falne out, at such a time, in such a rough and violent winde, sitting in such a point as to driue it vpon you, not from you. The Lord that knew the winds would then bee very boysterous and violent, and that they would sit fitly to carie the flame from house to house, euen til they had passed through al the places which he saw fit to strike, hee, I say, by his good providence, did order things so that the heedlessnesse of some or other should then giue occasion, to the breaking out of the fire, when the frosty winde had made each thing as dry almost as tinder to receiue fire, and when the present tempest was ready to scatter and disperse the fire . . . (the fire) came riding as it were in triumph, through your streetes, disdaining all resistance, till it had passed from end to end of your towne, and could not be restrained . . . The cry of fire, fire, came flying in at the church doores euen in that instant, when wee had newly begunne to celebrate the Lord's Supper; when some had receiued that holy Sacrament, and the greater number were to receiue, then was I compelled to request all of you (that had strength and ability to do seruice there) to make al haste to the place of danger, and the rest (that could haue but troubled others with their presence and outcries) to stay still at church . . . Thinke of the place also, where did the burning beginne? At a kilne, I say a kilne, a mault forge, the proper instrument of making that thing, which is the next and immediate worker of drunkennesse, that huge sinne, which is (as they say of the first matter) apt to take the formes of all sinnes, which by burying reason, and choking conscience, and setting loose all passions, doth turne a man into a beast, or rather into a Diuell, which makes a man for the time a meere Atheist, a very denyer of God, and thrusts out of his brest all remembrance, all feere, all loue of him . . . The Fire began in a kilne, it consumed twenty kilnes, it left no kilne standing that was within its walke, it leaped from one side of the street to the other, to fetch in kilnes, it spared none it came neere, it spoyled more mault, then of any other goods of one kind (so farre as I can learne). Say what you thinke, brethren, Is it not plain that the Lord doth admonish you of that fault (whereof the liquor of mault is the most common instrument) when he bare so hard a hand against kilnes and against mault? Give mine eyes leaue, therefore, to speake unto you in the language of teares, and seeing I heard so generall a cry for water, water, the other day: let me also cry water, water; and let all our eyes ioyne together, to powre forth a streame of water, sufficient to quench the remainder of those flames which are yet burning amongst you; yea, to quench the glowing fire of God's displeasure for our sinnes, which hath iustly kindled all these flames amongst us."

Note O.—Vol. I., page 54.

"There were no rates for the poor in my grandfather's days; but for *Kingston St. Michael* (no small parish) the Church-Ale of Whitsuntide did the business . . . The Church-Ale is doubtless derived from the 'Ἀγάπαι or Love Feasts, mentioned in

the New Testaments."—Aubrey's *Introduction to the Survey, &c.,
of Wiltshire.*

"It appears from a Sermon made at *Blanford Forum,* 1570,
by *William Kethe,* that it was the custom at that time for the
Church-Ales to be kept upon the Sabbath-day; which holy
day, says our author, the multitude call their revelyng day,
which day is spent in bulbeatings, bearebeatings, bowlings,
dicyng, cardyng, daunsynges, drunkenness, &c."—Brand's
Popular Antiquities, i. 278. London, 1849, Bohn's edition.

Stubbs, in the *Anatomie of Abuses,* 1585, p. 95, gives the following account of the manner of *Church-Ales* in England:—"In
certaine townes, where drunken *Bacchus* beares swaie, against
Christmas and Easter, Whitsondaie, or some other tyme, the
churchewardens of every parishe, provide halfe a score or
twentie quarters of mault, whereof some they buy of the
churche stocke, and some is given them of the parishioners
themselves, every one conferring somewhat, according to his
abilitie; whiche maulte being made into very strong ale or
bere, is sette to sale, either in the church or some other place
assigned to that purpose. Then when this is set abroche, well
is he that can gete the soonest to it, and spend the most at it.
In this kinde of practice they continue sixe weekes, a quarter
of a yeare, yea, halfe a yeare, together. That money, they
say, is to repaire their churches and chappels with, to buy
bookes for service, cuppes for the celebration of the Sacrament,
surplesses for Sir John, and such other necessaries. And they
maintaine other extraordinarie charges in their parish besides."

"On the *Coteswolds* is a customary annual meeting at Whitsuntide, vulgarly called an *Ale,* or *Whitsun-Ale.* Perhaps the
true word is *Yule,* for in the time of Druidism, the feasts of
Yule or the Grove, were celebrated in the months of *May* or
December. These sports are resorted to by great numbers of
young people of both sexes, and are conducted in the following manner. Two persons are chosen previous to the meeting
to be Lord and Lady of the Yule, who dress as suitably as
they can to the characters they assume. A large empty barn
or some such building is provided for the Lord's Hall, and
filled up with seats to accommodate the company. Here they
assemble to dance and to regale in the best manner their cir-

cumstances and the place will afford, and each young lad treats his girl with a ribband, or favour. The Lord and Lady honour the hall with their presence, attended by the steward, swordbearer, purse-bearer and mace-bearer, with their several badges and ensigns of office.

"They have likewise a page, or train-bearer, and a jester, dressed in a party coloured jacket, whose ribaldry and gesticulation contribute not a little to the entertainment of some part of the company. The Lord's music consisting generally of a pipe and tabor, is employed to conduct the dance.

"All these figures handsomely represented in basso-relievo, stand in the north wall of the nave of *Cirencester* Church, which vouches sufficiently for the antiquity of the custom.

. . . .

"I shall just remark, that the mace is made of silk, finely plaited with ribands on the top, and filled with spices and perfumes, for such of the company to smell to as desire it. Does not this afford some light towards discovering the original use, and account for the name of the mace, now carried in ostentation before the steward of the court, on court-days, and before the chief magistrates in corporations; as the presenting of spices by great men at their entertainments was a very antient practice?"—Rudder's *History of Gloucestershire*, p. 24. Cirencester, 1779.

"This is the agreement betwixt the inhabitants of the towns and parishes of *Elvaston, Thurlaston,* and *Ambaston,* of the one part, and the inhabitants of the town of *Okebrook* within the said parish of *Elvaston* in com. *Derby,* on the other part; by John Abbot of the Dale, Ralph Saucheverell, Esq., John Bradshaw, and Henry Tithet, gent.—*Witnesseth,* that the inhabitants as well of the said parish of *Elvaston,* as of the said town of *Okebrook,* shall brew four ales, and every ale of one quarter of malt, and at their own cost and charges, betwixt this and the feast of St. John the Baptist next coming, and that every inhabitant of the said town of *Okebrook* shall be at the several ales; and every husband and his wife shall pay two pence, every cottager one penny; and all the inhabitants of *Elvaston, Thurlaston,* and *Ambaston,* shall have and receive all the profits and advantages coming of the said Ales to the use and behoof of the said Church of *Elvaston*, and the inhabitants of the said towns of *Elvaston, Thurlaston,* and *Ambaston* shall brew eight ales betwixt this and the feast of St. John the Baptist; at the which ales and every one of them the inhabitants of *Okebrook* shall come and pay as before rehearsed; and if he be away at one ale, to pay at the t'oder ale for both, or else to send his money. And the inhabitants of *Okebrook* shall carry all manner of timber being in the Dale Wood now felled, that the said Prestchyrch of the said towns of *Elvaston, Thurlaston,* and *Ambaston,* shall occupye to the use and profit of the said Church.

"N.B. This appears to have been the old method of paying money for the repair of country churches.

"*From a MSS. in the Library of Robert Astle, Esq., F.R.S., F.A.S.*"—*Antiquarian Repertory,* vol. i. page 68.

Other Ales were also held, Bride Ales, Clerk Ales, &c. In the volume just quoted, we find: "In the *Easter* holidays was the Clerk's ale for his private benefit, and the solace of the neighbourhood."

NOTE P.—Vol. I., page 54.

"In every parish is (or was) a church-house, to which belonged spits, crocks, &c., utensils for dressing provision. Here the housekeepers met and were merry, and gave their charity. The young people were there too, and had dancing, bowling, shooting at butts, &c., the ancients sitting gravely by, and looking on."—Aubrey's *Introduction to the Survey, &c., of Wiltshire,* p. 32.

"In Sir Richard Worsley's *History of the Isle of Wight,* p. 210, speaking of the Parish of Whitwell, he tells us, that there is a lease in the Parish chest, dated 1574, 'of a house cald the Church House, held by the inhabitants of Whitwell, parishioners of Gatcombe, of the Lord of the Manor, and demised by them to John Brode, in which is the following proviso: Provided always, that, if the Quarter shall need at any time to make a Quarter-Ale, or Church-Ale for the maintenance of the Chapel, that it shall be lawful for them to have the use of the said house, with all the rooms, both above and beneath, during their Ale.' "—Brand's *Popular Antiquities*, i. 278. London, 1849, Bohn's edition.

Note Q.—Vol. I., page 56.

"A gatherer of notices respecting our pastimes says:—' The after-part of May-day is chiefly spent in dancing round a tall Poll, which is called a May Poll; which being placed in a convenient part of the village, stands there, as it were consecrated to the Goddess of Flowers, without the least violation offer'd to it, in the whole circle of the year.'[1] One who was an implacable enemy to popular sports relates the fetching in of 'the May from the woods.' 'But,' says he, 'their cheefest jewell they bring from thence is their Maie poole, whiche they bring home with greate veneration, as thus. They have twentie or fourtie yoke of oxen, every oxe havyng a sweete nosegaie of flowers tyed on the tippe of his hornes, and these oxen drawe home this Maie poole, which is covered all over with flowers and hearbes, bounde rounde aboute with stringes, from the top to the bottome, and sometyme painted with variable colours, with two or three hundred men, women, and children followyng it with great devotion. And thus beyng reared up, with handkerchiefes and flagges streamyng on the toppe, they strawe the grounde aboute, binde greene boughes about it, sett up Sommer haules, Bowers, and Arbours hard by. And then fall they to banquet and feast, to leape and dance aboute it, as the Heathen people did at the dedication of their Idolles, whereof this is a perfect patterne, or rather the thyng itself.'[2]

"It was a great object with some of the more rigid among our early reformers to suppress amusements, especially May-poles; and these 'idols' of the people were got down as zeal grew fierce, and got up as it grew cool, till, after various ups and downs, the favourites of the populace were, by the Parliament, on the 6th of April, 1644, thus provided against:—'The lords and commons do further order and ordain, that all and singular *May-poles*, that are or shall be erected, shall be taken down, and removed by the constables, bassholders,

[1] Bourne.   [2] Stubbes.

tithing-men, petty constables, and churchwardens of the parishes, where the same be, and that no May-pole be hereafter set up, erected or suffered to be set up within this kingdom of *England*, or dominion of *Wales;* the said officers to be fined five shillings weekly till the said May-pole be taken down.'

"Accordingly down went all the May-poles that were left. The restoration of Charles II. was the signal for the restoration of the May-poles. On the very first May-day afterwards, in 1661, the *May-pole* in the Strand was reared with great ceremony and rejoicing."—Hone's *Every Day Book.*

For a full description of the Morris-dance, said to be "a kind of Pyrrhic, or military dance," see Brand's *Popular Antiquities*, vol. i. pp. 247–270. Bohn's edition, London, 1840.

NOTE R.—Vol. I., page 58.

" In the Feast of *Christmas* there was in the King's House, wheresoever he was lodged, a Lord of Misrule, or Master of merry Disports, and the like had ye in the House of every Nobleman of Honour, or good Worship, were he Spiritual or Temporal. Among the which, the Maior of *London*, and either of the Sheriffs, had their several Lords of Misrule, ever contending, without Quarrel or Offence, who should make the rarest Pastimes to delight the Beholders. These Lords beginning their *Rule* at *Alhalloud* Eve, continued the same till the Morrow after the Feast of the *Purification*, commonly called *Candlemas* Day; In all which Space, there were fine and subtle Disguisings, Masks, and Mummeries, with playing at Cards for Counters, Nails, and Points; more for Pastimes than for Gain."—*Stowe.*

Previously to the Reformation, this functionary was styled *Abbot* of Misrule. See *Antiquarian Repertory*, vol. iv. p. 323.

NOTE S.—Vol. I., page 62.

" This yeare ended the dayes of *Mr. Arthur Hildersham*, born at *Steckworth* in the *County*, bred in Christ College in the *University* of *Cambridge*, whose education was an experimentall

Comment, on the words of David, '*When my father and mother forsake me, then the Lord taketh me up.*'

"*My Father*	*Thomas Hildersham*, a Gentleman of an ancient Family.
and Mother	*Anne Poole*, daughter to Sir *Jeffrey*, niece to Cardinall *Poole*, grandchild to Sir *Richard Poole*, and *Margaret*, Countess of *Sarisbury*, who was daughter to *George*, Duke of *Clarence*.
Forsake me	Quite casting him off because he would not be bred a Papist, and goe to *Rome*.
Then	An *emphatical Monosyllable*, just in that *nick of time*.
The Lord taketh me up.	Not immediately (miracles being ceased) but in and by the *hands* of *Henry* Earl of *Huntingdon*, (his honorable kinsman) providing plentifull maintenance for him.

"However, after he was entered in the Ministery, he met with many molestations, as hereby doth appear.

"1 ⎫   ⎧ The High Commission, 1590, in June.
 2 ⎬ Silenced by ⎨ Bishop *Chaderton*, 1605, April 24.
 3 ⎪   ⎪ Bishop *Neile*, 1611, in November.
 4 ⎭   ⎩ The Court at *Lecest.*, 1630, March 4.

 1 ⎫   ⎧ The High Commission, 1591, in January.
 2 ⎬ Restored by ⎨ Bishop *Barlow*, 1608, in January.
 3 ⎪   ⎪ Doctor *Ridley*, 1625, June 20.
 4 ⎭   ⎩ The same Court, 1631, August 2.

"And now methinks I hear the Spirit speaking unto him, as once to the Prophet *Ezechiel*, *Thou shalt speak and be no more dumb*, singing now with the Celestiall Quire of Saints and Angels. Indeed though himself a *Non-conformist*, he loved all honest men, were they of a different judgment, minded like *Luther* herin, who gave for his *motto*, *In quo aliquid* Christi *video, illum diligo.*

"He was minister of *Ashby de la Zouch forty* and *three* years. This putteth me in mind of *Theodosius* and of *Valentinian* (two worthy Christian Emperors) their constitution making those Readers of the Civil Law, *Counts* of the *first* order, *cum ad viginti annos observatione jugi, ac sedulo docendi labore pervenerint, when with daily observation and diligent labor of teaching they shall arrive at twenty years.* Surely the Readers of *God's Law* which *double that time* shall not lose their reward."—Fuller's *Church History*, vol. xi. p. 142. *London*, 1655.

"RANDALL BATES was a most holy man, an excellent preacher, and a zealous nonconformist, for which he was prosecuted in the ecclesiastical courts, and committed to the Gatehouse; where, after a confinement of twenty months, he died through the hardships of the prison. Mr. John Cotton, who was his contemporary, denominates him 'an heavenly saint;' and says, 'he suffered in the cause of nonconformity, being choked in prison.' Nor could his release be obtained, though Dr. Hering, a learned and excellent physician, earnestly solicited Bishop Neile for his enlargement, declaring that his life was in danger. But the suit of the physician was repulsed with reproaches, and the blood of his patient was spilt through the extreme rigour of his confinement. He died in the year 1613. During Mr. Bates' imprisonment he wrote a book, entitled, 'Meditations whilst he was prisoner in the Gatehouse, Westminster,' which shews him to have been a person of great humility and piety."—Brook's *Lives of the Puritans*, vol. ii. p. 244. *London*, 1813.

NOTE T.—Vol. I., pages 65, 98.

"Mr. Prynne of Lincoln's Inn hath lately set forth a book entitled 'Histriomastix, or the Players' Scourge,' the sale of which is prohibited, and he to appear at the high commission on Thursday next, where, when I have heard what is charged against him, I will, if you desire it, send you a more particular relation. His book is extraordinarily stuffed with quotations of old authors, which they say are his only arguments. He cites St. Austin who saith '*Si tantum modo boni et honesti viri in civitate essent, nec in rebus humanis Ludi Scenici esse debuissent.*' But I do not conceive this to be the only cause why he is called in question, but rather some exorbitant passage concerning ecclesiastical government; for I hear he compares the playing on the organ between the first and second lesson, to interludes and stage-play. It is observable that his book was published the day after the queen's pastoral at Somerset House."—*Justinian Paget, Esq., to James Harrington, Esq., at Walton-upon-Trent, January* 28, 1633: *Court and Times of Charles I.*

NOTE U.—Vol. I., page 76.

The Editor is indebted to Mr. Bruce for the following extract from the notes taken by Secretary Windebank in the Star Chamber on this case, from which it appears that A. B. was Sir Richard Shelton, who had been solicitor-general from 1625 to 1634. The note refers to the passage picked out from the *News from Ipswich.*

"Dom. Car. I. Vol. ccclxi. No. 77, p. 2.—Mr. Prynne. Sr. Rich. Shelton. Newes from Ipswich. What cold Belzebub had he ben the Archbp. have don more than in publishing the book agt. Sonday? Is it not high time to hang up such archtraytors?"

NOTE V.—Vol. I., page 120.

"The Jesuits perhaps will deny, they had any hand in that Invasion. But lest they deceive you, I will tell you some news from *Rome.* It is known there that the Pope tooke, and the Jesuits gave, the better halfe of the Colledge meanes, sold out-righte, to the use of that Fleet." — *Experience, Historie, and Divinitie, by Richard Carpenter, Vicar of Poling.* Printed by order of the House of Commons, 1642.

NOTE W.—Vol. I., page 132.

"The godlie here, in great numbers, meets oft in private houses, for in publick they dare not, fasts and prayes, and hears gracious sermons, for whole dayes, sundrie tymes in the week: truelie these heartie and humble prayers are our greatest confidence; in the adverse partie we hear of little devotion in the best of them." (January 1641.)

" . . . the godlie in the city, in diverse private societies, ran to fasting and praying: by these our old and best weapons, we are begining to prevaill, praise be to his holie name! London, Monday, March 15th [1641]."—*Robert Baillie's Letters and Journals.* Edinburgh, 1841.

" I pray God to heare all the praiers that are now put up for a happy issue of this Parliament." May 1, 1640.—*Letters of Lady Brilliana Harley. Camden Society.*

" How did the Lord (before this Parliament began, and hitherto ever since) *stir up* and *enflame* the fire of supplicating faith, on faithful supplication, and *fervent zeal* in private *humiliation* to seek the Lord in the face of Christ, for *mercie* and reconcilement to our poor *Land* and *Nation, so as the like* was never seen in this *Kingdom before.*"—Vicars' *Jehovah Jireh.*

Note X.—Vol. I., page 137.

" Upon *Saturday,* Nov. 7 [1640]. The First Petition which was preferred and read in the House was that of *Susannah Bastwick;* and afterwards, another of *Sarah Burton,* on the behalf of their respective Husbands, close Prisoners in remote Islands."—Rushworth's *Historical Collections,* part iii. vol. i. p. 20.

" First, upon the *petitions* of Mrs. *Bastwick,* and Mrs. *Burton,* the *pious,* but (then) most *disconsolate* and *too untimely widowed wives* of their *thrice noble and heroick husbands,* as also a *petition* exhibited in the behalf of most *precious* Mr. *Prynne,* . . . . the *pious Parliament,* like noble *Ebed-melechs,* redeemed those just *Jeremies* of the Lord out of their (otherwise) *perpetually captivating* most *remote* and *desolate dungeons.*"—Vicars' *Jehovah Jireh.*

" On Saturday Burton and Prin came through most of the citie triumphantlie: never here such a like show; about a thousand horse, and as some of good note sayes, above four thousand; above a hundred coatches, and, as manie sayes, above two hundred; with a world of foott, every one with their rosemary branch. Bastwick is not yet come from Sillie [Scilly]. This galled the Bishops exceedinglie. London, December 2nd [1640].

"Bastwick came into the City this day eight days; twentie-seven coatches, a thousand horse for his convoy, trumpetts sounding from diverse windowes, numbers of torches about him, and a world of people on all the way. London, December 12th [1640]."—*Robert Baillie's Letters and Journals.* Edinburgh, 1841.

NOTE Y.—Vol. I., page 139.

We will give a few extracts from a curious broadside, preserved among the *King's Pamphlets*, entitled "Time's Alterations, or, A Dialogue between my Lord FINCH and Secretary WINDEBANCKE; at their meeting in *France*, the eight of *Jan.* 1641. Brought up to *Billinsgate* the next Spring tyde following."

"*Windebancke.*—Well met, my Lord, it seems that you have taken flight over the great Pond, pray what newes in England?

"*Finch.*—Faith, I durst not stay to heare what newes, for I feare if I had tarried a little longer, my wings would have been clipt, and then I am sure, I had never come hither.

"*Windebancke.*—I commend your policy, for your being sure to flye, were sure to escape; but I pray, good my Lord, what do they say of me in *England?*

"*Finch.*—Newes more than I can relate; thinke you and I have bin the best benefactors to the ragged Regiment of Poets, that ever cam since *Noah's* floud?

"*Windebancke.*—Why, good my Lord?

"*Finch.*—Why I beleeve there hath bin more Impressions of severall kinds of lamentable Ballads and Pamphlets (made upon us two) then ever was of the *Practice* of *Piety*, or *Crums* of *Comfort*.

. . . .

"*Windebancke.*—The newes goeth in these parts, that in *England* they picture your Honour with wings.

"*Finch.*—'Tis true, good reason.

"*Windebancke.*—Thinks your honour so?

"*Finch.*—I am sure I know so, for had not my wings beene long, I am very certaine I had beene a shorter by a head ere this."

Note Z.—Vol. I., page 141.

Nov. 1640.—So numerous were the Complaints and Petitions touching Grievances that the whole House was divided, and subdivided into above Forty Committees to hear and examine them; But the main were reducible to these four General Heads:

I. Committees concerning Religion, Innovations in the Church, and Grievances by Ecclesiastical Courts.

II. Committees concerning publick affairs in general, and particularly concerning *Ireland* and *Scotland*.

III. Other Committees were relating to Ship-Money, Judges and Courts of Justice.

IV. Committees concerning Popery, The Popish Hierarchy, the Pope's *Nuncio*, Plots, Designs, &c.—*Rushworth*.

"It was the business of these Committees to prepare such measures as it might be supposed the house would think fit to adopt on these subjects. On the twelfth of the following month the Grand Committee for Religion appointed a sub-Committee of forty persons, which number, in the subsequent week, was increased to eighty, to enquire into the causes of the great scarcity of preaching ministers, and to consider of a way for removing scandalous ministers, and putting others in their places. This Committee was afterwards called, for brevity, the Committee for scandalous ministers."

Note AA.—Vol. I., page 141.

Extract from Sir Benjamin Rudyard's Speech.

"*Mr. Speaker*,—We are here assembled to do God's business and the King's, in which our *own* is included, as we are *Christians*, as we are Subjects: Let us first Fear God, then shall we honour the King the more: For I am afraid we have been the less prosperous in Parliaments, because we have preferred other matters before Him. Let Religion be our *primum quærite*, for all things else are but *et cæteras* to it; yet we may have them too, sooner and surer, if we give God his Precedence.

"We well know what Disturbance hath been brought upon the Church, for vain, *petty trifles :* How the whole Church, the whole Kingdom hath been troubled, where to place a *Metaphor,* an *Altar.* We have seen Ministers, their Wives, Children, and Families undone, against Law, against Conscience, against all bowels of Compassion, about not *Dancing* on *Sundays.* What do these sort of men think will become of themselves, when the *Master of the house shall come,* and find them thus beating their fellow-Servants? These inventions were but *Sives* made on purpose to *winnow* the *best men,* and that's the Devil's occupation; they have a mind to worry *Preaching;* for I never yet heard of any but diligent Preachers, that were vexed with these and the like devices. They despise Prophecy, and as one said, they would fain be at something like the *Mass,* that will not *Bite : A Muzzl'd Religion.* They would evaporate and dispirit the Power and Vigour of Religion, by drawing it out into solemn, specious *Formalites,* into obsolete antiquitated *Ceremonies* new furbish'd up: And this (be-like) is the *good work* in hand, which Dr. *Heylin* hath so often celebrated in his bold Pamphlets. All their Arts and Actions are so full of *mixtures,* involutions, and complications, as nothing is *clear,* nothing sincere in any of their Proceedings; let them not say, that these are the *perverse suspitions* and malicious interpretations of some few *factious* Spirits amongst us; when a *Romanist* hath bragged, and congratulated in Print, That *the face of our Church begins to alter, the language of our Religion to change.*

"*Mr. Speaker,* Let it be our principal Care, That these ways neither *continue* nor *return* upon us: If we secure our Religion, we shall cut off and defeat many Plots that are now on foot by them and others: Believe it, Sir, *Religion* hath been for a long time, and still is, the great design upon this Kingdom; it is a known and practised Principle, that they who would introduce another Religion into the Church, must first Trouble and Disorder the Government of the *State,* that so they may work their ends in a confusion, which now lyes at the door."

NOTE BB.—Vol. I., pages 146, 195.

The London Petition.

Twenty-eight grievances were enumerated in this Petition; which may be thus briefly stated.

1. Ministers were subjected to the Prelates, and thus exempted from the Temporal Power; hence,
2. Their faintheartedness to preach the Truth of God, (such as the doctrines of Predestination, Free Grace, Perseverance, Sin after Baptism, the Sabbath, Election, &c.) lest they should displease the Prelates.
3. Ministers were encouraged to despise the Temporal Magistracy, the Nobles, and Gentry of the land.
4. The restraint of many Godly and able Men from the Ministry.
5. Suppression of private patronage, Lectures, and Free Schools.
6. "The great encrease of Idle, Leud, and Dissolute, Ignorant and Erroneous Men in the Ministry, which swarm like the Locusts of Egypt over the whole kingdom; And will they wear but a Canonical Coat, a Surplice, a Hood, bow at the Name of Jesus, and be zealous of Superstitious Ceremonies, they may live as they list, confront whom they please, Preach and vent what Errors they will, and neglect Preaching at their pleasure without controul."
7. "The discouragement of many from bringing up their children in Learning, the many Schisms, Errors, and strange Opinions which are in the Church; Great Corruptions which are in the Universities," &c.
8. The wide circulation of bad books.
9. "The hindering of Godly Books to be printed, the blotting out or perverting those which they suffer, all or most of that which strikes either at Popery or Arminianism."
10. "The publishing and venting of Popish, Arminian, and other Dangerous Books and Tenets."
11. "The Growth of Popery and Encrease of Papists, Priests and Jesuits in sundry Places, but especially about *London* since the Reformation; the frequent Venting of Cruci-

fixes, and Popish Pictures both Engraven and Painted, and the placing of such in Bibles."

12. The multitude of Monopolies, Patents, increase of Taxes, &c.

13. The offices of Archbishops, Lord-Bishops, Deans, Archdeacons, being retained.

14. "The great conformity and likeness both continued and increased of our Church to the Church of Rome in Vestures, Postures, Ceremonies, and Administrations, namely as the Bishop's Rotchets and the Lawn-Sleeves, the Four-Corner'd Cap, the Cope and Surplice, the Tippet, the Hood, and the Canonical Coat; the Pulpits cloathed, especially now of late, with the Jesuites' badge upon them every way."

15. "The standing up at *Gloria Patri,* and at the Reading of the Gospel, praying towards the East, the Bowing at the Name of *Jesus,* the bowing to the Altar towards the East, Cross in Baptism, the kneeling at the Communion."

16. "The turning of the Communion-Table Altar-wise, setting Images, Crucifixes, and Conceits over them, and Tapers and Books upon them, and bowing or adoring to, or before, them; the reading of the second Service at the Altar, and forcing people to come up thither to receive, or else denying the Sacrament to them; terming the Altar to be the Mercy-Seat, or the place of God Almighty in the Church; which is a plain device to usher in the Mass."

17. "The Christ'ning and Consecrating of Churches and Chappels," &c.

18. The Liturgy being framed from the Romish Breviary, &c.

19. The multitude of Canons.

20. Plurality of Benefices, and Licenses for Marriages instead of Banns.

21. Profanation of the Lord's Day, and enforcing Sports on it.

22. "The pressing of the strict observance of the Saints' Days, whereby great Sums of Money are drawn out of men's Purses for working on them, a very high Burthen on most People, who getting their Living on their daily Imployments, must either omit them, and be idle; or part with their Money,

whereby many poor Families are undone, or brought behindhand," &c.

23. The great increase of Immorality.

24. "The general abuse of that great ordinance of Excommunication, which God hath left in his Church, as the last and greatest punishment which the Church can inflict upon obstinate and great offenders; and the Prelates and their Officers . . . . have made it, as they do all other things, a Hook or Instrument, wherewith to empty Men's Purses, and to advance their own greatness."

25. "The pride and ambition of the Prelates being boundless . . . . they . . . . exercise Ecclesiastical Authority in their own Names and Rights . . . . and take upon them temporal Dignities . . . . that they may sway both Swords."

26. "The putting of Ministers upon Parishes without the Patron's and People's consent."

27. Imposing of oaths upon Churchwardens and Sidesmen.

28. Inquisitorial proceedings against faithful Ministers; "only Papists, Jesuits, Priests, and such others as propagate Popery or *Arminianism*, are countenanced, spared, and have much liberty."

NOTE CC.—Vol. I., page 149.

In "A Large Supplement of the Canterbvrian Self-Conviction, opening to the World, yet more of the wicked Mysteries of that Faction from their own Writs—Imprinted 1641," the following passage occurs, describing one of the innovations and "strange doctrines" brought in by some of the adherents of Laud. One of them, Dr. Kellet, taught: "That the presence of Christ in the Sacrament, is such as the Eucharist itselfe must be adored. That in the adoration the bread would not be taken with the people's fingers, but in the hollow of the one hand, being supported by the other in the forme of a crosse, that upon the bread not a crosse onely but crucifixe may be drawne: that if any crumbe of this bread in the eating or handling fall to the ground, it is a grievous sinne against God."

NOTE DD.—Vol. I., page 149.

A curious Broadsheet, preserved in the *King's Pamphlets*, and entitled "A PROGNOSTICATION vpon W. LAVD, *late bishop of Canterbury, written Año Dom.* 1641, *which accordingly is come to passe*," contains some curious allusions to prominent persons of the day, who will be easily recognised, notwithstanding the orthography. The lines are addressed to Laud.

> "*My little Lord me thinks 'tis strange*
> *that you should suffer such a change*
> *in such a little space.*
> *You that so proudly t'other day*
> *did rule the king and country sway*
> *Must trudge to 'nother place.*

. . . .

> "*Wee scorne that popes with Crosier staues*
> *Miters or keyes should make us slaues*
> *and to there feete to bend.*
> *The pope and his malicious crew*
> *wee hope to handle all like you*
> *and bring them to an end.*

. . . .

> "*Within these six yeares six Eares haue*
> *bin cropt of worthy men and graue*
> *for speaking what was true.*
> *But if your subtil head and eares*
> *Can satisfie those six of thers*
> *expect but what's your due.*

. . . .

> "*The little ren that soard so high*
> *thought on his wings away to fly*
> *like finch I know not whither.*
> *But now the subtil whirly wind-*
> *debank hath left the bird behind*
> *you two must flock together.*

> " . . . . . *you will dye*
> *for churches good she riseth high*
> *when such as you fall down.*"

"That Lamb-skin'd Woolf the Archprelate of *Canterbury*, who had so long and so craftily and cruelly worryed Christ's

innocent lambs, was also impeached of high treason, and
thereupon forthwith, put into safe custodie under the Black-
rod, and afterwards lockt-up fast in the Tower of *London*, for
his future safe forth-coming, and thus all his former huge and
hyperbolicall puffe of ayrie honour and false windie reputation
among his clawing Pontificians, now at last tumbled into the
dust, yea besmired with the dirt of due disgrace, contempt,
and ignominie. *O then 'twas merry with harmlesse lambs, when
ravening wolves were shut up fast, and lambs at libertie.* As it is
recorded to be the speech of that blessed *Queen Elizabeth* of
ever-rarest memorie upon the Lord's delivering her from all
her unjust, great troubles, by the happy decease of her fierie
Sister, Queen *Marie*, when the Romish bloodie Bishop of her
clapt into prison, in her stead, and she delivered from their
devillish thraldom."—Vicar's *Jehovah Jireh*, 1644.

NOTE EE.—Vol. I., page 166.

From "Sr. Tho. Widdrington's Speech att a Conference
betweene Both Houses on Tuesday the 20 of July, 1641.
At the transmission of the impeachment against *Matthew
Wren*, Doctor in Divinity, late Bishop of *Norwich*, and
now Bishop of *Ely*. Printed by E. G. for R. Best at
Graye's Inne gate in Holborne, 1641."

"In the yeare 1635, this man was created Bishop of *Norwich*,
he is no sooner there, but he marcheth furiously . . . .

"He made a scourge, not of small cords, but of new Injunctions and numerous Articles tyed about with a strong twist
of a most dangerous oath; and with this he whips not out
buyers and sellers, but the faithful dispensers of the word out
of their Churches, out of their estates, out of their deare
Country . . . .

"(My Lords) in the time of King Rich. i. one of this man's
predecessors, a valiant Bishop, went into the holy warre, this
Bishop hath raised a warre at home in his own Dioces, a
warre not against *Sarazens, Barbarians, Turkes*, or *Infidels*, but
against good and well-disposed people, I know not what stile
to give this warre: without doubt (my Lords) this was no
holy warre.

"The weapons of this warfare were 28 Injunctions, 139 Articles, containing 879 questions.

"The souldiers were Chancellors, Commissaries, Officials, Commissioners, Rural Deans, &c.

"Himselfe commanded in chiefe. . . . .

"*Moses* led the children of *Israel* through the *Red Sea*; this man drives part of his flocks over the Sea, but went not himselfe. . . . .

"(My Lords) I cannot tell you all, but you can measure a Lyon by his paw. I am commanded to lay this great malefactour at your doores, one who hath been a great oppugner of the life and liberty of Religion, and who set a brand of infamy (to use his own words) upon *Ipswich* education.

"In summe, one who is a compleete mirrour of innovation, superstition and oppression, he is now in the snare of those articles, which were the workes of his own hands.

"The rod of *Moses* at a distance was a serpent, it was a rod againe when it was taken into his hands: this Bishop was a serpent, a devouring serpent in the Diocœs of *Norwich;* your Lordships peradventure will by handling of him make him a rod againe; or if not, I doubt not but your Lordships will chastise him with such rods as his crimes shall deserve."

See also, "Wren's Anatomy. Discovering his notorious pranks, and shamefull wickednesse; with some of his most lewd facts, and infamous deeds; both in his goverment of *Peter-house* Colledge, and domineering in three Bishopricks, to his perpetuall shame and infamy. Printed in the yeare, That *Wren* ceased to domineere, 1641."—Small 8vo. *King's Pamphlets.*

NOTE FF.—Vol. I., page 169.

"*There was a report of divers reasons to satisfy the Lords wherefore Bishops should not meddle in temporal affairs,*" &c.

"1. That it was a very great hindrance to the exercise of their ministerial function. 2. Because they do vow and undertake at their ordination, when they enter into Holy Orders, that they will give themselves wholly to that vocation. 3. Because Councils and Canons, in several ages, do forbid them to meddle with Secular Affairs. 4. Because the 24 bishops have a dependency upon the two Archbishops, and because of their oath of canonical obedience to them. 5. Because they are but for their lives, and therefore unfit to have a legislative power over the honours, inheritance, persons, and liberty of others. 6. Because of bishops' dependences and expectances of translations to places of greater profit. 7. That several bishops have, of late, much encroached upon the consciences and properties of the subjects; and they and their successors will be much encouraged still to encroach, and the subjects will be much discouraged from complaining against such encroachments, when they are judges of those complaints. The same reason extends to their legislative power, in any bill to pass for the regulation of their power, upon any emergent inconveniency by it. 8. Because the whole number of them is interested to maintain the jurisdiction of bishops; which hath been found so grievous to the three kingdoms, that Scotland hath utterly abolished it, and multitudes in England and Ireland have petitioned against it. 9. Because the bishops being lords of parliament, it setteth too great distance between them and the rest of their brethren in the ministry; which occasioneth pride in them, discontent in others, and disquiet in the church."—Cobbett's *Parliamentary History*.

NOTE GG.—Vol. I., pages 175, 210.

This was a small quarto pamphlet, pp. 51, entitled "The First Centvry of Scandalous, Malignant Priests, Made and admitted into Benefices by the Prelates, in whose hands the Ordination of Ministers and government of the Church hath been. Or, A Narration of the Causes for which the Parliament hath Ordered the Sequestration of the Benefices of severall Ministers complained of before them, for vitiousnesse of Life, errors in Doctrine, contrary to the Articles of our Religion, and for practising and pressing superstitious Innovations against Law, and for Malignancy against the Parliament.—It is Ordered this seventeenth day of *November* 1643, by the Committee of the House of Commons in Parliament concerning Printing, that this Booke Intituled [*The First Century of Scandalous*,

Malignant Priests, &c.] be printed by *George Miller*. JOHN WHITE: London. Printed by *George Miller*, dwelling in the *Black-Friers*. 1643."

NOTE HH.—Vol. I., page 176.

JOHN COSINS, Bishop of *Durham*, born in St. *Andrews* parish in *Norwich*, was brought up at the *free-school* here, sent thence to *Gonvile* and *Caius College*, where he was FELLOW . . . A. 1624 he was prebendary of the 10th stall in *Durham* . . . and lastly after the sequestration . . . was consecrated Bishop of Durham *Dec.* 2, 1660. He died at his lodgings in *Pall-Mall, Jan.* 15, 1671, aged 77, and was buried at *Bishop's Aukland* in his diocese, *April* 29, 1672, having settled a *rent charge* of £28 *per annum* by his *letters patent*, sealed as well with his *palatinate* as *episcopal* seal, issuing out of his hands and tenements in *Great Chilton*, in the *county palatinate* of *Durham*, out of which he founded three *scholarships* of 20 *nobles* apiece for three boys born in *Norwich*, and taught in the *publick grammar school* there.—Blomefield's *Norfolk*, iii. 416.

Rushworth assigns Monday, March 15, as the day on which the impeachment of Dr. Cosins was carried up to the Lords. It contained twenty-one Articles, some of which were as follows:—

1. That he was the first Man that caused the Communion-Table in the Church to be removed, and set Altar-wise; in the erecting and beautifying whereof, he (being then Treasurer) expended 200*l*.

2. That he used to officiate at the West-side thereof, turning his Back to the People.

3. That he used extraordinary Bowing to it.

5. That he converted divers Prayers in the Book of Common-Prayer into Hymns, to be sung in the Choir, and played with the Organ, contrary to the Ancient Custom of that Church.

7. That the first *Candlemas*-Day at Night that he had been in that Church, he caused three hundred Wax-Candles to be set up, and lighted in the Church at once, in Honour of our Lady, and placed threescore of them upon and about the Altar.

8. That in this Church, there were Reliques of divers Images, above which were remaining the Ruines of two Seraphims, with the Picture of Christ between them, erected in Queen *Mary's* time, in the time of Popery: All which, when Queen *Elizabeth* came to the Crown, were demolished by virtue of a Commission by her to that intent granted; which so continued demolished from that time, 'till Dr. *Cosins* came to that Church; who being Treasurer, caused the same to be repaired, and most gloriously painted.

10. That there was a knife belonging to the Church, kept altogether in the Vestry, being put to none but holy Uses, as cutting the Bread in the Sacrament, and the like, Dr. *Cosins* refusing to cut the same with any other but that; thinking all others that were unconsecrated, polluted; but that which he putting Holiness in, never termed but the *consecrated knife*.

11. That in a Sermon preached in that Church, he did deliver certain Words in disgrace of the Reformers of our Church: For instance, the Words were these: *The Reformers of this Church, when they abolished the Mass, took away all good Order; and instead of Reformation, made it a Deformation.*

12. That he seldom or never, in any of his Sermons, stiled the Ministers of the Word and Sacraments, by any other Name than *Priests*, nor the Communion-Table by any other Name than *Altar*.

13. That by his appointment there was a Cope bought, the Seller being a convicted Jesuit, and afterwards imployed in that Church, having upon it the Picture of the invisible and incomprehensible *Trinity*.

15. That he framed a superstitious Ceremony, in lighting the *Tapers* which were placed on the Altar, which for instance was this: A company of Boys that belonged to the Church, came in at the Choir-door, with *Torches* in their Hands lighted, bowing towards the *Altar* at their first entrance, bowing thrice before they lighted their *Tapers*; having done, they withdrew themselves, bowing so oft as before; not once turning their back-parts towards the *Altar*, the Organs all the time going.

17. That he used upon Communion-days to make the sign of the Cross, with his Finger both upon the Seats wheron they were to sit, and the Cushions to kneel upon, using some Words when he so did.

18. That one Sabbath-day there was set up an unnecessary company of *Tapers* and *Lights* in the Church; which Dr. *Hunt* being then Dean, fearing they might give Offence, being they were unnecessary, sent his Man to pull them down, who did so. But Dr. *Cosins* being therat aggrieved, came to the Fellow, and there miscalled him in a most uncivil manner, and began to beat him in the publick view of the Congregation, to the great disturbance of the same.

Note II.—Vol. I., page 189.

A specimen of the style of preaching of Vicar Squire shall here be given in his fourfold explanation of the etymology of Whitsunday. From "A Sermon appointed for the New-churchyard, by London, on Whitesunday," page 3. "Our countrey and custome call this feast by another name than Pentecost, viz., Whitsunday, that is Whitesunday; the attribute White being annexed to the Sunday for foure causes; from the time of the year, from the custome of the time, from the mercy of God to man, and from the mercy of man to man. 1. The time is *tempus albi solis*, a season of singular sunshine, the sun having now the clearest or whitest lustre: the time is therefore tearmed White-Sunday. The custome of the primitive time was, that this was *Dominica in Albis*: they used *albis vestibus post baptismum*; those who were baptized were accustomed to wear white garments about this time; the time, therefore, was called White-Sunday. 3. Through the mercy of God, the Holy Ghost came downe on man this day (a white, that is, a happy day for all Christians) rightly called White-Sunday. 4. Then also was it the guise of the church (in thanksgiving for this great gift from God) to give a small gift to man, white loaves, by way of alms to the poore: and hence also it is termed White-Sunday. Let your first care bee to practise this last point, by way of gratitude for this great gift, on this great day; give alms to the poore, as it were, white loaves; and (according to our homely proverb) White-Sunday shall make you white sonnes to God, obedient children unto your Father which is in heaven."—Ellis' *History and Antiquities of St. Leonard, Shoreditch.* 1798.

Note JJ.—Vol. I., page 191.

The Vicar defended himself in a quarto pamphlet, printed in 1641, entitled "The Vindication of the Vicar of Isleworth, in the County of Middlesex, from a scandalous Pamphlet, contayning one and twenty Articles; invented by some, closely: subscribed unto but by six, publiquely; presented but by one, openly; and now vented in print surreptitiously (in the name of the whole Parish) by a No-body.

"Whereunto are likewise added certaine notorious Impieties and Misdemeanours of *Gilbert Barrell*, Attorney, the Promoter: which shall be fairely and fully proved, upon just occasion."

Note KK.—Vol. I., page 213.

Court of Wards.—"A court first erected in Henry the Eighth's time, and afterwards augmented by him with the office of liveries. Hence it was called the Court of Wards and Liveries, till its suppression by Statute 12 Car. II.

"This was the most oppressive remnant of the prerogative which the Norman kings had claimed. Under the feudal system, every estate was considered a benefice, which, while the heir was a minor, or otherwise incapable of serving, reverted to the superior, who appointed another to perform military service in his stead. While this prerogative remained, the king, as feudal superior, gave or sold the wardship of a minor, or an idiot, to whomsoever he chose, with as much of the income as he thought proper. If the heir was a female, the king was entitled to offer her any husband of her rank, at his option; and if she refused him, she forfeited her land."—*Nares.*

Feb. 24, 1646. "A Message is sent up from the Commons for abolishing the Court of Wards, . . . to which the Lords Agree."—Parry's *Parliaments of England.*

"This act of grace and happines to the Kingdome, I conceive not to be inferiour to any of the former Acts or Votes passed by the *Parliament*, and must needs be extraordinary acceptable especially to the *Gentrie* of *England*, who by meanes of that Court were kept under in a mighty deale of homage and vassalrie in their children and estates."—Vicars' *Parliamentarie Chronicle*, part iv. p. 369. London, 1646.

APPENDIX

Note LL.—Vol. I., page 220.

"We desire .... to let the Reader understand what an evil savour such Patents and Monopolies granted by the King, had amongst the people of Better Rank, and which will best appear by a Speech made by Sir *John Culpeper*, of the County of *Kent*, Knight, immediately after the beginning of the Parliament, which met the third of *November*, and in regard it proceeded from him being a Person of very great repute in his Country, and also who afterwards, during the late Wars, was with the King in Person at Oxford, We think fit to communicate a *Branch* of his Speech, in reference to Monopolies, which the Author took with his pen at large, as he spoke the same.

"*Sir John Culpeper, his Speech in Parliament.*

"Mr. Speaker,—I have but one grievance more to offer unto you, but this one compriseth many; It is a Nest of Wasps, or Swarm of Vermine, which have over-crept the Land, I mean the Monopolies and Polers of the People; these, like the Frogs of *Egypt*, have gotten Possession of our Dwellings, and we have scarce a Room free from them. They sup in our Cup (*a*). They Dip in our Dish (*b*). They sit by our Fire (*c*). We find them in the Dye-Fat, Wash-Bowl (*d*), and Powdring-Tub (*e*). They share with the Butler in his Box (*f*). They have marked (*g*) and Sealed (*g*) us from Head to Foot. Mr. Speaker, they will not bate us a Pin (*h*). We may not buy our own Cloaths without their Brokage: These are the Leeches, that have suckt the Common-Wealth so hard that it is almost become Hectical . . . . . .

"Mr. Speaker, I have ecchoed to you the Crys of the Kingdom, I will tell you their Hopes. They look to Heaven for a Blessing upon this Parliament."

(*a*) Patent for 4*l. per* Tun on Wine.
(*b*) Licence to dress Meat in Taverns.
(*c*) Imposition on Coals.
(*d*) Patent for Soap.
(*e*) Tax upon Salt.
(*f*) Patent for Cards and Dice.
(*g*) Beavers, Belts, Bone-Lace, &c.
(*h*) Patent for Pins.

NOTE MM.—Vol I., page 221.

As an example of the arbitrary way in which these monopolies were granted, we may quote from Mr. Bruce's Preface to the volume of the Calendar of State Papers referred to in the preceding note. "On the western side of Great Yarmouth there lies a wide extent of marsh lands stretching inland almost to Norwich. These valuable marshes had at various and in some cases at far distant periods been won by the adjoining proprietors by embankment. In the time of Charles I. the manufacture of salt was a favourite branch of commercial industry, and, with a view to its promotion, various persons and companies obtained grants of extensive and valuable monopolies, for which they paid large sums to the Crown. Among these speculators there were two persons, named Nicholas Murford and Christopher Hanworth, whose salt-works were established in the immediate neighbourhood of Great Yarmouth. Murford and Hanworth looked with longing eyes upon the broad expanse of this adjoining marsh, and, alleging that it had been won from the sea, endeavoured to make it appear that it belonged to the King by legal right. An opinion was given by some of the King's counsel in favour of this pretended title, and the King was advised to write to the principal possessors of the marshes, including among them Sir John Wentworth, the owner of Somerleyton, and William Paston, the sheriff of Norfolk for 1636, apprising them that his Majesty had intended to settle these lands by Royal authority for the manufacture of salt 'against all such as pretend themselves to be owners,' but that finding Murford and Hanworth to be willing to yield some satisfaction to the present possessors, the King recommended them to treat with the salt-makers, lest otherwise he should use the power of his right.

"Startled by a claim enforced in a manner so peremptory, Sir John Wentworth and William Paston addressed the King by petition in a very calm and humble manner. They acknowledged the receipt of the letters in which he had called upon them to yield up their 'proper inheritance' upon terms of composition. They alleged the great prejudice that would result to the town of Yarmouth from the proposed application of their marshes, and the consequent want of pasture for horses and cattle. They denied that the marshes were ever overflown by the sea. They solicited the King to refer the business to some persons of quality in that neighbourhood to examine into the commodity pretended by the salt-makers, the unfitness of the place for such a work, and the prejudice that might ensue to the town, lands, and inhabitants. Finally, they prayed that in the meantime their marshes might not be disturbed. The King, whose foible it was never to see the real character of the positions in which he placed himself, treated the matter as if it had been a mere squabble between private persons. He directed the Council to call the parties before them and compose their differences, or otherwise to acquaint him with their opinions. The Council probably saw the matter in another light, for so far as we have gone we have found no more about it."

Note NN.—Vol. I., page 221.

"Upon Sunday last, the King and the council sat again upon the soap business: and now it is determined that the patentees for this new soap shall have power given to them to seize upon all such soap as hath been made since the middle of November last, or thereabouts; to seize upon the pans and all their other utensils belonging to the trade of soap-boiling, and, lastly, to commit the soap-boilers themselves to prison. It seems that the King and the Lords are well satisfied in the goodness of this new soap, and that part hath been adulterated by the procurement of the old company. Some allege, that by putting into a barrel of soap a small quantity of rhubarb or a glass of sack, either will make that barrel of soap unserviceable.

"It is granted that this new soap hath blistered the washers' hands, and done other mischiefs. But then again, it is believed that the soap was sophisticated with some obnoxious matter to work that mischief. It is said that there shall come forth a Proclamation concerning it. Then shall we know what to trust to."—*Court and Times of Charles I.*

Note OO.—Vol. I., page 221.

" It appears by p. 241 of the 20th vol. of the 'Fœdera' that the wine merchants and vintners of England having agreed to pay 40s. a ton to King Charles, for all the wines they should import; that the king, in return, 'prohibits the wine-coopers, who had already crept into the wine trade, from importing wines.' And by the same record it further appears that licences for retailing of wines were then under the management of the Vintners' Company, for his Majesty's benefit. The king also hereby directs that 'the custom of retailing of wines and bottles and other undue measures be laid aside, and that all wines be retailed by just measures alone.'"—Herbert's *History of the Twelve Great Livery Companies of England.* 1836.

Note PP.—Vol. I., page 223.

An " Ordinance of both Houses " was issued August 26th, 1642, "inhibiting the importation of Currans." The preamble states that "it is found by daily experience, that the Importation of Currans into this Kingdome (it being a Commodity of little or no use at all, but a meere superfluity, and may well bee spared) is a matter of great concernment, not only to the Merchant, but to this Nation, in regard the said Commodity cannot be had in the parts beyond the Seas, where the same are brought, without ready money, an hundred thousand pound *per annum* at least being bestowed in Currans, which otherwise would be brought into this Kingdome, is wholly diverted, whereas formerly (till of later yeares) the said Currans were bought for Commodities of this Kingdome, exported hence of small value."

Note QQ.—Vol. I., p. 241.

" Westminster Hall is a roome as long as broad if not more than the outer house of the High Church of Glasgow, supponing the pillars wer removed. In the midst of it was erected a stage like to that prepared for the Assemblie of Glasgow, but

much more large, taking up the breadth of the whole House
from wall to wall, and of the length more than a thrid part.
At the north end was set a throne for the King, and a chayre
for the Prince; before it lay a large wooll-seck, covered with
green, for my Lord Steward, the Earle of Arundaill; beneath
it lay two other secks for my Lord Keeper and the Judges,
with the rest of the Chancerie, all in their red robes. Beneath
this a little table for four or fyve Clerks of the Parliament in
their black gouns; round about these some furmes covered
with green freese, whereupon the Earles and Lords did sitt in
their red robes, of that same fashion, lyned with the same
whyte ermine skinnes, as you see the robes of our Lords when
they ryde in Parliament; the Lords on their right sleeve
having two barres of whyte skinnes, the Viscounts two and ane
half, the Earles three, the Marquess of Wincester three and
ane half. England hath no more Marquesses: and he bot one
late upstart of creature of Queene Elizabeth's. Hamilton goes
here bot among the Earles, and that a late one. Dukes, they
have none in Parliament: York, Richmond, and Bucking-
hame are but boyes; Lennox goeth among the late Earles.
Behinde the formes where the Lords sitt, there is a barr
covered with green: at the one end standeth the Committee
of eight or ten Gentlemen, appoynted by the House of Commons to pursue; at the midst there is a little dask, where the
prisoner Strafford stands and sitts as he pleaseth, together
with his keeper, Sir William Balfour, the Lieutenant of the
Tower. At the back of this is a dask, for Strafford's four
secretars, who carries his papers and assists him in writing
and reading; at their side is a voyd for witnesses to stand; and
behinde them a long dask at the wall of the room for Strafford's
counsell-at-law, some five or six able lawers, who were [not]
permitted to disputt in matter of fact, bot questions of right,
if any should be incident. This is the order of the House
below on the floore; the same that is used dailie in the Higher
House. Upon the two sides of the House, east and west,
there arose a stage of elevin ranks of formes, the highest touching almost the roof; everie one of these formes went from the
one end of the roome to the other, and contained about fortie
men; the two highest were divided from the rest by a raill,

and a raill cutted off at everie end some seatts. The gentlemen
of the Lower House did sitt within the raile, others without.
All the doores were keeped veire straitlie with guards; we
always behooved to be there a little after five in the morning.
My Lord Willoughbie Earle of Lindesay, Lord Chamberland
of England (Pembroke is Chamberland of the Court) ordered
the House, with great difficultie. James Maxwell, Black-Rod,
was great usher; a number of other servant Gentlemen and
Knights assisted. By favour we got place within the raile,
among the Commons. The House was full dailie before
seven; against eight the Earle of Strafford came in his barge
from the Tower, accompanied with the Lieutenant and a guard
of musqueteers and halberders. The Lords, in their robes,
were sett about eight; the King was usuallie halfe ane howre
before them: he came not into his throne, for that would have
marred the action; for it is the order of England, that when
the King appears, he speaks what he will, bot no other speaks
in his presence. At the back of the throne, there was two
roomes on the two sydes; in the one did Duke de Vanden,
Duke de Vallet, and other French nobles sitt; in the other,
the King, Queen, Princesse Mary, the Prince Elector, and
some Court ladies; the tirlies, that made them to be secret,
the King brake down with his own hands; so they satt in the
eye of all, bot little more regarded than if they had been
absent; for the Lords satt all covered; these of the Lower
House, and all other except the French noblemen, satt discovered when the Lords came, not else. A number of ladies
was in the boxes, above the railes, for which they payed much
money. It was dailie the most glorious Assemblie the Isle
could afford; yet the gravitie not such as I expected; oft
great clamour without about the doores; in the intervalles,
while Strafford was making readie for answers, the Lords gott
alwayes to their feet, walked and clattered; the Lower House
men too loud clattering; after ten houres, much publict eating,
not onlie of confectious, bot of flesh and bread, bottles of beer
and wine going thick from mouth to mouth without cups, and
all this in the King's eye."—*R. Baillie's Letters,* vol. i. p. 314.
Bannatyne Club, Edinburgh, 1814.

Note RR.—Vol. I., page 245.

There were some who held a different opinion from that of our author. Evelyn wrote on the same subject:—

"On the 12th of May, I beheld on Tower-hill the fatal stroke which severed the wisest head in England from the shoulders of the Earl of Strafford, whose crime coming under the cognizance of no human law, or statute, a new one was made, not to be a precedent, but his destruction. With what reluctancy the King signed the execution, he has sufficiently expressed; to which he imputes his own unjust suffering—to such exorbitancy were things arrived."—*Diary and Correspondence of John Evelyn.* London, 1850.

Note SS.—Vol. I., page 253.

"*Monday, May* 10, 1641.—An information was also given in, or at least so pretended, to render the Archbishop more Odious to the Populace, and to exasperate them against Him and the Rest of the Bishops, that there were great Stores of Arms and Ammunition laid up at *Lambeth*, in Order, as was buzzed about among the Faction, to promote some ill Designs against the Parliament; whereupon Sir *John Evelyn* and Mr. *Broxam* were Ordered to go over to *Lambeth*, to view what Arms were there; and some others were appointed to search about the Parliament House, lest any Plot should be secretly hid there; or rather in truth to amuse the People by these strange Fears and Jealousies, and keep them up in that Heat in which they were against the Government."—*Nalson's Collections*, vol. ii. p. 236.

"Information being also given to the Parliament, of store of Armes and Ammunition laid up by that Archplotter, the Arch-Prelate of *Canterbury*, at *Lambeth*-house, about 200 foot and a troope of horse were sent to search the said house; where they found excellent Armes for at least foure or five hundred men, which also were all taken thence, and brought into *Guild-hall* in *London*, and there safely laid up for better uses."—Vicars' *Jehovah Jireh*, 1644.

" . . . the greatest part of them being very new and compleat Arms."—*Certaine Speciall and Remarkable Passages for both Houses of Parliament.*

Note TT.—Vol. I., page 259.

I. e., "the *court military*, or, *court of chivalry*. The jurisdiction of which is declared by statute 13 Ric. ii. c. 2, to be this: 'that it hath cognizance of contracts touching deeds of arms or of war, out of the realm, and also of things which touch war within the realm, which cannot be determined or discussed by the common law; together with usages and customs to the same matters appertaining.' So that wherever the common law can give redress, this court hath no jurisdiction. .... The words 'other usages and customs,' support the claim of this court. 1. To give relief to such of the nobility and gentry as think themselves aggrieved in matters of honour; and, 2. To keep up the distinction of degrees and quality. Whence it follows, that the civil jurisdiction of this court of chivalry is principally in two points; the redressing injuries of honour, and correcting encroachments in matters of coat-armour, precedency, and other distinctions of families.

"As a court of honour, it is to give satisfaction to all such as are aggrieved on that point; a point of nature so nice and delicate, that its wrongs and injuries escape the notice of the common law, and yet are fit to be redressed somewhere. Such, for instance, as calling a man coward, or giving him the lie; for which, as they are productive of no immediate danger to his person or property, no action will lie in the courts at Westminster; and yet they are such injuries as will prompt every man of spirit to some honourable amends, which by the antient law of the land was appointed to be given in the court of chivalry .... it is the business of this court, according to Sir Matthew Hale, to adjust the right of armorial ensigns, bearing crests, supporters, pennons, &c., and also rights of place or precedence. ..... The marshalling of coat-armour, which was formerly the pride and study of all the best families in the kingdom, is now greatly disregarded; and has fallen into the hands of certain officers and attendants upon this court, called heralds."—Blackstone's *Commentaries*.

Note UU.—Vol. I., page 276.

"No setled peace was ever formerly intended, nor can now be futurely expected, in *England* or *Ireland*, without an universall publike toleration (at the least) of Popery, and a repeale and suspention of all Lawes against it; this being the very condition in the plot which the King must condescend to, ere the Papists would ingage themselves to assist him in these warres thus raised by them, for this end : and that none may doubt this verity; the late most insolent bold demands of the *Irish* rebels in the treaty with them, the most favourable *Articles* of *Pacification* granted to them, the present suspention of all lawes against Priests and Recusants in all Counties under his Majestie's power; the uncontrolled multitudes of Masses in his Armies' Quarters, *Wales*, the *North*, and elsewhere; the open boasts of Papists every where, the introducing of thousands of *Irish* Rebels, and other Fugitives, to extirpate the Protestant *Religion*, most really proclaim it."—Prynne's *Rome's Master-peece*, second edition, 1644.

Note VV.—Vol. I., page 283.

Articles of High Treason, and other Misdemeanours, against the Lord *Kymbolton*, Mr. *Pym, John Hampden, Denzil Hollis,* Sir *Arthur Haslerig*, and *William Strode*, being all Members of the House of COMMONS.

I. That they have traterously endeavoured to subvert the Fundamentall Lawes and Government of this Kingdome, and deprive the King of his Legall power, and to place on Subjects an Arbitrary and tyranicall power.

II. That they have endeavoured by many foule aspersions upon his Majesty and his Government, to alienate the afections of his people, and to make his Majesty odious to them.

III. That they have endeavoured to draw his Majestie's late Army to disobedience to his Majestie's commands, and to side with them in their Trayterous designe.

IV. That they have Trayterously invited and encouraged

a forraigne power to invade his Majestie's Kingdome of England.

v. That they have Traiterously indeavoured to Subvert the very Rights and Being of Parliaments.

vi. That for the completing of their trayterous designes, they have endeavoured as farre as in them lay, by force and terror, to compell the Parliament to joyne with them in their Trayterous designes, and to that end have actually raised and countenanced Tumults against the King and Parliament.

vii. That they have trayterously conspired to Leavy, and actually have Leavied, warre against the King.—From *An Exact Collection of all Remonstrances, Declarations, Votes, Orders, Ordinances, &c. which were formerly published either by the King's Majestie's Command, or by Order from One or both Houses of* PARLIAMENT. London, 1643.

NOTE WW.—Vol. I., page 283.

" *Die Lunæ*, 3 *Januar*. 1641.—It is this day ordered upon the question, by the Commons House of Parliament, That if any persons whatsoever shall come to the Lodgings of any Member of this House, and there doe offer to seale the Trunks, Doores, or Papers of any Members of this House, or to sieze upon their persons; That then such Members shall require the aid of the Constable, to keepe such persons in safe custodie, till this House doe give further Orders. And this House doth further declare, That if any person whatsoever, shall offer to arrest or detaine the person of any Member of this House, without first acquainting this House therewith, and receiving further Order from this House: That it is lawfull for such Member or any person, to resist him, and to stand upon his, and their guard of defence, and to make resistance, according to the Protestation taken, to defend the priviledges of Parliament."—*H. Elsynge, Cler. Parl. D. Com.*—*An Exact Collection, &c.*

Note XX.—Vol. I., page 284.

"*His Maiestie's Speech in the House of Commons*, 4° *Januarii* 1641.

" Gentlemen,—I am sorry for this occasion of comming unto you: yesterday I sent a Sergeant-at-Arms upon a very important occasion, to apprehend some that by my command were accused of high Treason, whereunto I did expect Obedience, and not a Message. And I must declare unto you here that albeit no King that ever was in England shal be more carefull of your PRIVILEDGES, to maintain them to the uttermost of his power then I shall be; yet you must know, that in cases of Treason no person hath a priviledge, and therfore I am come to know if any of those persons that were accused are here: for I must tell you, Gentlemen, that so long as these persons that I have accused (for no slight crime, but for Treason) are here, I cannot expect that this House can be in the right way that I do heartily wish it: Therefore I am come to tell you, that I must have them wheresoever I find them: well, sithence I see all the Birds are flown, I do expect from you that you shall send them unto me as soone as they returne hither: But I assure you, in the word of a King, I never did intend any force, but shall proceed against them in a legall and faire way, for I never meant any other.

"And now sithence I see I cannot doe what I came for, I thinke this no unfit occasion to repeat what I have said formerly; That whatsoever I have done in favour, and to the good of my Subjects, I doe mean to maintaine it.

"I will trouble you no more, but tell you, I doe expect as soon as they come to the House, you will send them to me, otherwise I must take my owne course to finde them."—*An Exact Collection, &c.*

Note YY.—Vol. I., page 291, and Vol. II., page 15.

" The carrying up these petitions to Westminster, and especially that of the London apprentices, occasioned great tumults about the parliament-house. The king was at his palace at Whitehall, attended by a great number of disbanded officers, whom his majesty received with great ceremony, and employed as a guard to his royal person. These officers insulted the common people, and gave them ill language as they passed by the court to the parliament-house, crying out, No bishops, no Popish lords! If the people ventured to reply, the officers followed their reproaches with cuts and lashes, which, says lord Clarendon, produced some wounds, and drew blood. Mr. Baxter says, they came out of Whitehall, and catched some of them. and cut off their ears. From these skirmishes, and from the shortness of the apprentices' hair, which was cut close about their ears, the two parties began to be first distinguished by the names of Roundhead and Cavalier."—Neal's *Puritans*, ii. 449.

See " A Trve Relation of the unparaleld Breach of PARLIAMENT by his Maiesty, as is conceived the 4 of *January*, 1641, Being instigated thereunto by unadvised Counsels, under pretence of a legall Proceeding. Together with a Relation of the Hostile intention upon the House of Commons, by Captaine Hyde, and those other Cavaliers and Souldiers that accompanied his Majesty in a warlike manner, armed with swords, Pistols and Dragonnes. And also a Relation of the free and Voluntary offers of the Trayned Bands of the City of London, of the Masters of Ships, Mariners, and Seamen, of the Apprentices of London, of the Trayned Bands of Southwarke, and of the Watermen upon the Thames, to defend the King and Parliament against malignant Councils, and plots of Papists. Likewise how certaine multitudes of Countreymen came to present their humble Petitions to the Parliament."—London, 1641.

NOTE ZZ.—Vol. I., page 301.

" The Irish nation is a people both proud and envious. The Commonaltie ignorant and illiterate, poor, and lazie: and will rather beg or starve than work; and therefore fit subjects for the Priests and Jesuits to spur on upon such bloudy actions and murtherous designes.

" It is too well known that the Irish have murthered of the Protestant party in the provinces of Vlster, Leinster, Connaght, and Munster, of men, women, and children, the number of fifty thousand as it is credibly reported by Englishmen, who have been over all parts of the kingdom."—From "Ireland's blood cries; A true Description of sundry sad and lamentable Collections, taken from the mouths of very credible Persons, and out of Letters sent from Ireland to this Citie of London, of the perfidious outrages and barbarous cruelties which the Irish Papists have committed upon the persons of the Protestants, both men, women, and children, in that Kingdom, since Anno Dom. 1641."—1646.

NOTE AAA.—Vol. II., page 6.

The Women seem to have taken a vivid interest in the politics of the day. This petition appears to have been presented after the noted one in which they approached the House " like the woman of Tekoah," seeking peace, security, and the reformation of religion, on which occasion the bearers of the petition received their answer from Mr. Pym, in the name of the House. We also find amongst others one with this title :—

"To the Right Honourable the House of Peeres Now Assembled in Parliament, The humble Petition of many thousands of Courtier's, Citizen's, Gentlemen's, and Tradesmen's Wives, inhabiting the Cities of *London* and *Westminster*, concerning the staying of the Queene's intended voyage into Holland, with many serious causes and weighty reasons (which they desire) may induce the Honourable House to detain Her Majestie.—*Presented and read in the House by the Lord* Mandevill, *the* 10*th of February*, 1641.—London. Printed for *T. Hale*, 1641."—*King's Pamphlets*.

Nor were the Women of London the only dames who came forward with their petitions. Those of Bristol, and of Leicester, represented the sorrows of their respective towns.

The Women of Leicester petitioned the King against " the turbulent carriages of Master *Hastings* (whom your Majesty hath lately made High Sheriffe) in assaulting our said Towne in the dead time of the night, with Troopes of Horse and armed men." The petition was presented to the King at

Leicester, July 24, 1642, " by many women of the best rancke there. London. Printed in the yeere 1642."

The London ladies were, however, the most resolute in the kingdom. Here is an account of another of their petitions:—

" On Tuesday the first of February . . . . also was another Petition delivered to the Lords by a company of Women, about the number of 400, desiring an answer of their petition delivered the day before, and attending there for the delivery thereof, the Duke of *Lenox* coming to the House, they presented him their petition, who answered: Away with these women, wee were best to have a parliament of Women. Whereupon some of the Women interrupting his passage, catched hold of his staffe, humbly desiring him to receive their petition, upon which the Duke being moved, offered to draw back his staffe, after which they delivered their petition to the Lord *Savage*, who presented it to the Lords, and upon reading, and some debate thereof, they gave orders that twelve of the petitioners should be called into the house, to declare their grievances, which was done accordingly."—*The True Diurnall Occurrences*, 1642.—*King's Pamphlets*.

It is not to be wondered at that this feminine activity afforded the wits of the day matter for fun and sarcasm; and a curious squib appeared, with the following title:—

" The Petition of the Weamen of Middlesex, Which they intended to have presented to the High Court of Parliament, but shewing of it to some of their friends they dissuaded them from it, until it should please God to endue them with more wit, and lesse Non-sence. Subscribed with the Names of above 12,000. 'We desire that Altars may be altered, and that haters of our petition may be haltered.' "— London. Printed for William Bowden. 1641.—*King's Pamphlets*.

NOTE BBB.—Vol. II., page 7.

"This Crosse in Cheapside was first erected as I have said, by *Edward* the first, in commemoration of his Queen whose name was *Ellenor;* Secondly, it was then builded for an Ornament to the City, being placed in the chiefest place or streete of the said City, and therefore was thought and held at that time for a glorious Fabricke, and would continue there, for antiquity sake, rather then to give an occasion of offence to any; It hath now stood near upon 400, or five hundred yeares, still repaired and beautified, but never suffered martirdome till now; it hath beene twelve severall times adorned and decored in all ages; and was ever held a gracefull Fabricke to London, till of late yeares; untill indeed many superstitious and foolish people have publickly adored and worshipped it as they have gone by it; which offence is the maine cause of its pulling downe and defacing.

. . . .

". . . therefore seeing no redresse or helpe for the suppression of it; the Common Counsell of London did Petition to the honourable Houses of Parliament for relefe in this case, which was soon granted, and had a warrant to take it downe, by all the faire meanes they could devise, calling to their ayd the Trained bands of the City for their defence, because no uproare might arise thereby, and that no blood might be spilt; because divers people had given out they would rather lose their lives then it should down; down it must, and it is so ordered to be taken downe that the materials may be made usefull other way, and that they should be sold for a valuable consideration; the materials being most lead, iron, and stones; some report divers of the Crownes and Scepters are silver; besides the rich gold that it is guilded with, which as it is reported, may be filed and taken off, and yield a good value; so that divers have offered some 400*l*., some 500*l*., but they that bid must offer 1000*l*. for it; and so this Tuesday it is a taking down with a great deal of judgement and discretion, and foure Companies of the Trane Bands of the City to guard and defend those that are about the worke, and to keepe others from domineering, and so I leave it to bee made levell with the ground this second day of *May* 1643."—From *The Downe-fall of Dagon, or the taking downe of Cheapside Crosse.*

" The House also tooke into consideration, the superstitious use of *Cheapside-Crosse*, and concurred with the Citie to have it removed; a very good worke when the chiefe Magistrates reforme, the adversary is silenced, but when things are reformed by the multitude, it begets clamour, and takes off the hearts of many from the Magistracy: If any say, it was needlesse, they are mistaken, ignorant people are much taken with babyes; and besides, the Papists seeing their gods throwne downe, will be out of hope, and so either be packing to Rome, or goe to Church."—From *Speciall Passages*, Numb. 38.

Note CCC.—Vol. II., page 42.

" For this Day a Message was brought from the House of Commons by *John Hampden*, Esq., to let their Lordships know, *That this Day there came a Man to the Door of the House of Commons, and sent in Word, That he had Matters of a high Nature to reveal, concerning some Lords and Members of the House of Commons;* Upon this the House sent forth some Members to speak with the Man, who acquainting the House with some Discourse they had with him, the Commons sent for him in, who beginning to relate the Business, the House of Commons would not suffer him to name any Person, lest the Parties hearing of it, should Fly. And because it concerned some Peers of this House, the House of Commons have sent the Man, who is now at the Door, ready to be Examined openly, or in what manner else their Lordships in their Wisdom shall think fit. Then *Thomas Beal*, a Taylor dwelling in *White-Cross* Street, was called in and made a Relation of the whole Matter, with all the Circumstances, which was as follows:—

" *That this day at Twelve of the Clock, he went into the Fields near unto the Pest-House, and walking on a private Bank, he heard some talking, but did not see them at first, but finding them by the Voice, he coming within hearing of them, understood they talked of State Affairs: and going nearer them, he heard one of them say, that it was a wicked thing that the last Plot did not take, but if this goes on, as is in Hand and intended, they shall be all made. And also heard them say That there was* 108 *Men appointed, to kill* 108 *Persons of the Parliament, every One his Man, some were Lords, and the others were to be Members of the House of Commons, all Puritans; and the Sacrament was to be Administered to the* 108 *Men for performing of this; and those that killed the Lords were to have* 10*l.* *and those that were to kill the Members of the*

House of Commons 40s. *That* Gorges *being the* 37*th Man, had taken the Sacrament on* Saturday, *to kill one of the House of Commons, and had received* 40s."—*Nalson's Collection.*

NOTE DDD.—Vol. II., page 53.

"Much about which time, a most impious and malicious-hearted fellow audaciously sent a Letter to the Parliament, directed and endorsed to that ever most highly honoured Member of the House of Commons, Mr. *Pim*, a most pious Patriot of his Country, and in it a filthy fresh plaster taken from the plague-sore, expressing in the letter what it was, and why 'twas sent, namely, in hope that the very sudden sight and thought on it (he being in the Parliament House) might and would damp and dead his heart with fear, and so have infected the worthy Gentleman to death with it. A Copy of which letter I have thought fit here to insert that the Reader may see the odiousness of it and this action more fully.

"The Copy of the Letter sent to Mr. *Pim*, in the Parliament House, with a filthy plague-sore plaster in it.

"*Master* Pim, *do not think that a guard of men can protect you, if you persist in your traiterous courses, and wicked designs. I have sent a paper messenger to you, and if this do not touch your heart, a Dagger shall, so soon as I have recovered of my plague-sore. In the mean time, you may be forborne, because no better man may be endangered for you.* "Repent Traitor.

"Which Letter was delivered, I say, as Mr. *Pim* went into the Parliament, But, contrary to the wicked intention of the master and message God preserved this noble Gentleman from the intended evil thereof. For this undaunted, and conscience-unspotted, courageous Worthy . . . this piously valorous-hearted Gentleman, Mr. *Pim*, was nothing at all disheartened or distempered at the sight of the plaster, nor with the wicked threats which that Atheistical wretch sent besides in the letter, to stab him with his Dagger if that plaster failed, God, having hitherto preserved him (and I trust so will) a most loyal subject to his Sovereign, and a most prudent and painful

promoter of the best good in Church and Commonwealth."—
Vicars' *Jehovah Jireh*. London, 1644.

Note EEE.—Vol. II., page 58.

" *Die Sabbati*, 26° *Martii*. 1642.

"Message from the Lords .... That the Lords are informed by the Relation of Sir *Philip Cartwright*, by Intelligence out of *France*, that Seven thousand Men are raising in *France*, in *Normandy*, and *Picardy:* And thereupon have appointed him to wait on this .... to make relation thereof: And

"Sir *Philip Cartwright* was called in: And Mr. Speaker acquainted him, that the Lords had sent them Word, that they had received Information from him of some Forces raised in *France*; of which Particulars the House desired from him a particular Information:

"Sir *Philip Carterett* said, He had received Informations from very good Hands, that there are Seven thousand Men raised in the Provinces of *Normandie* and *Picardie* besides the Five thousand Men formerly appointed to be raised: The which Five thousand Men were appointed to be transported by the 5th of *April*, according to our Computation; as, by former Letters, he had formerly acquainted the Parliament. .... To go to the Lord Admiral, to know of him in what particular State the Ships for this Summer's Fleet are."—*Commons' Journals*.

Note FFF.—Vol. II., page 63.

" There was a great Hurllyburly at Guild Hall in London on Munday last by a company of Malignants that came to the common Councell (then sitting) to gett their hands to a Petition which they pretended to be for peace, but in truth a very seditious and obusive thing as by any indifferent iudgement may easie be diserned a coppy whereof being extant in print, it is said to be framed by the Oxfordians, or as some thinke by that good instrument the Arch-Bishoppe of Yorke, and sent to the Citty to disturbe the proceedings of the Parliament, deceiving the Subjects with a pretence of peace when no such thing by the petition is really intended, unlesse such a peace as must force us yeald our selves slaves and vassalls to Traytors, Papists and Malignants if not in a little time prove the destruction of all Religion, Lawes, liberties, Parliament, and Kingdome. .... The Passages about this Petition was informed to the Parliament, and how the Petitioners upon their being in Guild-hall abused some of the Garrison Soldiers comming amongst them in an orderly manner, calling them Parliament Rogues and Roundheads, disarming and further abusing of them, and whiles one part of them cryed out *Peace, Peace*, another part cryed out *Peace and Truth together*, but that displeasing some of them they cryed out cursing and swearing, *hang truth lett's have peace on any termes and let trueth follow*, which words may well argue what desires these men have of an Honourable and lasting peace. ..... One of the chiefe Agents in that Businesse was the Master of the Baregarden .... the combustion about this Petition was so great at Guild-Hall, that two Troopes of Horse, and a great part of the Trained Bands were raised to allay the Tumult."—*A Continuation of certain Speciall and Remarkable Passages, &c., Number* 23.

"Information being given to Colonel *Randall Manwaring*, who is appointed by the Committee of the *Milicia* of the Citie of *London* to execute the place of Serjeant Major Generall *Skippon*, that a multitude of seditious persons and turbulent were assembled at Guild-Hall, London, under pretence of promoting a *Petition* for Peace, and that they were drawing Swords one among another: the said Col. directed Cap. *Harvey* to go with his Troop of horse to Guild-Hall to appease the said Tumult. And comming thither the said Cap. *Harvey* found a great multitude in the Porch and yard of the said Hall with their swords drawn fighting; where one *John Drury* was apprehended who was one of the Petitioners and had a drawne sword in his hand; very many of the rest retreated into the Hall with their swords drawne, shut the dores and barricadoed the same with Stooles, Formes and Tables and other Lumber, and refused to open the dore, or give any account of that uprore, but stood upon their guard. So that the said Colonel and Captaine were forced for the prevention of further mischiefe, and for the preservation of the Major, Aldermen, and Common Councell then sitting in the usuall place of the Hall beyond them, to bring two pieces of Ordnance, and caused the same to be planted by forcing the said Gate, And giving notice of their intention first to the said persons assembled within the Hall; they within desired a Parley, and declared by one *Charles Jennings*, That they were then willing all to depart quietly."—*The Image of the Malignants' Peace.*

" This day the Major of *London*, the Sheriffes and Aldermen, with many other Citizens came to the House of Commons and presented a petition in the name of themselves, and the whole City, it being directed to the Lords and Commons. .... In this petition of the City, they doe likewise disclaim the former crosse petition which was brought in a tumultous maner directed to the Lords, the same not being with the consent of the whole body of the City, but by some few disaffected persons that drew on some others under a sweet pretence of Peace, when it is justly suspected that the chief actours therein did secretly intende to increase the distractions in the City and whole Kingdome, and therefore they desire that the chief agents therein might be punished."—*A Perfect Diurnall, &c., Number* 28.

Die Lunæ. 12° *Decembris.* " Mr. *Whittacres* presents in Writing, the Examination in Writing, concerning the Words expressed by the Master of the *Beare Garden* " That he would cut the Throats of those that refused to subscribe a Petition: " Whereupon

It was *Resolved*, upon the Question, That Mr. *Godfrey*, Master of the *Beare Garden*, shall be forthwith committed to *Newgate*; there to remain during the Pleasure of this House.

Ordered, That the Master of the *Beare Garden*, and all other Persons who have Interest there, be injoined and required by this House, That for the future they do not permit to be used the Game of Bear-baiting in these Times of great Distractions, till this House do give further Order therein."—*Commons' Journals.* 1642.

"Another seditious Petition (I say) was hatched and contrived in Kent ... Which Petition being on the 29th of *April*, 1642, brought to the Parliament by some of the prime

Malignant-ones (the rest of that rout, being some certain thousands, remained at *Blackheath* for an answer, but were fair to depart with a flea in their ears) they received most foul (but most just) disgraces at their entrances into the City, the gate at the Bridge-foot was shut against them, they themselves were disarmed, their weapons being taken there from them, two of their prime Leaders having exhibited their Petition in Parliament, were committed to safe custody till fit opportunity of further examination of their high contempt and arrogancie. But immediately after, the truly religious, honest, and well-affected party of the said County of *Kent* unanimously also united themselves in an honest and loyal Petition, therein utterly disavowing and protesting against that other seditious and scandalous one, who were all, together with their Petition, most courteously and lovingly entertained, and dismissed with great thanks from the Parliament, for that their so honest and peaceable demeanour."—Vicars' *Jehovah Jireh*. London, 1644.

NOTE GGG.—Vol. II., page 70.

"And when the *Houses* issued out their *Propositions* for bringing in of *Money*, *Plate*, and *Horses*, to advance the Warre against His Majestie: what an unnecessary haste made the wealthy citizens to cast into the publike *Treasurie* as much as could be spared from their superfluities? How did the *Widows* presse to cast in their *Mites*, the married *Wives* their *wedding-rings*, the zealous *Virgins* their whole stocke, to their *Silver bodkins*?"—*Lord have Mercie upon us: or, A Plaine Discourse declaring that the Plague of Warre, which now wasts this Nation, tooke its beginning in and from the Citie of London.*

"The people from all parts, both in Citie and Country, set open the sluices and Floodgates of their affections to the cause, and came gushing in with their Contributions . . . to see, I say, the people like so many numerous and swifte swarmes of busie Bees in a *Mid-May*, and hot *June*, flocking and flying to and fro to carry honey (or rather Money, Gold and Silver Plate) to the hive or trustie Treasurie . . . was most admirable to behold by all spectators, who came daily

in innumerable multitudes to see and admire the same."—
Vicars' *Jehovah Jireh.* London, 1644.

Note HHH.—Vol. II., page 77.

Commissioners of Array.—" The assise of arms, enacted
27 Hen. 2, and afterwards the statute of Winchester, 13 Edw. i.
obliged every man, according to his state and degree, to provide a quantity of such arms as were then in use; and it was
part of the duty of constables under the latter statute to
see such arms provided. These weapons were changed by
4 and 5 P. & M. c. 2, into more modern ones; but both these
provisions were repealed by 1 Jac. I., 21 Jac. I. While
these continued in force, it was usual, from time to time, for
our princes to issue commissions of array, and send into every
county officers in whom they could confide, to muster and
array (or to set in military order) the inhabitants of every
district, and the form of the commission of array was settled
in Parliament, anno 5 Hen. 4 . . . the introduction of these
commissions of lieutenancy . . . caused them to fall into dis-
use."—*Blackstone.*

Note III.—Vol. II., page 79.

On this very day, July 11th, the King sent the following
message to both houses of Parliament, with a proclamation,
" *declaring our Purpose to go in our Royal Person to Hull, and
the true occasion and end thereof.*"

" By our former Declarations, and this our *Proclamation*
(which we herewith send you) you and all our good subjects,
may see the just Grounds of our present journey towards our
Town of Hull. Before we shall use force to reduce that
Place to its due Obedience, we have thought fit once more to
require you, that it may be forthwith delivered up to us, (the
business being of that nature, that it can admit no delay:)
wherein if you shall conform yourselves, we shall then be
willing to admit such Addresses from you, and return such
Propositions to you, as may be proper to settle the Peace of
this Kingdom, and compose the present Distractions. Do your

Duty herein, and be assured from us, in the *word of a King*, that nothing shall be wanting on our part, that may prevent the Calamities which threaten this nation, and may render our people truly happy. If this our gracious invitation shall be declined, God and all good Men judg betwixt us. We shall expect to receive Satisfaction herein by your Answer to be presented to us at *Beverly*, upon Friday next, being the 15th day of this present *July*.

"The two Houses of Parliament, before the Receipt of this message of the 11th of July, had prepared and concluded the [a] Petition to be presented to his Majesty, and therefore resolved not to return any other Answer thereunto. But lest his Majesty should think it a delatoriness in the Parliament to return an Answer, the two Houses sent the Author of these *Collections* Post to *Beverly*, to acquaint his Majesty, that the Earl of Holland, Sir John Holland, and Sir Philip Stapleton, were coming down with a Petition of both Houses, in answer to his Majesty's said Message of the 11th of July."[1]

The subject of this Petition was that the King would "be pleased to forbear and remove all Preparations and Actions of War, particularly the Forces from about *Hull*, from *Newcastle*, *Tinmouth*, *Lincoln* and *Lincolnshire*, and all other Places," also to recall the Commissions of Array, to dismiss extraordinary Guards by him raised; to come nearer to the Parliament, "and hearken to their faithful Advice," and contained the promise that they would be ready to lay down all those preparations which they had been forced to make for their defence. The King's reply entered minutely into the points contained in the petition; to the request to withdraw his forces from *Hull* he thus answers:—"For the Forces about *Hull*, his Majesty will remove them when he hath attained the end for which they were brought thither. When *Hull* shall be reduced again to his Subjection, he will no longer have an Army before it; and when he shall be assured that the same necessity and pretence of publick good, which took *Hull* from him, may not put a Garrison into *Newcastle* to keep the same against him, he will remove his from thence, and

---

[1] Rushworth.

from *Tinmouth;* till when, the Example of Hull will not be out of his Memory."

The following Proclamation was appended to the answer:—

"CHARLES R.—Our express Pleasure is, that this Petition of the Lords and Commons, with our Answer thereto, be read in all Churches and Chappels within the Kingdom of England and Dominion of Wales, by the Parsons, Vicars or Curats of the same."[2]

The Parliament published their reply in a similar manner:—

"Ordered by the Lords in Parliament, That the Petition of the Lords and Commons in Parliament, delivered to his Majesty the 16th day of July; together with his Majesty's Answer thereunto, and a Replication of the said Lords and Commons to the said Answer, dated the 26th of July, 1642, shall be read in all Churches and Chappels, within the Kingdom of England and Dominion of Wales, by the Parsons, Vicars, or Curats of the same.

"John Browne, Cler. Parliamentorum."[3]

"Mr. George, Vicar of Cople, Bedfordshire, having received two Declarations from Parliament, and one from the King, with a command from the Parliament that he should not publish that from the King, says, 'Judge, whether I am to obey God or Man. By God's Word I am commanded to obey the King. I find no such Command for the Parliament.' Upon which he threw away the two Declarations 'scornfully.' He is committed to Newgate, and fined £100."[4]

NOTE JJJ.—Vol. II., page 83.

"Mr. Hyde had been absent four or five days from the court, and came into the presence when the King was washing his hands before dinner; and as soon as the King saw him, he asked him aloud, 'Ned Hyde, when did you play with my band-strings last?' upon which he was exceedingly out of

[2] Rushworth. [3] Ibid. [4] Parry's *Parliaments of England.*

countenance, not imagining the cause of the question, and the room being full of gentlemen, who appeared to be merry with what the king had asked. But his majesty observing him to be in disorder, and to blush very much, said pleasantly, 'Be not troubled at it, for I have worn no band-strings these twenty years;' and then asked him whether he had not seen the diurnal; of which he had not heard till then; but shortly after, some of the standers by shewed him a diurnal, in which there was a letter of intelligence printed, where it was said that Ned Hyde was grown so familiar with the King, that he used to play with his band-strings. Which was a method of calumniating then, and shortly after prosecuted and exercised upon much greater persons."—*The Life of Edward Earl of Clarendon*, vol. i. p. 157. Oxford, 1827.

NOTE KKK.—Vol. II., page 110.

Tuesday, the fourth of *October* (1642).—"There was letters read from Manchester, declaring the Proceedings of that town, and the Lord *Strange*, who with 3000 souldiers have besieged the same seven nights and sixe dayes, duly assaulting and shooting to the same, that in all this time, none of the townesmen are slaine by the enemy, but foure or five which were slaine by the breaking of their Muskets which were overcharged; and that of the adverse party are slaine about 2100, Sir Gilbert Gerrat being one."—*Perfect Diurnall.*

"There was likewise information that the Earle of *Derby* had besieged the towne of Mancester, and great fear there was of his future claps; nevertheless he was peaceably suffered to raise his Forces towards the Towne; and on the sudden he was surrounded, and the Earle himselfe was hardly put to it; for he was well in reach of Captain *Skinner*, who reported afterwards, that he thought to struck him off his horse with his Patteson."—*Speciall Passages, &c.*

NOTE LLL.—Vol. II., page 110.

"The day before the King's arrival at Shrewsbury, he mustered his forces at Wellington, that being their first rendezvous. His Majesty caused military orders to be read there at the head of each regiment, and then mounting his horse, and placing himself in the midst, from whence he might be heard by all; he made the following speech to the soldiers:— 'Gentlemen—You have heard the orders read.'"—Phillips' *History and Antiquities of Shrewsbury.*

The whole speech has been preserved, as follows:—

"GENTLEMEN,

"You have heard these Orders read; It is your part in your severall places to observe them exactly: The time cannot be long before Wee come to Action, therefore you have the more reason to be carefull; And I must tell you, I shall be very severe in the punishing of those, of what condition soever, who transgresse these Instructions. I cannot suspect your Courage and Resolution; your Conscience and your Loyalty hath brought you hither to fight for your Religion; your King, and the Laws of the Land; you shall fight with no Enemies, but Traitours, most of them Brownists, Anabaptists, and Atheists, such who desire to destroy both Church and State, and who have already condemned you to ruin for being Loyall to Vs. That you may see what use I mean to make of your valour, if it please God to blesse it with successe, I have thought fit to publish my Resolution to you in a Protestation, which when you have heard me make, you will believe you cannot fight in a better Quarrell; in which I promise to live and die with you."—*Collection.*

NOTE MMM.—Vol. II., page 118.

"Prince *Rupert's* Brigade quartered at *Henley*, and of them a Regiment of Horse at my House at *Fawley-Court.*

"Sir *John Biron* and his Brothers commanded those Horse, and gave order that they should commit no Insolence at my House, nor plunder my Goods; but Soldiers are not easily govern'd against their Plunder, or persuaded to restrain it, for there being about 1000 of the King's Horse quartered in and about the House, and none but Servants there, there was no

Insolence nor Outrage usually committed by common Soldiers on a reputed Enemy, which was omitted by these brutish Fellows at my House . . . they spent and consumed 100 Load of Corn and Hay, littered their Horses with Sheaves of good Wheat, and gave them all Sorts of Corn in the Straw: Divers Writings of Consequence, and Books which were left in my study, some of them they tore in Pieces, others they burnt to light their Tobacco, and some they carried away with them, to my extreme great Loss and Prejudice, in wanting the Writings of my Estate, and losing very many excellent Manuscripts of my Father and others, and some of my own Labours.

"They broke down my Park Pales, killed most of my Deer . . . and let out all the rest, only a tame young Stag they carried away and presented to Prince *Rupert*, and my Hounds, which were extraordinary good. They eat and drank up all that the House could afford, broke up all Trunks, Chests, and Places; and where they found Linen or any Householdstuff they took it away with them, and cutting the Beds, let out the Feathers, and took away the Ticks. They likewise carried away my Coach, and four good Horses, and all my saddle Horses, and did all the Mischief and Spoil, that Malice and Enmity could provoke barbarous Mercenaries to commit, and so they parted.

"This is remembered only to raise a constant Hatred of any thing that may in the least tend to the fomenting of such Unhappiness and Misery."—Whitelock's *Memorials of the English Affairs*, page 65.

The Mayor of Reading fared no better. "He invited Prince Robert to a very sumptuous dinner, providing for him all the severall sorts of dainties he could get, but especially a Woodcock, which he brought in himselfe, with many complements to shew his courtly entertainment. Prince Robert gave him many thanks for his good cheere, and asked him whose was all that plate that stood upon the cupboard, the Maior had set out all his plate to make a shew, and besides had borrowed a great deale of his neighbours to grace himselfe withall, replied, and please your Highnesse, this plate is mine; no quoth the Prince, this plate is mine, and so accordingly he tooke it all away, bidding him to bee of good cheere, for he tooke it as the Parliament did upon the publique faith, but the Maior of Redding lookt as if he would for very griefe have hanged himself in his guilded chaine, and wisht he had never feasted Prince *Robert's* chops."—*Certain Speciall and Remarkable Passages.*

NOTE NNN.—Vol. II., page 125.

"Mr. *Boys*, a Citizen of London, went lately downe into Hamshire to see his Father, and to effect some other affaires, but returning back he found that Country overspread with the Cavaliers, whom to avoyd, he turned into Berk-shire, and being there misinformed that the Cavaliers had left Reding, he made into that Town, where being stayed and examined by one of their Sentinells, he gave satisfaction and was suffered to passe on, but coming to an other Sentinell a wicked fellow laid hold on him for a spie, and brought him to Sir *Arthur Aston* the Governour there, and deposed that he saw him at Edge Hill, where he was taken for a spie and escaped from them; whereupon the Governour in a Councell of War condemned him to be hanged, and on Friday last he was there executed accordingly, but no doubt his Innocent blood cryeth for vengeance against that false accusation and execution."—*England's Memorable Accidents, from the 12th of Decemb. to the 19th of the same*, 1642.

"It is informed the Houses from the Lord General's army, that the Cavalliers in Redding have taken one Master Boyce, whom they pretended to be a spye, a Citizen, a very honest and religious man, and one of good worth, and they have adjudged him."—*Perfect Diurnall.*

NOTE OOO.—Vol. II., page 127.

This chapter is an abridgement of a quarto pamphlet preserved in the *King's Pamphlets* in the British Museum. The title-page runs thus:—

"MARLEBOROVVE'S MISERIES,

or, ENGLAND turned IRELAND, by The
{ Lord *Digby* and *Daniel O'Neale.*

READE and JVDGE, This Being A Most Exact and a true Relation of the Besieging, Plundering { Pillaging, and Burning part of the said Towne.

Written by T. B. W. B. O. B. J. H. who were not onely Spectators, but also Sufferers in that most unchristian action. Dedicated to all ENGLAND, and directed to the city of *LONDON*, to shew the abuse of the Subjects, Liberty, and Priviledges of their own goods.

Printed by one that Prints the Truth, 1643."

The pamphlet concludes thus:—

" Thus have we made a rude but true relation, out of which you may collect what you please, and omit what you thinke not convenient to be printed: And so we leave you.

"*All of them your friends.*
"*T. B. W. B. O. B. J. H.*

"*Reader, the reason why this came no sooner in print was, the first copy was intercepted by the Cavaliers.*"

NOTE PPP.—Vol. II., page 150.

" We must hansell the beginning of this week with the observation of what was seene the night before, which was a most unusuall light, which continued all the night, and by the attestation of a thousand witnesses, was nothing inferiour to that *Diaphanum*, when the Moon shines forth in her perfect Orbe; That such a light should be seen in the absence of the two great Luminarie Bodies is so neere a Miracle, that I believe the most exact *Meteorist* can neither according to Reason or Philosophy define the cause. No Conjunction of the Planets could effect it, nor any union of the starres, should all the starres (which is impossible) crowd themselves together to make all one Hemisphere, but one milky way. Nor could it be an exhalation, for every exhalation that takes fire in the ayre, as it is cleare, so it is suddaine and violent; but this was beheld to continue in the same degree of light all the time of the Night. We must therefore looke upon a higher cause, and taking comfort to our selves, believe with comfort that GOD will not forsake us, who extraordinarily hath pleased to afford us light in a Land of darknesse."—*The Weekly Accompt, Numb. 9, Novem. 1.*

NOTE QQQ.—Vol. II., page 156.

See the varying accounts of the battle, given in Rushworth's *Historical Collections*, part iii. vol. ii. pp. 33–38, entitled "A Relation of the Battels fought between Keynton and Edgehill, by his Majesty's Army and that of the Rebels: Printed by his Majesty's Command at Oxford by Leonard Lichfield, Printer to the University, 1642;" and "A Relation of the Battel between his Majesty's Army and the Parliament Forces, under the command of the Earl of Essex, at Edghill near Keynton in the County of Warwick, Octob. the 23rd, 1642, as it was communicated to the Speaker and Commons assembled in Parliament, and by them ordered to be printed and published."

NOTE RRR.—Vol. II., page 161.

" . . . . though they intended to burne the Towne utterly, as may be known by their laying lighted Match, with Powder and other combustible matter, at the other end, which fired in divers places, and divers was found out and prevented, so that we may truely say that the flames . . . . made a difference between those that feared God, and those that feare him not. But this is remarkable in their vilenesse, that all these Houses saving two were fired in their cold blood, at their departure, wherein they endeavoured to fire all, and in the flames they would not suffer the people to carry out their good, or to quench it, triumphingly with reproaches rejoyced that the wind stood right to consume the Towne, at which present the Lord caused the Winds to turn, which was a token of his notice of their insultation."—*A True Relation of Prince Rupert's*

Barbarous Cruelty against the Towne of Brumingham. (Letter from R. P., dated Coventry, April 8, 1643; printed in black letter.)—London, Printed for *John Wright* in the Old-baily, April 12, 1643.

NOTE SSS.—Vol. II., page 165.

See "A true and most sad Relition of the hard usage and extreme cruelty used on Captain *Wingate* .... with others of the Parliament Souldiers, &c. Prisoners at OXFORD, under the custody of one *Smith*, Provost-Marshall Generall to the KING's Army: Written by one of the same Prisoners in behalf of them all, to a Worthy and eminent Citizen of LONDON. Dated 9th of *February*, 1642.—*London*, Printed for GEORGE HUTTON, at the Turn'd-Style in Holborne, *Feb.* 13, 1642." Also, "The trve Copie of a Letter written by Captaine Wingate, &c. London. Printed for WILLIAM LEY, at Paul's-Chaine. *October*, the 7th, 1642;" and "Englande's Wolfe with Eagle's Clawes; or the cruell Impieties of Bloudthirsty Royalists, and blasphemous *Anti-Parliamentarians*, under the command of that inhumane Prince *Rupert*, Digby, and the rest." London, 1646.

"Others finde fault with the committing of Malignants to prison; but they are used like men, not as Smith the Provost Marshall useth them; not as Captain *Lilburn*, Captain *Wingate*, Captain *Walton*, &c., are used, like dogs rather than Christians; almost pined to death for the want of sustenance, eaten with vermin, for want of help, and shifts of cloaths; loaded with fetters of iron, debarr'd the company of their wives, children or friends, debarr'd of the charity that friends would relieve them with; cannot have the favour which Christians have of Turks, for those blood-thirsty Cavaliers, who use them like Hackny-Jades, nay worse, than dogs; for though it is true the King allows six pence a day; But Smith detains four pence three farthings of it; here is cruelty indeed, unspeakable cruelty; what would these men do, if he should subdue us?"—*A Complaint to the House of Commons.* Oxford. Printed by Leonard Lichfield, *Printer to the Vniversity.* 1642.

Note TTT.—Vol. II., page 173.

"Touching the perfidious revolt of King's *Lyn* in *Norfolk*, you heard in part the last week, and since that further certified, That after they could no wayes prevail to procure their own ends, under a seeming pretence of Neutrality, though they offered 10,000*l.* composition to the Parliament, That no Garrison but their own, might be placed amongst them, they then soon declared themselves the true sons of Rebellion, and hung out a flag of defiance; upon which the Earl of *Manchester*, drew his Forces neerer to them, besieged the Town with a considerable force of Horse, and Foot, possesseth himself of Old *Lyn*, stops all the passages, that no provisions can be brought unto them by Land; the Earl of *Warwick* in the like manner blocking them up by Sea, so that there is no doubt, but in short time their own exigency and want of provisions, will compel their reducing to the obedience of King and Parliament, if no other course be taken, though for the present they remain obstinate, under a supposed vain hope to be relieved by the Earl of *Newcastle*, whom it is said they have sent unto for aide: But the Earl of *Manchester* is resolved to make short work of it, and by his Batteries from Old *Lyn* doth so terrifie them, they cannot be many dayes able to hold out: In the mean time the Earl understanding that there are divers Papists and Malignants in *Norfolk* and *Suffolk*, that have secured themselves in that Town, and are the chief causers of their revolt, with their Malignant Recorder, and one or two others of the Townsmen, his Lordship, and a Committee that sits now at Saint *Edmund's Bury* to that purpose, spare no pains to inquire out, and sequester their estates, which will amount to a very considerable value, for the service of the Parliament."—*A Perfect Diurnall of some Passages in Parliament, Numb.* 8.

"This present Tuesday (Sept. 19th, 1643), we heare good and true news from *Lyn* in Norfolk, that that Towne which stood so much upon its strength, hath now within 3 dayes past submitted themselves to the King and Parliament, so that my L. of Manchester hath quiet possession thereof, and

30,000 pound composition: and that by my Lord's appointment the towne to be garrisoned: besides many new forces come to my Lord daily in abundance.

"My Lorde entered the Towne on Saturday last on these conditions, the common soldiers to have a month's pay, the Troopers a fortnight's pay, the Gentlemen to be at my Lord's disposall, with their Armes and Magazine; the women of the Towne being very angry."—*The Weekely Accompt of Certain Special and Remarkable Passages, &c.*

NOTE UUU.—Vol. II., page 199.

Soon after the Norman Conquest, this castle was given by William the First to his kinsman Roger de Montgomery, whom he at the same time created Earl of Arundel and Shrewsbury; but he took his title from this place, where he resided. During the civil wars of the seventeenth century, this castle did not answer the expectations that were formed of its strength and situation. It had been in the possession of parliament from the beginning of the war, and was esteemed a principal bulwark in those parts. About the end of 1643, Lord Hopton, with a view to compensate an unsuccessful summer's campaign, brought his forces suddenly before it, and reduced it on the first summons; but in less than two months Sir William Waller re-took it as suddenly. In neither siege its strength was tried, the garrison in each instance being intimidated. From this period Arundel Castle continued to decline, and at last became little better than a mass of ruins. The circumference of the whole site of the castle is 950 feet by 250, enclosing five acres and a half, but, with its appendages, said to have been formerly a mile in circumference, and the walls are from three to four feet in thickness. The ground-plan nearly resembles that of the royal casde of Windsor. It has a circular keep[1] in the middle, raised on a mount, chiefly artificial, and the elevation is not dissimilar to that royal abode.—Allen's *History of Surrey and Sussex*, 1830, p. 522.

[1] A fine collection of owls is kept in this building. They were a present to the late Duke of Norfolk from North America, and are uncommonly fine specimens, some measuring across the wings, when extended, from eight to ten feet.

Note VVV.—Vol. II., page 222.

"At this period Liverpool was a small and inconsiderable place; its fortifications, however, together with the Mersey, strongly environed the town, and as the river afforded a depth of water sufficient for the reception of vessels of the largest burthen, the garrison were readily supplied with provisions and military stores: but the adjacent high lands, on which the besiegers were encamped, rendered its reduction speedy and inevitable. This last consideration induced the Prince, as he approached nearer to the town—its low situation towards the river being partly hidden from his view—to compare it, sarcastically, to a *crow's nest;* but ere he became master of its works, the courage and intrepidity of the garrison obliged him to acknowledge that an *eagle's nest*, or even a *den of lions*, would have been a more proper denomination."—*History of Liverpool*, pp. 57, 58. Liverpool, 1810.

"Liverpoole cost a hundred barrels of munition, which makes Prince Rupert march ill provided."—*Letter from Arthur Trevor to the Marquis of Ormonde, dated Chester, June 29th,* 1644. Baines' *History of Liverpool*, p. 315. London, 1852.

Note WWW.—Vol. II., page 241.

Built by Sir Baptist Hickes, who was a Mercer. "Son of *Robert Hickes*, a Mercer also, keeping a shop in *Cheapside* . . . at the *White Bear;* and of *Juliana*, Daughter and Heiress of *Arthur de Clapham in Comitat*, Somerset.

"This *Baptist*, upon K. *James's* coming in, was sworn his Servant, *Anno* 1602, and soon knighted; and before his Death was created Viscount *Campden*. He supplied the Court with Silks, and rich Mercery Wares, when King *James*, with his bare *Scotch* Nobility and Gentry, came in: By which means he got a great Estate.

"He was one of the first Citizens, that after knight-hood kept their Shops.

"An Epitaph made in his Memorial.

" *Reader, know,*
Whoe'er thou be,
Here lies Faith, Hope,
And Charitie :

" Faith *true*, Hope *firm*,
Charity *free* ;
BAPTIST *Lord* Campden
Was these Three.

" Faith *in* GOD,
Charity *to Brother*,
Hope *for Himself* ;
What ought He other ?

" Faith *is no more* ;
Charity *is crown'd* :
'Tis only Hope
Is under Ground."

NOTE XXX.—Vol. II., page 250.

" *Die Jovis* 24 October 1644.

" At this time the Lord *Macguire* and *Hugh Oge Mac Mahone* Esquire were first brought upon their Tryals; the Bills against them being this day found by the Grand Jury. And though the former by reason of his Plea of Peerage was not Executed till some Months after, yet I shall here together set down the whole Story of them both.

" These Gentlemen were two of the Principal Contrivers of the *Irish* Rebellion, and Massacre of the Protestants in that Kingdom; and taken upon the first Discovery *October* 22, 1641, at *Dublin.* . . .

" . . . About *July* 1642, They were sent over into *England*, and Committed to the Tower, And by means of the multiplicity of Affairs wherein the two Houses were involved, and the difficulty of having the Witnesses against them from *Ireland.* they continued there in Custody till *Saturday* the 17th of *August* 1644. And then by Confederacy with two Priests that belonged to the *Spanish* Ambassador, and one Mrs. *Leviston* over against the *New Exchange* in the *Strand*, in whose House the *French* Agent lay, They having got a small Steel Saw, therewith in the Night saw'd asunder the Door of their Chamber, which was above two Inches thick, and so with Cords got over the Tower-wall, and swam over the Ditch; Whereupon the Parliament set forth an Order for their Apprehension, *promising* 100*l.* to any that should bring them in, or either of them, Dead or Alive; And that whosoever should harbour or relieve them, should be prosecuted as Traitors.

"No News was heard of them till the 19th of *September*, and then they having got Lodgings in a Contable's House in *Drury Lane*, and one of them looking out of the Window or Balcony to call a Woman that cryed Oysters, it happen'd at that instant a Servant of Sir *John Clotworthy's* espyed him, and instantly gave notice to his Master and the Lieutenant of the Tower, who came and seiz'd them, and carryed them back to the Tower; Mrs. *Leviston's* Room was also searcht and she taken into Custody, but because the *French* Minister had Lodgings in her House, to prevent any occasion of Offence, a declaration was drawn up to give his most Christian Majesty satisfaction touching this Affair.

"This breaking Prison put the two Houses upon expediting their Tryal; And the Bill being found *November* 11th, on the 13th they were Arraigned at the King's Bench Bar.... *Mac Mahone* pleaded *Not Guilty* and put himself for Tryal upon God and his Country; But *Macguire* alledged he was a Peer of *Ireland*, and ought to be tryed there by his Peers, desiring that he might be allowed Council therein for matter of Law and Form, which was granted accordingly. *Mac Mahone* on *Munday November* 18th on full Evidence was found Guilty, and received Judgement as in Cases of Treason; and on the 22nd was Executed accordingly at *Tyburn;* refusing to make any Confession, and being ask'd, if he desired any to pray for him, Answered, *None but* Roman *Catholicks*.

"The same Day the Lord Macguire brought in his Plea signed by Council; The purport of which was,

"That by the Statute of *Magna Charta* 10 *February* 9 *Hen.* 3, It was Enacted that none should be Tryed or Condemned but by the lawful Judgement of his Peers; And that by the

Statute of 10 *Hen.* 7, It was Enacted, That all the Statutes made in *England*, should thenceforth be in force in *Ireland*. .... After it had several Days been Argued, both by the Defendant's Council, and the King's; Judge *Bacon* at the beginning of *Hillary Term* over-ruled the Plea, and delivered his Judgement, That a Baron of *Ireland* is triable by a Jury in this kingdom .... on *Thursday February* 20th he was drawn on a Sledge from the *Tower* through *London*, and so to *Tyburn*."—Rushworth's *Historical Collections*, part iii. vol. ii. p. 783.

Note YYY.—Vol. II., page 256.

"This day the House of Commons being informed, that *Rupert* before he came from North Wales, had hanged 13 honest Protestants, Countrey-men, that lived about Shropshire, because that there were 13 Irish Rebels hanged at Shrewsbury, the House had some debate thereon, and ordered, that a letter should be sent to *Rupert*, the substance whereof is thus: Letting him know how much both Houses resent his crueltie, in hanging of 13 of our English Protestants; because wee hanged so many of the Irish Rebels. That there is a great difference between those Rebels and the English Protestants; the King and Parliament having by divers Acts of Parliament proclaimed them Traytors, that if hee shall proceed to hang up more of our prisoners in cold blond, wee must and shall retaliate."—*Perfect Passages of Each Daye's Proceedings in Parliament, Numb.* 24.

THE END.

www.ingramcontent.com/pod-product-compliance
Lightning Source LLC
Chambersburg PA
CBHW020227240426

43672CB00006B/447